PRAISE FOR DYLAN HOWARD

"Dylan Howard is the rare combination of cutting-edge journalist, true crime commentator, and relentless investigator."

—Dr. Phil McGraw, host of TV's #1 daytime talk show, *Dr. Phil*

"Renowned."

—*Nancy Grace*

"A wunderkind Hollywood gossip reporter."

—*Columbia Journalism Review*

"Big-name producer."

—*Vanity Fair*

"Howard is a throwback to an older age of journalism."

—Anne Helen Petersen, BuzzFeed

"One of my favorite people in American media."

—Anthony Scaramucci

"A tabloid prodigy."

—Jeffrey Toobin, staff writer at the *New Yorker*, CNN senior legal analyst, and *New York Times* bestselling author

"The king of Hollywood scoops."

—Ad Week

"The go-to guy for authoritative showbiz news and analysis on cable and over-the-air television."

— Los Angeles Press Club

"When Dylan Howard focuses his attention to investigating a case, you can be sure he will uncover sensational new information that we, as readers, viewers, or listeners, will find astonishing."

—Dr. Drew Pinsky, *New York Times* bestselling author and TV and radio personality

OTHER BOOKS BY DYLAN HOWARD

Epstein: Dead Men Tell No Tales
Aaron Hernandez's Killing Fields
Diana: Case Solved
The Last Charles Manson Tapes: Evil Lives Beyond the Grave
Billion Dollar Hollywood Heist

OTHER BOOKS BY ANDY TILLETT

The Last Charles Manson Tapes: Evil Lives Beyond the Grave

ROYALS
AT WAR

ROYALS
AT WAR

The Untold Story of Harry and Meghan's
Shocking Split with the House of Windsor

DYLAN HOWARD
& ANDY TILLETT
with Arsalan Mohammed

Skyhorse Publishing

Skyhorse Publishing books may be purchased in bulk at special discounts for sales promotion, corporate gifts, fund-raising, or educational purposes. Special editions can also be created to specifications. For details, contact the Special Sales Department, Skyhorse Publishing, 307 West 36th Street, 11th Floor, New York, NY 10018 or info@skyhorsepublishing.com.

Skyhorse® and Skyhorse Publishing® are registered trademarks of Skyhorse Publishing, Inc.®, a Delaware corporation.

Visit our website at www.skyhorsepublishing.com.

10 9 8 7 6 5 4 3 2 1

Library of Congress Cataloging-in-Publication Data is available on file.

Cover design by 5mediadesign

ISBN: 978-1-5107-6119-3
eBook ISBN: 978-1-5107-6273-2

Printed in the United States of America

TABLE OF CONTENTS

AUTHOR'S NOTE   *x*

PART ONE

THE DIVISIVE DUCHESS   1
A COMMONER PRINCESS LIKE NONE BEFORE   6
FORCED TO FLEE   10
"A BIT OF TENSION"   15
"DEEPLY HELD DIFFERENCES"   18
UNHAPPY BIRTHDAY   25
THE $500,000 WOMAN   38
GOD BLESS THE CHILD   43
ZOOMING AROUND THE WORLD   48
GOING ROGUE   53
A COSTLY WITHDRAWAL   68

PART TWO

THE MAKING OF MEGHAN   77
A TALE OF TWO COMMONERS   84
CAROLE MEETS HER CAPTAIN   88
POOR LITTLE CHAP   91
"I PUSHED HER DOWN THE STAIRS"   95
CHARLES AND THE SWEET-CHARACTERED GIRL   97
WASTING AWAY   102
THE FURIOUS BRIDE   106
THE HEIR AND THE SPARE   112

ROYAL AFFAIRS   114

MISERABLY EVER AFTER   123

"YOU'LL BE KING, I WON'T!"   132

THE DEATH OF DIANA   138

"A TIDAL WAVE OF GRIEF"   142

CASE CLOSED   147

PART THREE

ROYAL WELCOME FOR THE OTHER WOMAN   157

WILLIAM WEATHERS THE STORM   160

THE REIGN DOWN IN AFRICA   163

"WOW, KATE'S HOT!"   165

BETTER STAND BACK   174

THERE'S SOMETHING ABOUT KATE   178

WAITY KATIE   184

LEARNING TO FLY   190

THE SPLIT AND THE REUNION   199

WILL AND KATE GET HITCHED   208

THE DIAMOND JUBILEE   215

ANOTHER PAIR OF HEIRS   219

THE PRINCE'S PARTNERS IN CRIME   223

OUT BACK OF THE PUBLIC EYE   226

DIRTY HARRY   228

PART FOUR

A STAR IS BORN   239

MEGHAN: STEPPIN' OUT   245

INTELLIGENT HOT MESSES   248

SOUTHERN SOJOURN, HUSTLE TO HOLLYWOOD   253

ONE-WOMAN PITY PARTY   256

"THIS IS THE ONE"   260

THE RING RETURNED TO SENDER   262

PART FIVE

WHEN HARRY MET MEGHAN 273

THIS IS NOT A GAME 282

"WHAT MEGHAN WANTS, MEGHAN GETS" 302

TEARS AND TIARAS 307

THE WEDDING WALK THAT WASN'T 310

THE POWER OF LOVE 314

WINDSORS & LOSERS 320

EPILOGUE 327

AUTHOR'S NOTE

Over the past few centuries, the British monarchy has been sailing onward in a generally stately manner. Impediments—deaths, divorce, and natural disasters—have rocked its course at times, sometimes perilously, but for the most part, there have been only a few really ugly and destabilizing icebergs in its path.

But as 2019 came to an end, a year Elizabeth II, the ninety-four-year-old Queen of the United Kingdom, herself expressed as being somewhat "bumpy"—that's Royal-speak for what you and I would describe as an absolute nightmare—two ominous clouds heaved into full view of the monarchy's serene path.

One was the astonishing self-immolation of the Queen's favorite son, Prince Andrew, Duke of York, as he took to television to present a thoroughly disgraceful defense of his association with the late pedophile and Israeli spy Jeffrey Epstein. The resulting collapse of what was left of his credibility mired the Royals in controversy, but just as that was dying down, in the opening days of the new decade, the Duke and Duchess of Sussex—Prince Harry and Meghan Markle—sensationally announced that they would be "stepping back" from their duties. In other words, they quit the House of Windsor, the reigning royal house of the United Kingdom and other Commonwealth realms, a dynasty founded in 1917.

To underline their new "brand," the pair launched a glossy website, sussex-royal.com, and announced they would be eschewing their Royal duties and income to become "financially independent" and focus their time on their charity commitments. It certainly is a laudable goal: Harry has done a tremendous amount of sterling work in promoting awareness of mental health issues in young people, among impoverished people in Africa via his Sentebale charity, and in organizing the Invictus Games, a magnificent initiative that encourages young disabled military veterans to participate in an Olympiad, a celebration of the human spirit, endurance, and resilience.

But to many in the country at large, the blame for the schism could be squarely laid at the feet of the Duchess, Meghan Markle. The British media are no strangers to xenophobia and hostility to change. With varying degrees of bile, Meghan, a cipher of progressive modernity, diversity, and social awareness, was seen as being utterly at odds with the staid, traditional, duty-bound structure of the Royal Family. Her perceived control over Harry has been at the root of disagreements with his brother, Prince William, the Duke of Cambridge, and their wider network of old friends. And her conflicts with Catherine, the Duchess of Cambridge, only intensified speculation that Meghan was shaping her marriage and status to fit her needs above all.

It was hardly surprising, therefore, that the Royals were incandescent with outrage at the couple's defection, the Queen said to be "furious." "They want to become the world's biggest lifestyle brand," one Palace insider told me. "If they are allowed to do so, the monarchy as we know it will cease to exist and a new 'celebritized' Royal Family is about to take over. They want to have their cake and eat it, too. This is all about money."

Not since the abdication crisis of 1936, when Edward VII renounced the throne to marry the American divorcée Wallis Simpson, had the monarchy faced a situation of such gravity. It was a crisis that exceeded the near-catastrophic fallout from Diana, Princess of Wales's death in 1997. The decision of the young couple to extrude themselves from "the Firm," as the Royals wryly refer to themselves, was a colossal rejection of the values, traditions, and beliefs that have kept the Crown afloat for countless generations. Now, as we watch Harry and Meghan begin the process of establishing themselves as professional ex-Royals in North America, William and Kate have been left in the United Kingdom to be the face of the future Royal Family, as it embarks on an epochal new decade. Unless medical science exerts a hitherto unimaginable miracle, the odds of the incumbent being on the throne in 2030 are remote. Therefore, it will either be Charles or William who will be King a decade hence—and a new dynamic and purpose to the family will be in place.

The relationship between William and Harry and, by extension, Meghan and Kate will be fundamental in this new era. But as we enter 2020, those relationships are at their lowest ebb to date.

"I've put my arm around my brother all our lives and I can't do that anymore; we're separate entities," Prince William told a friend. "I'm sad about that. All we can do, and all I can do, is try and support them and hope that the time comes when we're all singing from the same page. I want everyone to play on the team."

Royals at War combs through the rich history of the Royal Family from its position and relevance to society today, to its German paternal descent and scandals—and takes an unprecedented look inside a divided Buckingham Palace to provide the definitive account of the current abdication crisis:

- Has Prince Harry ever really recovered from the death of his mother, Diana—and the resentment he feels against the institution that tried to destroy her?
- Why did Meghan, once hailed as a breath of fresh air, rile up the monarchy?
- Why did she refuse to conform to royal conventions in the way that Catherine did before her?
- Did the public and media criticism of Meghan go too far? And just how valid are the accusations of racism?
- How did these modern royals treat the tabloids differently from tradition? And did it backfire?
- How did we get to this and how can the Royals hope to restructure themselves and retake their place in our hearts?

In this book, we will answer what is next for Harry and Meghan. What's more, how will they—and the institution they've turned their backs on—react to their new lives outside the confines of the Palace and free from the strict codes and conventions that bind all members of the Royal Family?

An intimate portrait of a couple trapped in a gilded cage, *Royals at War* sets out to answer these questions and more to provide you, the reader, a chance to form your own opinion on right- and wrongdoing in this unprecedented crisis, as we reveal how Harry's infatuation with Meghan began, and how it could yet end in disaster.

—DYLAN HOWARD & ANDY TILLETT

PART ONE

THE DIVISIVE DUCHESS

The Duchess of Sussex tried to live up to expectations on a royal tour of South Africa in September 2019. In Cape Town, she gamely danced with local children on the beach. She gave impassioned speeches for female empowerment and against gender-based violence. She even introduced her adorable infant son, Archie, to South Africa's Archbishop Desmond Tutu. Surely, even her late mother-in-law, Princess Diana, couldn't have represented the Crown better.

The royal tour offered a perfect opportunity for the American-born Meghan to begin to rehabilitate her embattled image. It was a chance for the television actress, who made her name playing brash, sultry attorney Rachel Zane on *Suits*, to prove that she was more Buckingham Palace than Hollywood. But it was always going to be an uphill battle. "When she first started dating [Prince] Harry, she was hailed as the 'American sweetheart,' but it didn't take long for the tide to turn," a friend of Meghan's told these authors. "Meghan just couldn't seem to escape from the negative press that seemed to always surround her."

Meghan's honeymoon with the British public began to sour shortly after she and Harry announced in November 2018 that they would be leaving Kensington Palace to move to Frogmore Cottage, an hour outside London. Gossips claimed the move was due to a rift with the future king, Prince William, and his wife, Duchess Kate.

Onlookers noted a coolness between the couples, and insiders whispered that "Duchess Difficult"—Markle—had made her sister-in-law, Kate, cry during a fitting for Princess Charlotte's bridesmaid dress. The Palace, when it finally commented, called the rumors of a feud overblown, but tellingly they did not deny it entirely. An insider said they're not without basis. "Meghan and Kate have extremely different outlooks on life. They are far from best friends. There's still tension between them and a sense of competition," said the confidante.

"They are civil to each other but don't have much in common."

The public seemed to enjoy the royal spat as a sport, with many still supporting Team Meghan—until it came out that it cost British taxpayers some three million pounds to renovate Frogmore Cottage to Meghan's lavish expectations.

"During the renovations, floor plans and designs changed constantly because Meghan's such a perfectionist," noted the friend. "She's a keen interior designer and worked closely with architects to ensure their new home was built with all the essentials and more. There's a fully equipped yoga studio, screening room, his and hers walk-in-closets, a huge kitchen—and the nursery is out of this world. Even Archie has a walk-in closet!" (Harry and Meghan, for their part, have denied their renovations were as glam and luxe as reported.)

The pal, who asked not to be identified, added Meghan felt that the old building needed a lot of work: "If she had her way, she would've torn down some of the property and started from scratch—but the Queen would've gone ballistic."

Many called it outrageous. "Quite a cottage, that, for a couple. You could build twenty council houses for the amount that has been spent on the royals," sniffed Kevin Maguire, associate editor of the *Daily Mirror*, referring to British public housing. "I think they have lost the plot. There is a sense of entitlement, or privilege, in that family."

The birth of Archie on May 6 should have calmed the brewing storm and been a cause for national celebration—but many were upset by the couple's refusal to pose for the traditional family photo outside the hospital where their son was born.

Royal commentator Victoria Arbiter called it a missed opportunity for Meghan and Harry to generate some goodwill. "That first photograph has the potential to be incredibly valuable," she said. "It is when you see royals take control of the narrative. They (effectively) say, 'We'll give you this picture, but in exchange you've got to leave us alone and respect our privacy.'"

Meghan, however, doesn't seem to understand the benefits of following tradition. "Meghan refused to conform to royal ways," another friend told us. "She has a strong personality, and sadly her ideas of modernizing the monarchy have back-fired. She has continued to break protocol, time and time and time again."

In September 2019, for example, Meghan and Harry declined an invitation to visit Queen Elizabeth at Balmoral, the monarch's summer home in Scotland. Instead, the Duchess traveled solo to New York City to watch her best friend, Serena Williams, play tennis—a move that many viewed as disrespectful to the Queen. Meghan's choice to leave her infant son behind also ruffled royal feathers.

"I would have thought twice about leaving my firstborn at home at the tender age of just four months in order to fly 3,500 miles to watch Serena Williams play in the US Open final," sniped the *Daily Mail*'s Sarah Vine, who called Meghan's actions "insensitive" and suggested that the young Royal get her priorities straight. "Serena is no relation. The Queen, by contrast, is baby Archie's great-grand-mother—not to mention being in her ninety-fourth year."

At least Meghan saved herself a headache by flying on a commercial jet to New York City. She and Prince Harry, who have long expressed their support for envi-ronmental causes, suffered a public relations disaster after they traveled via pri-vate plane four times in eleven days while on vacation in Spain and on the French Riviera the previous August. Commentators called them hypocritical for not considering how their private flights impacted climate change.

Friends such as music legend Elton John, who provided a plane for their use, tried to defend them. But the storm of negative publicity only grew worse when Prince William, Kate, and the children were spotted boarding a commercial flight to Scotland, en route to a visit with the Queen. (Some sensed a feud-related photo opportunity.)

Harry tried to deflect some of the heat during a speech in Amsterdam. "We can all do better, and while no one is perfect, we all have a responsibility for our own individual impact," he admitted. "The question is what we do to balance it out." He announced that he had purchased carbon offsets to soften the damage done by their private flights.

While Meghan tried to ignore the furor, she couldn't. Over the past year, she's been harshly judged on everything from her wardrobe choices to the way she holds her infant son. Her decision to guest-edit an issue of British *Vogue* was called "cheap" and "vulgar" by her blue-blooded detractors. "Everyone thinks Meghan is thick-skinned, but underneath the tough exterior, she's incredibly hurt by the constant criticism," a friend explained. "She said she doesn't read the negative stories written about her, but the reality is she can't avoid them—they're everywhere, and she makes front page news on a daily basis. Of course she's hurt."

To add insult to injury, many of the stories originated with Meghan's estranged family members. Her stateside relatives—most notably, her estranged father, Thomas Markle, and her sister, who referred to Meghan as "Princess Pushy"—served as a dial-a-quote service to media outlets looking for commentary and headlines.

It's all been quite embarrassing. A poll published in August 2019 indicated that Queen Elizabeth was Britain's favorite member of the Royal Family, with a whopping 73 percent favorability. Duchess Kate ranked fourth, behind Prince Harry and Kate's husband, Prince William. Meghan came in at number seven, after the wildly mocked Prince Philip and her father-in-law, the famously unloved Prince Charles. Indeed, Meghan's popularity had dropped six percentage points from the previous year.

"Part of the problem seems to be Meghan and Harry's perception about their place in the world," a source said. Critics chastised that they acted like VIPs, not public servants. "Do they want to be American celebrities or hard-working members of the British Royal Family?" asked Princess Diana's former private secretary, Patrick Jephson. It seems we now have our answer, as the pair have turned their backs on the Royal Family and relocated to Los Angeles.

Harry's mother, Princess Diana, would have been "appalled" by the young couple's behavior, claimed Lady Colin Campbell, a royal commentator. "She was very aware of how important it was to be gracious, while Meghan—and Harry to an extent—trot out the charm when it suits them but are otherwise graceless." She felt Meghan, "a very proud hustler," should keep in mind that being a member of the Royal Family is about service, not "hustling your way from the bottom to the top."

In a damning op-ed, British television host Piers Morgan, a former CNN anchor, went so far as to accuse Meghan and Harry of "exploiting" the tragic death of Princess Diana for their own financial gain.

Morgan—an outspoken critic of Meghan's since her engagement to

Harry—slammed the couple over their reported appearance at a JP Morgan event in Miami, Florida. Referring to Harry's ongoing struggles with grief in the wake of his mother's death, he wrote, "There's a big difference between talking about it to raise public awareness of grief-related mental health issues—and doing it privately for a big fat fee to a bunch of super-rich bankers, business tycoons, politicians and celebrities."

Fortunately, the Duchess has some strong supporters in the Royal Family—chief among them Prince Harry, of course. In 2019, he publicly sprang to her defense by condemning the "ruthless" treatment she had encountered in the media. "I cannot begin to describe how painful it has been," Harry said in a statement, adding that he had been "a silent witness to her private suffering for too long." Comparing Meghan's plight to what his mother, Princess Diana, encountered, Harry announced that he was taking legal action against a British tabloid newspaper that printed one of Meghan's private letters.

At that moment in time, Queen Elizabeth was said to be a source of strength for Meghan. "The Queen had been supportive, despite what others were saying," said the friend. "At the end of the day, HRH (Her Royal Highness) is a reasonable woman and accepts that marrying into the Royal Family isn't easy and mistakes are going to be made."

The successful royal tour of South Africa was widely seen an excellent first step toward becoming more respected in the public eye.

Even Lady Colin, who has been one of Meghan's most ardent and outspoken critics, admitted that there was still time for the young royal to turn things around. "I'm rooting for Meghan," she said after the visit. "But I think the verdict is out at the moment."

A COMMONER PRINCESS LIKE NONE BEFORE

As the sun rose over Windsor on the morning of Saturday May 19, 2018, the rays pushed away the swathes of early morning mist to reveal hundreds of forms huddled on the pavement and along the famous Royal Mile. They emerged from sleeping bags, set up deckchairs, and organized those first, essential flasks of tea.

As the trains from London began arriving—the 0518 from Paddington being the first—a steady stream of jubilant revelers in party attire waved Union Jacks, the national flag of the United Kingdom. The streets were filled with that peculiarly British sense of shared anticipation and excitement that appears only in times of national crisis or celebration.

It was the wedding of Prince Harry and Meghan Markle—a day that would transcend even the traditional pomp and pageantry of a British Royal wedding and instead become a true moment of world history. Not only had the third in line to the British throne chosen to marry a commoner, he had chosen a tough, confident, biracial American actress to be his wife and helpmeet. In doing so, he had turned centuries of tradition upside down.

As the morning wore on, the sun blazed down on the crowds. As with any occasion in Britain, this elicited a vast communal sigh of relief among spectators—but clearly, even a torrential downpour wouldn't have dampened the spirits. Thousands of well-wishers now stretched along the two-and-a-half-mile length leading up to the historic St George's chapel, where the nuptials would take place. They were six, seven deep along the tree-lined Long Walk, Castle Hill, and Windsor High Street.

Shortly before 10 a.m., Harry and Meghan's guests began arriving, an uncommonly cosmopolitan collection of superstars, nobles, and dignitaries. Cheers of recognition went up as Oprah Winfrey, Idris Elba, Earl Spencer (the brother of Diana, Princess of Wales), George and Amal Clooney, and David and Victoria Beckham made their way to St George's chapel.

The couple had extended invitations to six hundred VIPs and a lucky two thousand members of the public to view the ceremony from the grounds of the castle, chosen for their work with charities and good causes. They were invited into the most exclusive fold, directly in front of the chapel itself, where they not only enjoyed a front-row view of the arriving guests and the ceremony, but even received official goody bags—totes branded with Harry and Meghan's initials and stuffed with special commemorative chocolate, shortbread, a magnet, a bottle of Windsor Castle water, and a wedding program. When some of the privileged special guests took their wedding swag to eBay within hours of the wedding, frantic bidding saw bags being sold for five-figure sums.

That morning, the Queen, Elizabeth II, as is traditional on such occasions, blessed the impending union by bestowing official titles upon the couple. Now, like his brother, Harry was a Duke and Meghan, like her counterpart Catherine, a Duchess.

Referring to Harry by his real first name, palace said, "The Queen has today been pleased to confer a Dukedom on Prince Henry of Wales. His titles will be Duke of Sussex, Earl of Dumbarton, and Baron Kilkeel. Prince Harry thus becomes His Royal Highness The Duke of Sussex, and Ms. Meghan Markle on marriage will become Her Royal Highness The Duchess of Sussex."

"Today will be the most amazing party on the planet," said one spectator. "Harry is marrying an American—if that's not reason for a global celebration, what is?"

Little did anyone suspect at that time the Prince and his new bride would be made to stop using their Royal Highness titles less than two years later.

When Harry announced his engagement to Meghan in November 2017, the world collectively whooped with joy and then immediately began to consider what it meant for a biracial woman to marry a prominent British royal. Markle was celebrated by some as Britain's first "black princess"—a milestone for a Royal Family that had presided over centuries of slavery and colonialism. (The House of Windsor was formed after the monarchy changed its name from Saxe-Coburg and Gotha to the English Windsor because of anti-German sentiment in the United Kingdom during World War I.) The union of Harry and Meghan wasn't just a coming together of two young, adorable lovebirds. A more profound occurrence was to take place—a reconciliation and uniting of two very different histories. Lineages that had enjoyed privilege and nobility would entwine with those that had suffered oppression and slavery. The modern day Black-American experience would penetrate the fusty walls of Buckingham, Windsor, Balmoral, and Sandringham.

Past the headlines, the truth of the matter was more complex. Harry is a cocktail of bloodlines, reflecting the tangled ancestral history of the British Royal Family. Meghan can trace her ancestors back to slaves and British nobility. *This was going to be one hell of a marriage.*

In the outpouring of media analysis and commentary in the wake of the couple's announcement, much was speculated about the heritage of Prince Harry's future wife. One eminent genealogist sought to allay the fears of the more wary British by uncovering a distant link between Meghan's family and the Royals. According to genealogist Gary Boyd Roberts, Meghan is a direct descendant of England's King Edward III, who ruled from 1327 until 1377—which would technically make her and Harry seventeenth cousins. (The link was discovered to be through a certain Rev. William Skipper, a royal descendant who arrived in New England in 1639 and a distant forebear of Thomas Wayne Markle). Another expert discovered that, in the 1500s, one of Harry's ancestors, the notorious King Henry VIII, ordered the beheading of Lord Hussey, first Baron Hussey of Sleaford and another Markle ancestor. (One wonders whether this topic has ever come up during Christmas reunions at the Buckingham Palace dinner table.)

Born in Los Angeles in 1982 to parents Doria Ragland and Thomas Markle, Meghan enjoyed a happy and successful childhood, due in no small part to her innate sense of self-worth, determination, ambition, and guts. She was nicknamed "Flower" by her family for her sunny disposition and charismatic personality, but the question of her heritage and identity dogged her through her formative years, as her parents split and she grew up with her mother. As she encountered racial prejudice in school and from the world at large, she was never sure if she identified as "black" or "white." She often tells a story of a childhood dilemma in which she was asked to complete a registration form, ticking a box for "white" or "African-American" and not knowing what to do, for fear of upsetting one of her parents—she instead followed her father's advice, when she told him what had happened. "Make your own box, Meghan," he said.

That sunny morning, as a vintage Rolls Royce Phantom IV from the Queen's personal stable of luxury British cars drove Meghan and her beaming, tearful mother to the ancient Windsor chapel, where her Prince stood in military regalia waiting for her to marry him and become one of the most admired women in the world, Meghan must have reflected on that pivotal moment from her childhood. That moment when she decided that if there was no box for her to fit into—well, she would make that box herself.

FORCED TO FLEE

It was supposed to be a real-life royal fairy tale.

Britain's own Prince Charming sweeping an American actress off her feet and pledging a life of service to the Crown. Unlike Harry's mother, Meghan hit the ground running. Having learned valuable lessons from the tumultuous time Princess Diana spent as a member of the Royal Family, the Queen was determined that Meghan would have every support to help her navigate the first few months of her life as a Royal.

The country was in a haze of love for the new recruit to the family. An estimated 1.9 billion viewers had tuned in around the world to watch the couple exchange vows, and the wedding had pumped about 3.5 billion pounds into the British economy. She was clearly a valuable asset to the Firm.

The Queen had formed a bond with the American in the run-up to the wedding. Still, she shrewdly loaned her one of her most trusted aides, Samantha Cohen, in order to ensure that an old hand be present to keep an eye on Meghan. She didn't want her making any major blunders along the lines of Sarah, Duchess of York's un-royal missteps and meltdowns. Those ranged from topless tabloid photos while her husband was away serving in the royal navy, to selling out access to her ex-husband, to taking a three-million-dollar contract with Weight Watchers after being cruelly dubbed the "Duchess of Pork."

The fact that Harry was still dazed with love and devotion to his new wife made things much easier all round. Meghan naturally took the lead in the marriage and embarked on her new life with tail-wagging enthusiasm, while in public, Harry skulked awkwardly in the background, happy to let her get on with it.

Weeks after the wedding, Meghan undertook her first joint engagement with the Queen—a monumental ascension within the Firm's ranks. Notably, this came far sooner than Kate's first public visit with Her Majesty. The pair opened the Mersey Gateway Bridge in Cheshire and the Storyhouse Theater in Chester, and attended a lunch at the Chester Town Hall. Against all odds, the event was a success. Traveling to Chester in the Queen's private train—another very high honor indeed, seeing as not even William and Harry have been permitted to use it— Meghan and her then ninety-two-year-old grandmother-in-law laughed, joked, and chatted with each other. The Queen was sufficiently chilled to indulge Meghan a slight mix-up about who should get in a car first (clue: not Meghan). Meghan made sure that she was deferential and polite to the monarch and behaved with immaculate elegance. For her part, the Queen was seen nattering happily to Meghan throughout the day and even roaring with laughter at one point. As a gift, the Queen gave her a pair of diamond earrings to mark the occasion.

Video from the event shows Meghan was also working hard to ditch her California twang and instead adopting a slightly wobbly British accent as she greeted rambunctious crowds. One woman yelled out to Meghan asking how she was enjoying her new role. "It is wonderful, I'm really enjoying it," Meghan said, sounding like a tipsy Sloane—a British reference to a young woman from a rich upper-class background. The woman then told her to "give our love to Harry," to which the Duchess replied: "Ay will do. That means an orful lot to us. He's the best husband evah."

But inside Buckingham Palace, and behind the scenes, things weren't as they seemed. Following whispers of tension between the pair, all eyes were on Kate and Meghan as they attended the Women's Singles Final of the US Open on July 14. Meghan's close friend, Serena Williams, was facing down Angelique Kerber, a three-time German Grand Slam champion who'd unwittingly been cast in the most-watched event in the world . . . and it wasn't because of what happened on the court. Given her close friendship with Serena, Meghan had chirpily offered to get Kate a courtside seat, to which Kate politely replied that actually, the Royal offices could sort that out for them, according to a source. The two sat by each other in VIP seats, making polite small talk. There was no roaring laughter or diamond earrings in this case.

The wariness felt by some of Harry's older friends began to make itself known that summer. "Skippy" Inskip, a pal, felt he was being distanced from the Duke of

Sussex. Perhaps it was because of his rather juicy speech at the wedding, full of racy tales and fond memories of bad behavior, such as the infamous time when Harry was caught on camera cavorting naked during a game of strip billiards at a "high rollers hotel suite" in Las Vegas in 2012. What happened in Vegas on that occasion certainly didn't stay there, and pictures of Harry naked and hiding his modesty were circulated around the world.

While embarrassing for Buckingham Palace originally, with the passage of time, it became somewhat of a folklore story.

Six weeks after their own wedding, Harry and Meghan and the Windsors were back at St George's Chapel, this time for the wedding of Princess Eugenie and Jack Brooksbank, a British wine merchant and brand ambassador who married the youngest daughter of Sarah, Duchess of York, and Prince Andrew, Duke of York. Onlookers were astonished at the change in Harry in such a short period of time. Far from being the cheeky life and soul of the party, he looked tense and unhappy. They sat next to a beaming William and Kate, looking as if they'd just had a major fight. At one point, Meghan even turned to Harry and snapped at him. Using film from the event, body language expert Judi James noted: "For some reason Harry looks distracted and fidgety as they wait in the pews, while Meghan sits facing front and looking demure and impervious, with a polite social smile on her face."

She added, "Harry mutters something to Meghan and her eyebrows raise before she turns her head towards him, using what looks like an emphatic gesture with each word of her reply." Meghan continued her conversation with Zara Tindall (the daughter of Princess Anne and Mark Phillips and the eldest grand-daughter of Queen Elizabeth II) on her other side, leaving Harry looking visibly upset and discombobulated, as if he had been told off by an angry parent. "Harry rubs his face, chews his lips, and leans into the side of his seat like a child that has just been told to sit still," observed James.

To the family, the unease they had felt about Meghan's control over Harry was now becoming stronger. While his discomfort with the press and being watched all the time like a hawk was known and understood, he was a dutiful young Royal, good-looking, charismatic—and a brave soldier. What's more, he was known as a clown who could laugh easily at himself. Within his trusted circle of friends and family, Harry's company was usually a riot of cackles and giggles. But now—suddenly—it appeared that Meghan had changed him.

Later on at the reception Meghan put her foot in it when she decided that it would be the ideal moment to announce that she and Harry were expecting their first child. This was a huge social gaffe, even if you were not a Royal—stealing the limelight from Eugenie, who was furious, as was her mother, Sarah.

Harry would have been only too painfully aware just how big a no-no this would be, yet he went along with Meghan's wishes. Following the wedding and the premature announcement, there were also some concerned discussion within the family about the speed at which Meghan had gotten pregnant, ensuring her connection with the family was now irrevocable and ceding even more power to her.

The next day, Harry and Meghan departed for Sydney, Australia, for the first stop of their first royal tour, where, on arrival, they announced their pregnancy to the world at large. The Australians—for whom the Queen serves as the nation's sovereign and head of state—were thrilled for the couple, as Meghan played the perfect part of newlywed Duchess. As Harry bumbled and wilted in the periphery of the spotlight, Meghan shone.

Throughout the two-week tour, Meghan got up at 4 a.m. to do yoga and baked banana bread late at night. A week into the trip, Harry appeared at the opening of the Invictus Games, a sporting event where injured servicemen from around the world compete. The launch was usually one of his favorite commitments, and his past appearances had been exuberant. This year, he caused concern when he showed up looking drawn and tense, grinding his teeth and seeming bewildered and exhausted. The Australians whooped and cheered him, which seemed to bring a smile to his face, and pregnant Meghan, in yet another dramatic and costly outfit, clutched his arm.

If the previous six months had shown signs of fundamental changes taking place within the new royal household, when the couple returned from Australia, there was a shock in store for everyone. The less than effusive welcome Meghan believed William and Kate had shown her was irritating and annoying her, according to a source. Things had to change. Having only lived a few weeks next door to his brother and his family, Harry now announced that he and Meghan would be moving out. They would move to Frogmore Cottage in Windsor, over twenty miles away on the outskirts of London. Meghan wanted to renovate the property—built in 1801 at the direction of Queen Charlotte, the wife of King George III—to her specifications.

"Windsor is a very special place for Their Royal Highnesses and they are grateful that their official residence will be on the estate," Kensington Palace said in a statement.

Yet at this moment, British tabloids had picked up on the simmering tensions with William and Kate—and knew that the decision to move to Frogmore was in fact a direct snub to the couple. Insiders claimed Meghan and Harry had been "forced to flee."

"The initial plan was for Harry and Meghan to move out of their cottage in the grounds of Kensington Palace and into one of the main apartments. But there was "too much tension between the brothers," a source said. The regal writing was on the wall.

"A BIT OF TENSION"

By the end of 2017, Harry and William's infamously tight bond was not so much suffering a "bit of tension," but said to be "almost irretrievably broken," according to Palace insiders. "William is used to being head of their joint household," said a source, adding it was apparently he who suggested Meghan and Harry consider moving to Frogmore Cottage, rather than staying next door to the Cambridges at Kensington.

"Harry didn't think William was rolling out the red carpet for Meghan and told him so," a source said of the brothers' rift. "They had a bit of a fallout, which was only resolved when Prince Charles stepped in and asked William to make an effort." But even with paternal intervention, the relationship between the two became frostier. One source insisted the problem was "only between the brothers," yet another palace insider confided, "Meghan and Kate are just simply very different people."

At the same time, the third of Meghan's close aides at the Palace quit. To lose one aide in upper Royal circles is notable, but to lose three within six months is alarming. Harry's longtime private secretary, Ed Lane Fox, stepped down just before the wedding, after five years working alongside the Prince. It was rumored that Meghan distrusted his closeness to Harry and felt he wasn't sufficiently on her team. He was replaced by Samantha Cohen, private secretary to both Harry and Meghan, who had been specially appointed by the Queen. She announced in turn that she would leave their service after the birth of the baby. Samantha— also known as "Samantha The Panther," one of the most trusted advisors to the monarch—had worked with the Royal Family for seventeen years before six months at Meghan's beck and call, when she decided to try other career options years.

In *The Times* newspaper, a source close to Meghan said diplomatically: "Going forward, Meghan might need someone cut from a slightly different cloth to traditional courtiers, someone who is not a career civil servant or royal insider. Sam will be a huge loss."

Samantha's departure came hot on the heels of the rapid resignation of Melissa Toubati, a personal assistant to Meghan, who abruptly quit after just six months on the job, thanks to what courtiers had jokingly referred to as "Hurricane Meghan." It was the Duchess' "particular brand of 'up and at 'em West Coast energy" and routine of "getting up at 5 a.m. [and] bombarding aides with texts, and her eyebrow-raising fashion" that pushed the aide over the edge, a source explained. "Meghan put a lot of demands on her and it ended up with her in tears. Melissa is a total professional and fantastic at her job, but things came to a head and it was easier for them both to go their separate ways."

Finally, in an unprecedented move, Kate had to step in to tell off Meghan over her strict attitude toward her own staff members. They had been receiving the full force of the Californian despite not even technically working for her. "That's unacceptable," Kate is said to have warned Meghan. "They're my staff and I speak to them." Tensions were rising.

"Meghan can be difficult. She has very high standards and is used to working in a Hollywood environment," a royal insider explained to *The Sun*. "However, there's a different degree of respect in the royal household and Kate has always been very careful about how she has acted around staff."

Another source within the Palace revealed, more succinctly: "Her and Kate fell out when she lashed out at Kate's staff." On the Sussexes' move to Frogmore and the allocation of Palace staff to the new household, the source said: "Staff would be lying if they said they didn't hope they end up with Kate and William because Harry and Meghan have developed a reputation of being demanding, temperamental—and, at times, rude."

The speculation over the move prompted renewed analysis of the brothers' close relationship and how their marriages had changed their internal dynamic. "Harry knows he will always be in William's shadow and for many years he has felt like a bit of a spare wheel, dragging along behind his brother and then later,

Kate," a diplomatic friend revealed. "Now he has a life of his own and a family of his own. It is perfectly natural to want to be more independent."

While Harry tried to keep on top of all the internal disputes with the family, Meghan's high-profile charity causes were at the top of her agenda. Immediately after the marriage, she dived in, naming various charities that would henceforth benefit from her patronage. A Palace insider claimed: "It was all too rushed, without proper research."

Her first priority was supporting the victims of the recent Grenfell Tower fire in London, the tragic disaster that saw a housing block go up in flames, leaving seventy dead, with many victims from ethnic minorities and disadvantaged backgrounds. The government's own response to the calamity was deemed too little, too late. In contrast, the Queen's genuine concerns and sadness for the victims of the tragedy had been widely applauded in the media; she was praised for her low-key visits to the site. Meghan made numerous visits to the community kitchen that had been set up on site and eventually produced *Together: Our Community Cookbook* in September 2018. The book was well-intentioned, but it somehow forgot to include a single recipe of British origin, something that wasn't unnoticed by Kensington Palace staff.

Another chosen charity was Smart Works, which used quality second-hand clothes and coaching to help women from low-income backgrounds attend job interviews. All was well until Meghan showed up for a public meeting with clients of the charity in a £6,000 outfit. The calamity caused more than a few winces in the press, but the media was still in love with Meghan, and the matter barely caused a ripple.

With swelling public support, Harry and Meghan were on their way to Frogmore Cottage with their first-born on the way, and life on the surface was perfect.

Meghan had also promised Harry he would emerge in his own right, his own man, away from William's overbearing judgment and constant advising, recalled a source. Just because their mother had married in haste and repented in leisure, that didn't mean that he and Meghan were facing the same fate. And why did William have to keep voicing his "concerns"—couldn't they see how happy he was?

"DEEPLY HELD DIFFERENCES"

Frogmore Cottage, Harry and Meghan's new house, was beautiful. There was no denying its legacy: from Queen Charlotte, the history books have noted that theologian Henry James Sr. lived with his family at the cottage in the 1840s. After their tenure, Abdul Karim, personal secretary to Queen Victoria, moved in, with his wife and father in 1897, before the exiled Russian Grand Duchess Xenia Alexandrovna stayed there in the 1920s. At the start of the twenty-first century, the cottage was broken up into five separate units for Windsor estate workers.

The Duke and Duchess of Sussex could renovate the garden cottage how they liked. This would make Meghan happy—and that, in succession, made Harry happy, too. Things had gotten off to a bit of a shaky start, with the Palace staff acting hoity-toity around Meghan—"but that was just because they didn't get her," said a source. She was, after all, a bona fide television star who "had so much to impart and so much love to give," said one Meghan pal. But a royal aide had hinted that Meghan was the royal equivalent of Yoko Ono, the wife of John Lennon blamed for breaking up the Beatles. Here the Sussexes' closest aides were comparing Meghan to an ambitious, foreign-born older woman who was accused of exploiting a needy, confused, world-famous young man and breaking him off from his friends? It all sounded too familiar.

But so what if a few haters and stick-in-the-mud old traditionalists didn't like the way they did things—what was it Meghan had said in an old blog post? "Be the change you want to see in the world." That, of course, was a repost of one of the more famous quotes from Mahatma Gandhi, an Indian lawyer, anticolonial nationalist, and political ethicist. Meghan had no vehicle presence to preach—at least not now. But she and Harry had talked about relaunching their personal online branding presence imminently, and it would then only be a case of when, not if, Meghan could get back to inspiring and sharing her learnings and journeys with their millions of fans worldwide.

***

Harry and Meghan also underwent a few more teething problems as they settled into Frogmore. Two more staffers had quit, bringing the total to a remarkable five since the wedding. The latest casualties: an assistant to the personal assistant, Amy Pickerill, and Meghan's senior female protection officer from Scotland Yard. The latter was said to be exasperated because Meghan had ignored advice about venturing into risky crowd situations and had ended up needing to be yanked out of a chaotic scrum. The *Sunday Times* claimed wanting to be seen as "one of the people" presented challenges to her protection team, "unlike someone who has grown up in the Royal Family and has been used to having close protection from an early age, it can be quite constraining." In October 2018, the protection officer was with the couple on a Pacific tour when she was forced to rush the Duchess out of a solo visit to a market in Fiji, cutting it short because of the crowds and sweltering conditions.

There were also considerable rumblings over Meghan's appearance. In the early days of Meghan's pregnancy, insiders told the *Mail on Sunday* that Meghan had earned a stern telling-off for her shorter hemlines above the knee, constant shout-outs to non-British designers, and her fashionista fondness for black, which royals traditionally only don when they are in mourning.

"Meghan was being told she needed to start dressing less like a Hollywood star and more like a Royal," recounted a well-placed insider from within the fashion team. This was after Meghan made the controversial decision not to wear a hat during her first official appearance with the Queen back in August . . . despite being told to.

It's also believed, according to one source I spoke with, that Meghan's rotating door of Hollywood friends such as Serena Williams, Idris Elba, and George and Amal Clooney were also raising eyebrows with some of the more traditional members of the family who preferred to mix with fellow aristocrats with less pizzazz.

The dramas and alarms, the nerves and tensions, the tears and tiaras—all reached boiling point in December 2018, when Kate was seen visiting the Queen for a discreet conversation. It's rumored that Kate was seeking advice from her grandmother-in-law, a long and staunch ally of hers, over how to deal with the unpredictable and troublesome new Duchess. Despite the Queen's extraordinary efforts to get along with Meghan, she too knew something had to give. According to an aide, she recalled when her youngest son Edward's new wife, Sophie, Countess of Wessex, married into the family in 1999 and had a somewhat bumpy entry to the clan. But then, with goodwill on all sides and ensuring she was in regular contact with the monarch, Sophie went on to build an "incredibly close" relationship with the Queen and remains one of her favorites.

Following Kate's meeting, the Queen was keen to lend Meghan her support, Palace sources said. "Her Majesty has seen it all and could offer the duchess some helpful advice at the moment," one source said, adding: "[Meghan] would do well to nurture that relationship and pop over for the occasional cup of tea with the Queen. That is what Sophie Wessex has quietly done so well. She will go over for a chat or take the children to watch some TV with her. She has built up that relationship, now they are incredibly close and discuss everything. Meghan doesn't need an invitation—this is a family, after all."

A few days later, Kate was overheard bringing up the latest Royal pregnancy at an engagement at Leeds University. Asked if she was excited about the new baby, she enthusiastically cried: "Yeah, absolutely!" "It's such a special time to have little kiddies," she added.

Traditionally, each step of a senior Royal pregnancy is logged and noted by an adoring press and excited public. A baby who will be in line to the throne is still a big deal, no matter how far down the line of succession. People want to know—and are always told—where the baby will be born, who the medical team overseeing the birth will be, how the mother is preparing herself, and who the godparents will be. It's been a cherished part of the public's relationship with the Royals for decades, and is important for the family, as it makes the population feel invested in the Royal tot, to welcome it to the national family and celebrate it suitably.

Unsurprisingly, things were to be different in the case of Baby Sussex. But as the country and the world celebrated the couple's happy news, no one could have predicted how different things would be in just a few months.

As the couple hunkered down for Meghan's pregnancy Frogmore Cottage was undergoing a breakneck three-million-pound renovation.

The cottage, nestled on the picturesque grounds of the Windsor Estate, is also home to the Mausoleum, the royal cemetery, where Victoria is buried with Prince Albert. Ironically, it's also where Harry's great-great uncle, the abdicated King Edward VIII, is buried with his wife and Meghan's spiritual forebear, Wallis Simpson. All of them were keeping a ghostly eye on proceedings and "no doubt, would have had plenty to say about it all," joked one royal aide. (Like Harry, King Edward VIII dramatically abandoned his birthright—giving up the Crown for the woman he loved.) Just like Edward and Wallis Simpson, the catalyst for the scandal here was an ambitious, controversial American woman. In 1931, then known as the Prince of Wales, Edward met and fell in love with American socialite Wallis Simpson. After George V's death, the prince became King Edward VIII. However, because his marriage to Simpson, an American divorcée, was forbidden, Edward abdicated the throne after ruling for less than a year.

Plans for Frogmore submitted to the local council showed that the Sussexes installed, among other things, an "eco-boiler"; a yoga studio with a custom-built spring floor; a nursery with nontoxic, vegan, organic paint; and a studio for Meghan's mother, Doria, when she came to visit her new grandchild. The new residence would also soak up approximately five million pounds a year on security for the couple and their baby. (For their part, in court papers, Meghan and Harry described the reporting on their renovations of Frogmore Cottage as "made up," "false," and "misleading.")

Harry and Meghan also defended their decision to split from William and Kate by saying they were moving for the sake of their unborn child.

"The Cambridges have their garden in the back, which is nice, but there is no real other space for children to play in," said one source. "Frogmore, which is inside the Windsor security zone [where the main house is only open to the public for a couple of days a year] is secluded, peaceful, tranquil and, most importantly, private. No one will see them coming or going."

There would, of course, be a trade-off: Harry and Meghan were now twenty-five miles out of London, so official engagements would require some travel.

"Frogmore is just lovely," reiterated the insider. "It will be a beautiful place for the Sussexes to bring up their child. Harry and Meghan are incredibly happy and deservedly so."

In December, Meghan's grueling lifestyle and endless haranguing (as she saw it) by the media boiled over.

That month, a royal insider told these authors that Meghan was "fed-up" with the rumors and her inability to "stand up for herself" on social media. Since *The Tig*, her lifestyle blog, had gone offline, Meghan had not had a forum to share her daily thoughts, whims, and opinions. The pressure of not being able to tell everyone what she was feeling at any given moment was getting to her.

"It's just been frustrating and stressful to have no voice," the source said, at the time.

"She's always relied on her own voice to stand up for others, and for herself. So not being able to say anything is a debilitating feeling. She's always been so independent, her entire life, and that's all been taken away from her. She's always been able to clap back on social media and now she can't." The Royals were taken aback—Kate especially was said to be severely unimpressed.

The Royals, as it happened, were all keen on social media, with even the Queen having her own Twitter account (although it was unlikely she was up until 4 a.m. at night getting involved in online spats). The Palace appreciated the role of social media in forging and maintaining relationships across its numerous channels and the ability to smoothly churn out family news, feel-good items of gossip, pictures, and approved messages in line with prearranged guidelines. What was considered off-limits were spontaneous, off-message, opinionated tweets and posts that bypassed the Palace's well-oiled press machine. Meghan's pre-Harry opinions on issues relating to feminism, global politics, and climate change were so vigorously expressed that she found it more or less intolerable to be silenced.

As Christmas 2018 loomed, the Royals sent out their cards. Usually, a cheery family image would dominate these, nothing especially avant-garde or esoteric. This year, however, The Sussexes sent out a card that, instead of cheery toothy grins and chunky knit jumpers, looked like an ad for a new Netflix psychodrama. Taken on the night of their wedding in high-contrast monochrome, the photo showed the pair standing silhouetted from behind, looming up from the ground, in high contrast monochrome staring at a fireworks display. It might have looked splendid on the photographer's portfolio, but "the public felt Harry and Meghan were—literally—turning their backs on them," according to another royal watcher. Meanwhile, Catherine and William released a picture of their family of five, all dressed down, perched on a tree trunk outside their country home in Norfolk. The three youngsters, Prince George, five, Princess Charlotte, three, and Prince Louis, seven months, were seen cuddling up to their parents. Everyone looked ecstatic, as if they were in an upmarket leisurewear catalogue.

But as far as Christmas went, all talk of rivalries was put to one side. The year before, Meghan had charmed and twinkled her way through her first Royal Christmas, like a character in a romcom, making cute little gaffes and being cheerily forgiven by charmingly understanding, yet eccentric, Royals. This year, things were a little different. Despite everyone bringing their festive A-game to the Sandringham table, brothers William and Harry were noticeably cool with each other. That Christmas morning, they were all photographed walking to church together. Royal body language expert Judi James examined the photographs of the foursome as they arrived at St Mary's church to provide a peek into what was really going on.

"It's interesting to note that while Meghan and Harry walked arm-in-arm, which is just standard PDA for them, Kate and William simply walked side by side. But take another look at William and Harry. Apart from having very rigid, fixed smiles on their faces, I didn't see anything in the way of glances or exchanges between them," James said.

"They've always been seen laughing and sharing jokes, they usually have lots of 'tie-signs' [gestures that signal closeness] between them. They've both got their hands stuck in their pockets and I didn't see any connection signals between them at all."

Following the traditional lunch blowout, everyone gathered as usual, to watch the Queen's speech. To nobody's surprise, her 2018 speech included a message that was intended for a country bitterly divided over Brexit. But many felt it also had a pointed relevance much closer to home.

"Even with the most deeply held differences," she intoned in her prim manner, "treating the other person with respect and as a fellow human being is always a good first step towards greater understanding."

As the Royals watched the broadcast, in silence, not a few furtive looks were cast over to where the newest additions to the family were seated.

UNHAPPY BIRTHDAY

If 2019 was going to start on a positive note, any dreams of harmony were shattered when Meghan received a clear and indubitable snub from her sister-in-law.

Kate celebrated her thirty-seventh birthday at home with family on January 9, 2019. "Kate had a gathering for her thirty-seventh birthday at Kensington Palace," a source said. "The guest list consisted of her, William, the kids, her mum, dad, sister Pippa and her husband James Matthews. Noticeably, Harry and Meghan were not invited."

Meghan was said to be furious. But not as angry as her husband, who couldn't control his rage and contacted William, a source close to the prince said. It was at this moment William told his brother that he felt Meghan was tearing the Royal Family apart. "Even though they don't get on, the Queen and Prince Charles had asked that William and Harry make a good public show of trying to make nice," confided an insider. "Poor Kate was so nervous about her own birthday and how to handle the family drama, she was almost in tears."

Leading royal commentators were now openly predicting things would only get worse between the brothers and their wives. Lady Colin Campbell—a close friend of the boys' late mum—claimed Harry was "beguiled by Meghan" and added she had "considerably changed him" as a man.

"William was quite concerned that the relationship had moved so quickly and being close to Harry, probably the only person close enough to voice his concern," observed the noted royal author Katie Nicholl. "What was meant as well-intended brotherly advice just riled Harry. He saw that as criticism. I don't think things have been quite right ever since."

Worse was to come when it was leaked that Meghan had told Harry she wanted to return to the small screen as an actor. In the past, her acting career was limited only by her talent and her ability to persuade people to give her a break; now that more sizable and weightier roles would no doubt be available to her, she was excited at the prospect of transitioning to the silver screen, and possibly even winning an Oscar.

"It's always been her secret ambition—as it is any actor," revealed a source, who added that Meghan's former showbiz agent, Gina Nelthorpe-Cowne, had confirmed an eventual return to acting by saying, "I'm sure she'll make a movie again."

Harry was supportive of the idea and in January of 2020 was filmed pitching his wife's talents to former Disney CEO Bob Iger in a face-to-face meeting on a red carpet.

"You know she does voiceovers," Harry told Iger.

"Oh, really?" Iger replied.

"Did you know that?" Harry appeared to say, with the interaction caught on camera.

"Ah, I did not know that," Iger replied.

"You seem surprised," the Duke said and then pointed briefly at Meghan, who was standing right near them, chatting with Beyoncé and Jay-Z. Harry added: "But yeah, she's really interested."

"Sure," Iger replied. "We'd love to try."

William, on the other hand, was firmly against the idea.

"William has always thought it'd be tacky and he knew he'd have the support of the Queen in this opinion," said a source. "Everyone was worried this will spark a new chapter in Harry and William's clash over Meghan."

A Palace informant expressed dismay over Harry's impromptu pitch session: "For the Queen, there's an element of cringe factor. To watch Harry groveling to the boss of Disney is nothing short of uncouth. She is embarrassed at this debacle. How could she not be asking herself, 'Why are members of my family selling themselves off to the highest bidder?'"

Speaking to the *Daily Star*, Meghan's half sister, Samantha, said it seemed her sister was using the Royal Family as "a launch pad for high places that *Suits* [her final TV acting role, which she left when she met Harry] couldn't get her."

"The Disney movie would have been fine if initiated after leaving royal roles but seems inappropriate prematurely. And disrespectful of royal protocol," Samantha said. "It's like cheating on a spouse and giving a phone number for a dinner date before being divorced."

While Royals offering themselves up for promotional gigs isn't unprecedented—another of the Queen's grandsons, the lesser-known Peter Phillips, has been advertising milk in China—no one as close to the inner sanctum, sixth in line to the throne, has actively solicited work in such a brazen way while still a working royal.

"Senior members of the Royal Family are looking at this and wishing it had never occurred," said a source connected to the Palace. "What happens next is even more worrisome. Within the establishment, there were controls. But a rogue Royal could be a disaster, as history has proven."

"Prince Charles has privately told people he wishes Harry hadn't have taken this step."

Before any more scandal could occur, an extraordinary intervention took place. Apparently motivated by a fierce sense of collective outrage, five of Meghan's "closest friends" offered to speak to America's *People* magazine. It was a jaw-dropping piece of public relations puffery, designed to show that caring, sharing Meghan was still the same as ever.

The strange thing was that the women all asked to remain anonymous, in order to "protect the private relationships they all hold dear."

"After maintaining their silence for nearly two years, five women who form an essential part of Meghan's inner circle have spoken with *People*," trumpeted the magazine. They speak to "stand up against the global bullying we are seeing and speak the truth about our friend," said a "long-time friend and supposed former costar."

The "friends" all sang from the same hymn sheet, praising Meghan for her warmth, her love of kids, her relentless selflessness, her simple joy and happiness at their wedding, her love of Harry and his family, her attention to her husband—cooking nightly for him—and her abiding adoration of muddy dogs.

It was a masterstroke of timing. With almost uncanny timing, *People*'s article "set the record straight" on the topics that were making the headlines daily.

The interviewees' anonymity, and the uniform, bland, scripted tone of their words, indicated that chances were slim, to say the least, that Meghan wasn't somehow behind the "spontaneous" outburst of concern.

"We've all been to their cottage," said one close confidante. "It's small and she's made it cozy, but the perception of their lifestyle and the reality are two different things. Meg cooks for herself and Harry every single day."

The "friend" warmed to their theme and got into their stride, much to *People*'s delight.

"Meg has silently sat back and endured the lies and untruths, we worry about what this is doing to her and the baby. It's wrong to put anyone under this level of emotional trauma, let alone when they're pregnant."

The article went on: "A 'selfless' friend who writes thank-you notes for reasons big and small and is 'the best listener,'" said a former colleague. "We talk daily. And the first thing out of her mouth is, 'How are the kids? How are you?' I'm not even allowed to ask about her until she finds out about me."

As if Meghan's chakras weren't thrumming enough, Royal documentary film-maker Nick Bullen, who had already made a couple of Markle-related films and had interviewed each of the main players in the drama, publicly described the difficult state of the family's internal dynamics.

"I think the biggest question is what's going to happen with the Markles," said Bullen, speaking to FOX News in December. "That to me is the biggest issue. William and Harry . . . things will ultimately resort itself. But how can [the Markles] repair what they have done? That's pretty tricky. Thomas and [sister] Samantha have both been speaking to the press, nonstop. We even interviewed Samantha recently for a program and her view is that this is not going to get fixed anytime soon."

It was unlikely to be resolved anytime soon, as long as Samantha and Meghan's half-brother Thomas Jr. could keep making lucrative media appearances about their estranged relationship. As a former tabloid editor, this author can attest they'd get hundreds—if not thousands—for a couple of quotes, or more if encouraged to stage a scene such as gate-crashing Buckingham Palace with camera in tow. Her own blood both veered between bitter character assassinations (Meghan was a "shallow social climber," according to Samantha and "a jaded, shallow, conceited woman," said her half brother) and mawkish sentimentality about their apparently happy childhoods together (Samantha also recalled Meghan as "very animated, very charming, very lively," and "absolutely lovely" [at times]).

But at the heart of the matter was Meghan's inner reluctance to contact her father. Meghan had no compunction about cutting people out of her life; she isolated herself from her embarrassing dad, a broken, tragic figure. As he repeatedly made the rounds of breakfast television sofas or did interviews with tabloids, he sadly recounted, time and again, how he had not heard from or seen his daughter for an eternity.

Following the wedding, in August 2018, Meghan had written an impassioned letter to her father, expressing her hurt and pain at his ongoing interviews with the press and for his "victimizing" of her. A friend had summarized the letter in the *People* feature: "She's like, 'Dad. I'm so heartbroken. I love you, I have one father. Please stop victimizing me through the media so we can repair our relationship.'"

With that quote, Meghan may have overplayed her hand. In response to the *People* article, Thomas Markle sold the letter to Britain's *Mail on Sunday* newspaper, in a supposed effort to show that Meghan and Harry "misunderstood" him. The letter did show one thing: Meghan must have shared the contents of the private communication with her friends before mailing it, as they appeared to have quoted directly from it in *People*.

Meghan almost evaporated with fury, according to a source. In addition, the world could see what she had shared in private with her father. Her begging him to stop the damaging revelations, the reiteration of what she considered lies, his ignoring her anguished concern for his health:

> *Daddy,*
>
> *It is with a heavy heart that I write this, not understanding why you have chosen to take this path, turning a blind eye to the pain you're causing.*
>
> *Your actions have broken my heart into a million pieces—not simply because you have manufactured such unnecessary and unwarranted pain, but by making the choice to not tell the truth as you are puppeteered in this. Something I will never understand.*

You've told the press that you called me to say you weren't coming to the wedding—that didn't happen because you never called.

You've said I never helped you financially and you've never asked me for help which is also untrue; you sent me an email last October that said: 'If I've depended too much on you for financial help then I'm sorry but please could you help me more not as a bargaining chip for my loyalty.'

I have only ever loved, protected, and defended you, offering whatever financial support I could worrying about your health . . . and always asking how I could help.

So, the week of the wedding to hear about you having a heart attack through a tabloid was horrifying. I called and texted . . . I begged you to accept help—we sent someone to your home . . . and instead of speaking to me to accept this or any help, you stopped answering your phone and chose to only speak to tabloids. If you love me, as you tell the press you do, please stop.

Please allow us to live our lives in peace.

Please stop lying, please stop creating so much pain, please stop exploiting my relationship with my husband . . .

I realize you are so far down this rabbit hole that you feel (or may feel) there's no way out, but if you take a moment to pause I think you'll see that being able to live with a clear conscience is more valuable than any payment in the world.

I pleaded with you to stop reading the tabloids. On a daily basis you fixated and clicked on the lies they were writing about me, especially manufactured by your other daughter, who I barely know.

You watched me silently suffer at the hand of her vicious lies, I crumbled inside.

We all rallied around to support and protect you from day one, and this you know.

So to hear about the attacks you've made at Harry in the press, who was nothing but patient, kind and understanding with you is perhaps the most painful of all.

For some reason you continue fabricating these stories,

manufacturing this fictitious narrative, and entrenching yourself deeper into this web you've spun.

The only thing that helps me sleep at night is the faith and knowing that a lie can't live forever. I believed you, I trusted you, and told you I loved you.

You haven't reached out to me since the week of our wedding, and while you claim you have no way of contacting me, my phone number has remained the same.

This you know. No texts, no missed calls, no outreach from you—just more global interviews you're being paid to do and say harmful and hurtful things that are untrue.

The betrayal, to Meghan, was breathtaking. So too was the *Mail*'s analysis, via a handwriting expert who, the paper claimed, showed the Duchess as a "narcissistic showman whose self-control is wavering."

Ignoring Meghan's desperate requests that he stop speaking to the papers, Thomas then gave a number of interviews to promote the release of the letter. He contended it spelled out Meghan telling him their relationship was done.

Thomas also claimed he had issued the letter because he felt the *People* story was false, one-sided, and frantically skewed against him. Thomas had claimed he couldn't reach Meghan, and one of *People*'s sources claimed that was false. "He knows how to get in touch with her," said Meghan's friend. "He's never called; he's never texted. It's super-painful."

Robert Jobson, author of *Charles at Seventy: Thoughts, Hopes and Dreams*, noted that Thomas was not in the best of health and felt his daughter Meghan should "make contact with him and to try and build bridges."

"I understand (there are) many people who feel he is a sad and attention-seeking figure. But I believe Meghan is playing a dangerous game," he told the *Daily Express*. "Thomas Markle has been stupid and naive in his dealings with the media. But why should he be an expert? He is reaching out to her and sounded desperate."

Once Thomas published the letter, this time in London's *Mail on Sunday*, Meghan had had enough. She announced she was suing the newspaper for publishing the highly personal note, and her solicitors (lawyers) filed papers early in

October 2019, claiming publishing the letter was a breach of copyright, infringed her privacy, and was a breach of the Data Protection Act.

In January 2020, lawyers for the newspaper stated that Meghan "knowingly" allowed her friends to leak details of the letter to the media. She "caused or permitted" five close friends to speak anonymously to the US magazine *People*, to attack Thomas. The court filing also insisted that Meghan had never denied that she gave her consent to *People* magazine's five sources. The meaning and effect of the "one-sided and/or misleading" account in *People* "was to suggest Markle had made false claims about his dealings with his daughter."

In other words, Meghan was now, unbelievably, being accused of invading her *own* privacy.

The *Mail on Sunday*'s defense also stated: "The *People* interview stated that Mr. Markle had responded to the letter with a letter of his own in which he asked for a 'photo op' with [Meghan], with the implicit suggestion that he was seeking to make money from a photograph of him with [her]. This was false."

The media organization's legal eagles added, "Mr. Markle had in fact written, 'I wish we could get together and take a photo for the whole world to see. If you and Harry don't like me? Fake it for one photo and maybe some of the Press will finally shut up!' None of Mr. Markle's account of events or feelings about those events was mentioned in the *People* interview."

The lawyers said it was apparent from Meghan's neat handwriting and immaculate presentation of the letter that she anticipated it being read by others—or possibly disclosed to the media. In legal papers obtained for this book, the newspaper argued far from being a private and personal communication, Meghan actually meant for it to be disclosed to the public: "It is apparent from the Letter that the Claimant [i.e., the Duchess] took great care over its presentation. The Letter appears to have been being immaculately copied out by the Claimant in her own elaborate handwriting from a previous draft. There are no crossings-out or amendments as there usually are with a spontaneous draft. It is to be inferred also from the care the Claimant took over the presentation of the letter that she anticipated it being disclosed to and read by third parties."

Meghan went on to claim the British tabloids had waged a three-year campaign against her, printing a litany of falsehoods. In court filings, obtained by this author, she set out an extensive list of "false" and "absurd" stories. She disputed spending five thousand pounds for a copper bath, five hundred thousand pounds on soundproofing, and building an entire new wing of their home at Frogmore—and charging it to taxpayers. She told the court this was all "completely untrue." She also complained about a "deliberately inflammatory" story that connected her enjoyment of avocado toast to "murder" and "human rights" abuses, and another that linked a community kitchen project she supports to Islamist jihadists. (For its part, the newspaper said: "These allegations are nonsense. As we have said before, we will be defending this case vigorously. We do not intend to provide a running commentary on it.")

***

However, an examination of the court filings shows just how distraught Meghan felt, at least at the time, about the coverage. It also raised the specter of whether the British media's coverage of Meghan is racist and stoked by entrenched attitudes that the Royals are a white, hereditary monarchy.

The *Mail:* "Harry's girl is (almost) straight outta Compton: Gang-scarred home of her mother revealed—so will he be dropping by for tea?"
Markle: "The statement that the Claimant lived or grew up in Compton (or anywhere near to it) is false. The fact that the Defendant chose to stereotype this entire community as being 'plagued by crime and riddled with street gangs' and thereby suggest (in the first few days of her relationship being revealed) that the Claimant came from a crime-ridden neighborhood is completely untrue as well as intended to be divisive. The Claimant will also refer to the fact that the article cites her aunt as living in 'gang-afflicted Inglewood' in order to bolster this negative and damaging impression of where this (black) side of her family is said to come from. In fact, Ava Burrow (said to be 'the actress' aunt') is not her aunt or any blood relation at all, a fact which if correctly stated would have undermined the narrative which the Defendant was intended to convey."

The *Mail:* "Kitchen supported by Meghan's cookbook is housed inside mosque 'which has links to 19 terror suspects including Jihadi John.'"

Markle: "The connection made between the Hubb Community Kitchen (in which the Claimant worked with those affected by the Grenfell tragedy as part of a cookbook project which became a *New York Times* best-selling book) and the Al Manaar Muslim Cultural Heritage Centre (supposedly 'linked to 19 Islamic extremists') is at best a highly tenuous and deliberately inflammatory one. The characterization of these victims as being linked to terrorism, in the same way as the Claimant is said to be supporting or endorsing jihadi terrorists through her participation in a cookbook for victims of Grenfell, is as false as it is offensive."

The *Mail*: "How Meghan Markle's Australian aide Samantha 'the Panther' Cohen rose from a Brisbane home to Buckingham Palace—before becoming the second aide to walk out on the 'difficult Duchess.'"

Markle: "The suggestion that Samantha Cohen (who was private secretary for both the Duke and Duchess of Sussex) walked out on the Claimant or that she did so because the Claimant was 'difficult' to work for (a word used six times in this article) is untrue, as well as 'damaging.' Ms. Cohen, who was a highly respected and dedicated member of Her Majesty the Queen's staff for sixteen years, personally chose to come out of retirement in order to work for the Claimant.' Far from walking out on her, Ms. Cohen even extended the original year which she had intended to work for as she wanted to carry on helping the Duke and Duchess with their office. Further, the Claimant's 'personal assistant' was in fact assistant to both the Duke and Duchess, and, contrary to what the Defendant stated in the article, she did not 'quit.'"

The *Mail*: "How Meghan's favorite avocado snack—beloved of all millennials—is fueling human rights abuses, drought and murder."

Markle: "The connection made between the fact that the Claimant likes eating avocado and made avocado on toast for a friend who visited her with human rights abuses, murder and environmental devastation is another highly tenuous and deliberately inflammatory one . . . The suggestion that by liking avocados she is fueling or supporting these extreme occurrences, and therefore is disingenuous about her 'campaigning for racial equality and female empowerment,' is again as absurd as it is offensive."

The *Mail*: "Doria Ragland spotted alone in LA while daughter Meghan Markle parties with famous friends at her $300k baby shower."

Markle: "The suggestion that the Claimant deliberately left out her mother from her baby shower and ditched her in favor of her famous friends is untrue and offensive to her. The Claimant's mother was of course invited, and the Claimant also offered to buy her airline tickets. However, her mother was unable to attend due to work commitments. It was also untrue and offensive to suggest, as the article does, that 'not a single guest had known [the Claimant] for more than a decade.' In fact, the true position was that the baby shower (which actually cost a tiny fraction of the $300k falsely stated in the article) was organized and hosted by one of her best friends from university; the fifteen guests who attended the shower were close friends and included long-term friendships some of which had existed for over twenty years."

In all, it was a sad chapter for everyone involved, noted biographer Angela Levin: "For a daughter and a father to be fighting each other in a court of law is most unpleasant. I mean, it's very unedifying. I think airing dirty laundry of yourself and your family is absolutely awful in public . . . but she's a very determined woman."

At the time of publication, Meghan had suffered a major setback in her legal fight. In a pre-trial victory for the tabloids, a judge struck out key requirements that Meghan would need to prevail: That being, determining whether the Mail on Sunday acted dishonestly, deliberately stirred up conflict between the Duchess and her father, or pursued a deliberate agenda of publishing offensive or intrusive articles about the Duchess. Touting the court's findings as a win, counsel for the newspaper raised a "curious" alarm: If the Mail on Sunday was being accused of manipulating Thomas when Meghan hasn't spoken to him since she married Prince Harry, it said, how could she have "verif(ied) these allegations with him or obtaining his consent. It is therefore highly unlikely that she has any credible basis for these allegations of impropriety towards him." The court's surprising ruling ensured the case will rest solely on the claims that the Mail on Sunday infringed on Meghan's privacy, breached copyright, and violated data protection laws—still a strong case, according to many legal observers.

As for Meghan, despite the finding, she was unrepentant. A spokesperson for Schillings, acting on behalf of the Duchess, said: "(It's) very clear that the core elements of this case do not change and will continue to move forward. The Duchess' rights were violated; the legal boundaries around privacy were crossed. As part of this process, the extremes to which The Mail on Sunday used distortive, manipulative, and dishonest tactics to target The Duchess of Sussex have been put on full display."

Meghan and Harry's tete-a-tete with the tabloids opened up the world to an even darker underbelly. Maya Goodfellow, an academic who holds a PhD from the School of Oriental & African Studies in London, the University of London, concluded the media coverage of Markle has been undeniably racist. Writing for VOX , she deduced:

The Royal Family is historically a white institution. So when Markle, a biracial woman, became a member, some heralded it as "progress." But in late 2016, the same year it was announced she and Prince Harry were dating, the prince put out a statement condemning the "wave of abuse and harassment" Markle had already been subjected to. That included "the racial undertones of comment pieces" and "the outright sexism and racism of social media trolls and web article comments." Three years later, Markle talked about the difficulty of dealing with tabloid coverage more broadly, saying it had been "hard," and that adopting "this British sensibility of a stiff upper lip" was difficult.

For example, the press has talked about her "exotic DNA"; described her as "(almost) straight outta Compton"; attacked her for the very things that Kate Middleton, Prince William's white wife, has been praised for; and compared the couple's son to a chimpanzee. But in TV studios around the country, commentators seem to have peculiarly missed all of this. The coverage of Markle has been welcoming and warm, they say. And when confronted with the evidence that shows that certainly hasn't always been the tone of reporting, they ask: Is it really racism, though?

Not all racism is overt. Much of it is subtle, quietly shaping the way people are seen, talked about, and treated. Some, like Piers Morgan, have argued it's not racist to talk about Markle's DNA as "exotic," but this term has colonial roots, long working as a form of othering. Acknowledging this would mean really grappling with the insidious ways racism operates in the UK, undermining the notion that it is fundamentally a "tolerant" and "progressive" country.

In the days following the Sussexes' announcement that they would be "leaving" the Royal Family, the racist—not to mention, sexist—attacks continued. One poll suggested a significant proportion of people thought it was Markle's decision, not one made jointly or by Prince Harry. We don't know, and might never discover, all the ins and outs of what prompted their departure from their frontline "duties." But in this telling, Prince Harry's previous admission that he didn't want to be a "traditional royal" disappears, and all the power, responsibility, and blame seems to lie with Markle.

There's little doubt that racism in the British media was—in some part—a driving force behind Meghan and Harry's decision to "step back."

THE $500,000 WOMAN

In better times, the team of Harry, Meghan, William, and Kate had been dubbed the "Fab Four"—successors to the Beatles—by the British media. They had collaborated on charity events and public appearances together, maintaining a facade of friendship and warmth. But by spring of 2019, the truth had become too hot to handle. On March 13, a telling statement was issued by Kensington Palace:

> Queen Elizabeth II has agreed to the creation of a new household for The Duke and Duchess of Sussex, following their marriage in May last year. The household, which will be created with the support of the Queen and The Prince of Wales, will be established in the spring. This long-planned move will ensure that permanent support arrangements for the Duke and Duchess' work are in place as they start their family and move to their official residence at Frogmore Cottage.

While the news came as no surprise to many observers within the inner circle, there was immense sadness that the Sussexes and Cambridges had publicly acknowledged their incompatibility—one the torchbearers of a new monarchy full of hope and promise—and had formally split their households. To many, the impenetrable bond between Harry and William that had endured so much over the years was now in tatters.

But the move was approved of—and enabled by—senior staff at the Palace and at the very top of the family. Clearly, they understood that Meghan was a big draw, and, as their postwedding tour of Australia and the Far East had shown, the couple was extremely popular and would continue to be a huge asset to the family.

Compared to the rather staid Kate, Meghan was an exciting addition—entertaining, inspiring, and unpredictable. She had tapped into the mood of the young around the world and connected with them in a way nobody since Diana had managed to. The rift with William had to be managed and not allowed to deteriorate further. The Firm knew they had to act—and fast, before Harry and Meghan did something unthinkable. From what they had seen of her so far, she obviously would pursue any route she deemed necessary, Royal or not.

Suitable roles for the couple were discussed, roles that would keep them within the family structure but allow as much as possible their tricky balancing act of self-promotion and privacy.

There was talk of allowing the couple to assume a role in Africa that would combine their "rock star" appeal with work promoting Commonwealth interests as well as keeping up their charity work on the African continent.

Other ideas floated included making Harry the Governor-General or Deputy Governor-General of Australia or Canada, member nations of the Commonwealth. But these were soon dismissed, according to one royal aide. Another idea was that the couple become trade envoys for post-Brexit Britain. It enjoyed support from senior figures in the government, but it was ultimately rejected.

According to a report in London's *Times* newspaper, a great deal of work at the very highest circles was involved, to manage the crisis. "The plan has been drawn up by Sir David Manning, the former British ambassador to the U.S. and special adviser on constitutional and international affairs to the two princes," reported the paper. "Lord Geidt, the Queen's former private secretary, has also been involved in the discussions. He is chairman of the Queen's Commonwealth Trust, an organization that champions young global leaders, of which Harry and Meghan are president and vice-president."

The article added, "The proposal would give the couple the chance to enjoy a break from the divisions that have riven the royal household in recent months while 'harnessing' their global appeal for Britain."

Everyone had *hoped* that this would be a workable solution to the problem and that once Meghan had given birth, the matter could be resolved to everyone's satisfaction.

***

In the meantime, Meghan was blossoming. As her pregnancy continued, she cocooned herself in a nest of self-care and healthy living, while Harry fussed and fretted around her, ensuring she was as comfortable as possible. During this time, she took a number of healing therapies, including sessions with a celebrity acupuncturist at an exclusive herbal wellness center in London (where treatments can come in at £6,200 for a year of forty-five-minute sessions).

The couple also visited Ilapothecary in Notting Hill, for a twelve-week course of numerology readings, costing £2,520, to ensure that everything was A-OK on the spiritual front. The couple then went on a joint "babymoon" together to the luxury Heckfield Place spa, in Hampshire. Reported to have cost £33,000, the three-night stay included three security staff, who presumably also got a chance to enjoy organic mani-pedis and salt body scrubs along with the Duke and Duchess. Back at Frogmore Cottage, tabloid reports suggested they were taught hypnobirthing techniques, as well as Meghan insisting on preparing with chanting, aromatherapy, and massage therapies, in the hope of reducing any need for an epidural or pain relief during the birth. She was also convinced her unborn child was already a feminist.

"I had seen this documentary on Netflix about feminism and one of the things they said during pregnancy is, 'I feel the embryonic kicking of feminism,'" Meghan said during an International Women's Day panel on March 8. "I loved that, so boy or girl, or whatever it is, we hope that's the case."

But it was Meghan's maternity wardrobe—or wardrobes—that drew gasps of horror from the notoriously frugal Royals. The royal fashion blog UFONoMore tallied up all the new items that the thirteen royal women—including Meghan, Kate, Eugenie, and Beatrice—added to their closets last year. Topping off the list was the Duchess of Sussex, who spent a whopping $508,258 during 2018—excluding her wedding gown! Compare that to Kate, whose new clothes in 2018 cost $85,097, a mere fraction of Markle's wardrobe, while Princess Eugenie, a noted contemporary fashion icon, spent $39,818, which also excluded her own wedding gown.

Even before money spent on birthing, baby clothes, equipment, and numerous other sundries, this was shaping up to be one of the most expensive babies of 2019!

The fact that Meghan splashed so much cash rang alarm bells with the traditionally conservative Queen Elizabeth. Growing up in the war left the monarch with a built-in sense of frugality and economy, despite being one of the richest women in the world. Away from the spotlight and the pomp and circumstance, the Queen is an unassuming character. This was amply demonstrated to the world when in 2002, a British tabloid journalist managed to sneak undercover into the Palace and gain a job as a footman. The journalist tried to dish dirt on the Queen living an extravagant existence when the truth was far more boring. Her Majesty, it was discovered, ate her breakfast out of Tupperware boxes, often thriftily using up leftovers. HRH even used to feed her beloved corgis scraps under the table.

What's more, the Queen hates excessive jewelry and dislikes people standing on ceremony. There was no entourage of servants at her beck and call, and her day-to-day life is based in a somewhat humble part of Buckingham Palace.

As the rogue footman discovered, she insisted on calling all her employees staff, not servants—and took pains to put people she met at ease. Such was the down-to-earth ordinariness of Elizabeth: the newspaper's great idea for uncovering a sensational scandal about a spoilt, imperious, icy woman had backfired dreadfully, and instead there was an outpouring of anger from the public at the Queen's privacy being compromised.

So it would not have been a surprise to learn that the Queen was monitoring Meghan's reckless spending with a shrewd eye. "The fact that Meghan spent more than half a million pounds on clothes for public events during 2018, with £111,000 just on her trip to Africa alone, as well as further costs for her private life—the jewels, the renovation of Frogmore, the allowance for [her mother] Doria, her private trips (with bodyguards) back to the US and Canada—the lavish extravagance was the gossip of the Palace staff and insiders, especially as it was known that in the same time frame of 2018, Kate, the future Queen Consort, had spent only £85,000," said one family insider.

One of those extra costs Meghan had incurred came about after she snubbed the Queen yet again in rejecting her offer of the usual, all-male doctor team of Alan Farthing and Guy Thorpe-Beeston, specialists in high-risk births—and amongst the most highly-regarded birthing doctors in the world. Despite the fact that Kate had gratefully accepted their help and support, Meghan informed the

Palace that she would be choosing (and paying for) her own delivery team, led by a female doctor.

A Royal source revealed: "Meghan said she doesn't want the men in suits. She was adamant that she wanted her own people. It did leave a few of us a little baffled."

"It is slightly surprising," said another insider. "The Queen's doctors are the best of the best and when it comes down to it, their role would actually be very limited in the birth itself, assuming all goes to plan."

Another firm decision was Meghan's choice of venue for the birth. It was rumored that she would have a home birth, with a doula on hand to ease her child into the world with a natural birth, and not posing with a blow-dry and a full face of makeup on the steps of the Lindo Wing in front of the world's media, as Kate and Diana before her did. Harry and Meghan informed the media that they would not be sharing details of the birth with an expectant world—until *they* were ready.

As it happened, the birth ended up taking place not at home, but at the private Portland hospital in central London. No media or cheering crowds were welcomed, breaking another British tradition. Kensington Palace's communications team was ready with another firm statement to that effect.

"The Duke and Duchess look forward to sharing the exciting news with everyone once they have had an opportunity to celebrate privately as a new family," the statement read. There was a collective rolling of eyes over at Anmer Hall when a friend of Meghan's told the media that the Duchess "felt bad" for Kate having to look impeccable and face the world's media mere hours after giving birth.

In her defense, as Meghan's pregnancy progressed, the embarrassing noises from Thomas Markle continued. Her father continued to protest he had repeatedly tried to contact Meghan, had tried to reach out and communicate but was consistently rebuffed with silence.

"Markle says the estrangement from his daughter is affecting his health, causing 'massive stress,'" reported the *Daily Mail*. Thomas was quoted as saying: "I want nothing more than to sort this mess out. I would ask her and Harry to contact me. All it would take is one phone call and most of this craziness would stop."

But it was nowhere near stopping.

GOD BLESS THE CHILD

At 5:26 a.m. on the morning of May 6, Archie Harrison Mountbatten-Windsor was born, in the opulent surroundings of a private hospital in central London. The latest Royal weighed seven pounds, three ounces. Until the very last minute the night before, Meghan had planned on a natural home birth. But when Archie finally decided to make his appearance a week after his due date, the couple's security detail drove her to the clinic, under such confidentiality that even senior Royals weren't told.

Only Harry and Meghan's Mom, Doria, were present as Meghan went into labor and for the birth, however.

Within hours of the dawn birth, the couple was back at Frogmore, where Harry, thirty-four, gave an impromptu press conference to break the news to the world. Dazed and delighted, the Prince addressed a gaggle of mics and cameras, saying, "How any woman does what they do is beyond comprehension. But we're both absolutely thrilled. This little thing is absolutely to die for, so I'm absolutely over the moon."

Later that day, Meghan's father Thomas weighed in from Rosarito, Mexico, where he lives, with his congratulations, having heard of the birth on the news. He told *The Sun*: "I am proud that my new grandson is born into the British Royal Family and I am sure that he will grow up to serve the Crown and the people of Britain with grace, dignity, and honor. God bless the child and I wish him health and happiness, and my congratulations to my lovely daughter Duchess Meghan and Prince Harry, and God save the Queen."

The birth prompted a new wave of speculation about the family's future plans. A source revealed that Meghan wanted a place in Los Angeles, a city whose life-style and climate she loved. "Hollywood is in her DNA and I think it is where she has always wanted to keep a solid footing," the source said. "Spending time there would also allow her some freedom and independence from both the Palace and the Press—and more control over her life and the people around her. She also has friends in LA with babies and will want to have that interaction and bring up her child in a less restrictive environment—similar to how she grew up."

Other reports at the time hinted a move to South Africa was in the cards. The public, already baffled and hurt at Meghan's reticence to share the news of the birth as soon as it happened, was growing irritated. Especially since this came on top of the news that taxpayers had forked out millions for Frogmore's renovations, right down to the organic vegan paint in the nursery.

A couple of days after the birth, Meghan unveiled Archie to the world in a tightly controlled press appearance. According to a source, Kate (and her friends) watched with a mixture of envy at Meghan's perfect choreography of the event and annoyance at her implication that Kate's media appearance had been forced upon her, hours after giving birth. Rather than the customary appearance on the steps of the Lindo Wing at St Mary's Hospital, Meghan appeared in a fashionable trench-style dress by Grace Wales Bonner, the London high society designer of the moment, at Buckingham Palace, shadowed by her adoring spouse and holding her little bundle of joy up for the world's media.

The decision to skip the traditional baby photo call outside of the hospital made Meghan and Harry appear "more regal" than William and Kate, speculated the world's foremost Royal biographer, Andrew Morton.

"It played out very well," he said. "They controlled the narrative, they controlled the photo call. We've had far more pictures than we would have had if it had just been outside of the hospital because we've had that lovely picture of the Queen and Doria Ragland." He added, "That ground-breaking photo really is a celebration of this new multiethnic Royal Family. This is about a new age of social media engagement."

But behind the smiles, another category-five storm was brewing. Insiders at the Palace had expressed concern that the pair had not undertaken the usual post-birth photo call and instead waited to micromanage the photographs following the birth. After it was announced that the baby would take the name Archie—not a traditional Royal name—all eyes turned to the little fellow's first major engagement, his christening. This is usually a time when Royals gather, celebrate the new arrival, and joyfully share him with the public, who as taxpayers and loyalists expect to see their new national treasure being inducted into the Firm and the Church of England, a Protestant Anglican church.

Pointedly, the Queen and Prince Philip stayed away. They had been generous and understanding at their best. But they simply now felt publicly embarrassed by Meghan's controlling behavior, said a well-placed Palace insider. That meant only twenty-five people (plus the holy man) were allowed into the couple's presence for the christening. But Doria, Charles and Camilla, Kate and William, and the brothers' former nanny under their late mother, Diana, Tiggy Legge-Bourke, were all present and correct, while the padre did his stuff at the font.

During the course of royal history, some pretty fast work has been pulled at the font in terms of naming. But the baby received his moniker with equilibrium, barely breaking a doze for the anointing. Meghan and Harry had turned down the Queen's offer to name Archie HRH or bestow upon him the title the Earl of Dumbarton.

By now, decisions like this were everyday occurrences, and the family was wondering just how much a part little Archie would be playing in their all-important evolution as the era of King Charles III hovered faintly, but very evidently, on the far horizons.

By the expressions of one couple in particular, this was a question that was clearly in need of urgent clarification. William and Kate had played it by the Royal book. Each of their three kids had been born and exhibited in the manner accustomed, and a proper family christening was part of that deal. Now, the couple was adamant that they would be asserting their authority in the near future when it came to having their say on Archie's destiny. As if signaling to the world that she was very much going to be present in her nephew's life, Kate was spotted after the ceremony wearing the same earrings Diana had worn to Harry's christening, in 1984. Admittedly, while Kate's jewelry collection was dwarfed by Meghan's, she certainly would have had plenty of others to choose from. Fans on social media noted the subtle gesture. One typical example read:

In all honesty, I think Kate was a tad bit disrespectful and spiteful. She

didn't have to come there sporting Princess Diana's earrings. I believe
she did that intentionally to upstage Meghan's special moment.

Meanwhile, William, always reliably jovial and jolly at such family occasions, here looked shockingly grave and stern. Body language experts pored over the pictures from the christening, noting his aloof stance, his folded arms, and tense facial expression.

His unhappiness at the situation was public, and clearly he was no longer worried about hiding it.

This had been exacerbated by his and Kate's reportedly feeling offended that Harry and Meghan had not invited them to see Archie until a week after his birth.

Meghan had already confused the British media by withholding updates on her birth (according to some, this was to ensure news broke with maximum impact on US morning news networks). Now she had managed to further alienate her husband's brother and wife in the bargain. According to reports at the time, "royal higher-ups" had advised Meghan and Harry to be more "forthcoming" about access to Archie with pictures. But the couple "pushed back," said a source.

William and Kate dutifully publish photographs of their children occasionally, but it's a precedent that Meghan and Harry would not be following.

Filmmaker Nick Bullen, who has over twenty years' experience with the family, had spoken that spring to confirm the chasm that had opened up between William and Harry. It was "really, really sad" that Harry and William had had a "rift," he explained. "You don't want to hear this, but again, it goes back to them being real people. We forget that they are people. We've all fallen out with our brothers and sisters over the years, and hopefully, it'll be fine," he said.

Bullen added: "I think the Prince of Wales and the Queen are working incredibly hard to try and make sure everybody reunites."

Around the same time, TrueRoyalty.tv host Tim Vincent commented on a "well-placed" guest on his show, who had admitted: "It's the two princes that don't get on. The actual wives actually are still finding their feet or have found their feet, and they're very happy in the situation they find themselves, but it's the brothers themselves who have been closer than anybody up until now."

That month, Meghan made her first postbirth appearance in public without

Archie, at the gala of *The Lion King* in Central London. As crowds cheered, she trotted up and down the red carpet, soaking up the adulation. In a video shared by a Twitter account named Royal Suitor, a conversation between Meghan and US singer Pharrell was overheard. "So happy for your union," the singer gushed. "Love is amazing. It's wonderful. Don't ever take that for granted but what it means in today's climate. We cheer you guys on."

"Thank you," replied Meghan, before adding pointedly, "They don't make it easy." It was unclear whether she was referring to the Royals, the media, or the crowds of cheering fans wishing her well.

ZOOMING AROUND THE WORLD

After all the excitement over the new arrival, it was time for the couple to take a well-earned holiday abroad. In August, Harry and Meghan, with baby Archie, decided to jet off to Ibiza before looking in on the south of France. That choice caused many critics to label the royals as hypocrites, for preaching about environmentalism and conservation, while choosing a method of travel that is proven to be terrible for the environment.

The venerable Royal commentator Ingrid Seward was one of many who bitterly rebuked the couple for their "hypocrisy . . . zooming around the world in private jets, pausing only to deliver a barefoot lecture at Google's eco camp in Sicily, where Harry piously moralized about climate-harming behavior."

In an "embarrassing" press conference in the Netherlands, Harry defended his actions for taking private jets as a security measure to protect his family, which Ingrid Seward dismissed angrily: "To claim he used them to protect his family was simply ludicrous."

When he rushed to defend his family's choice of transport, Harry put his foot in it by saying that 99 percent of the time he flew commercial flights. That proved something of an exaggeration when records—reviewed by these authors—proved he had spent about half his recent flying time, since marrying Meghan, in private or chartered jets. That didn't include extravagances such as Meghan's private jet, a gift from a Canadian friend, to New York for her luxury baby shower party at five-star The Mark Hotel in Manhattan, an occasion that cost a significant sum, not least because of all the security that was obliged to accompany her.

To commemorate Archie's imminent arrival, Meghan's friend Serena Williams had booked and paid for the elite hotel's insanely luxurious penthouse suite. It was spread over two floors that incorporated five bedrooms, four fireplaces, six bathrooms, and two powder rooms, plenty of room for the guests, including friend Jessica Mulroney, actress and close pal Abigail Spencer, Priyanka Chopra, Amal Clooney, Misha Nonoo, and Markus Anderson, among others.

The matter would have most likely been ignored—after all, we are all used to pictures of Royals tripping daintily in and out of private jets and baby showers are a fact of life now, accepted by all but the most puce-faced, retired colonel living in the sticks. But the effect was somewhat ruined by the couple's efforts to inform anyone who would listen of the risks that flying posed to the environment. What's more, Harry also had the very laudable sentiment that his father had spent decades preaching, that we need to curb climate change: "With nearly 7.7 billion people inhabiting this Earth, every choice, every footprint, every action makes a difference."

In the eyes of many around the world, the Sussexes' busy travel schedules seemed to say that the rules didn't apply when it came to the couple themselves. As they toured the south of France, it emerged that one of their jets, at least, had been sent by Elton John, who had invited them to stay at his house. The pop pianist defended them on Twitter when it all subsequently kicked off.

"To support Prince Harry's commitment to the environment, we ensured their flight was carbon neutral, by making the appropriate contribution to Carbon Footprint™. I highly respect and applaud both Harry and Meghan's commitment to charity and I'm calling on the press to cease these relentless and untrue assassinations on their character that are spuriously crafted on an almost daily basis," said Elton, who, after Lady Diana's death, released "Candle in the Wind 1997," a ballad about a life extinguished early that would go on to become the most successful single since the introduction of the charts.

But just as the media furor over the private jets began to subside (not before William and family had pointedly used a commercial budget Easyjet flight to travel to Ireland), another controversial episode came sliding down the track.

The debacle convinced Meghan that it was time to supercharge the Sussexes' public relations operation, one insider close to her told me. To her thinking, Buckingham Palace's advisers and communications teams—as charming, reliable, and experienced as they were—simply could not deliver the wall-to-wall positive coverage Meghan craved, especially in US media, which had been a rather low priority for the Palace team. To this end, she auditioned a number of firms, before settling on Hollywood and Manhattan heavyweights Sunshine Sachs. Despite their cheery name, Sunshine Sachs are PR badasses. They had previously represented clients such as Harvey Weinstein in his bid to counter the accusations of sexual assault that had been piling up, as well as Michael Jackson, when he was attempting to clear his name following his child abuse trial. Now, the firm had the task of rebooting Meghan's public image, to her specifications.

Palace staff were said to be "shocked" at the hiring of an external agency not related to the Firm, especially as the couple had been represented by the Royals' global public relations chief, Sara Latham. Latham's former clients include Hillary Clinton, with whom she worked during Clinton's 2016 presidential run. Now she was being passed over in favor of a high-powered crisis management firm.

With very British understatement, an insider at the Palace mused that "Hiring a Hollywood firm to represent you for PR while a member of the Royal Family is unorthodox to say the least."

That September, Meghan had the chance to promote herself even further when she was asked to guest-edit the September edition of the British version of *Vogue*, a major coup for both *Vogue* and for the Duchess.

Kate herself had appeared on the cover of the centenary edition in 2016, wearing a tweed jacket and hat and leaning cheerfully on a gatepost. There were acerbic comments from some quarters; the writer Hilary Mantel sneered that Kate looked as if "designed by a committee and built by craftsmen, with a perfect plastic smile and the spindles of her limbs hand-turned and gloss-varnished." But Kate's self-effacing and lack of ego offended some feminists and equal-rights opportunists, who felt she should have used her platform more wisely. When Meghan was offered the chance, she grabbed it with both hands.

For the cover, she forewent a picture of herself in favor of fifteen women, mostly models and actors, but also the author Chimamanda Ngozi Adichie and New Zealand's prime minister, Jacinda Ardern.

"The line-up is evidence that, in 2019, a new metric for global success is in play," ran the breathless unattributed commentary to the shoot. "First, attract visibility. Then, convert visibility into a platform. Finally, use your platform to effect change."

If the text hadn't been written by Meghan, it was the product of someone who had clearly spent a lot of time talking to her.

The Meghan edition of *Vogue*—including interviews with a range of figures across her political and social portfolio—offered up a feel-good bible of wokeness and inspiration. But the project also underlined Meghan's limits. She could chuckle with Michelle Obama about how cute their babies were when asleep, she could commission a poem from author Matt Haig that included a daring "fuck," she could send Harry off to interview Dr. Jane Goodall, an eminent ecologist and climate expert. During that conversation Harry let slip that due to "environmental" reasons, the couple planned to have only two children.

But, ultimately, as a Royal, Meghan wouldn't be able to do much about any of the problems she discussed, the key challenge she faced. In her role as Duchess, Meghan could flag up injustices and inequalities, causes she held close to her heart and, as a lifelong campaigner and outspoken advocate of feminism and racial equality, always had, ever since childhood. But, in the gilded Royal cage, she quickly realized that her impact was limited, something that seemed to drive her crazy. Anyone who knew Meghan knew she had always wanted to speak up for the causes close to her heart. Thinking that her new position might allow her to be more effective in solving the issues she highlighted would prove a serious mistake. This paradox at the heart of Meghan's new existence was generating a huge amount of frustration for her, and for some of those who were following her.

The acclaimed author Helen Lewis explored this question at the root of Meghan's public position, her inability to do little more than signaling, for an article in *The Atlantic*.

"Too often, feminism—even when not championed by a beautiful, wealthy aristocrat—gets stuck in this toothless, villain-free zone," she wrote. "Markle can talk about marginalized women who struggle to find clothes for job interviews—and the charity SmartWorks, which she supports—but she cannot address the causes of poverty. The cookbook she oversaw to help victims of the Grenfell Tower fire in 2017, in which seventy-two Londoners died, can raise money for those affected. But there is a tacit agreement not to engage with discussions about the inadequate cladding on the apartment building, overseen by the local authorities, which made the fire so lethal."

That autumn, the Sussexes began a major trip abroad to Africa. They were accompanied by the four-month-old Archie, who set a new royal record as the youngest Royal to make an international tour. Prince William was nine months old when he joined his parents on the road to Australia in 1983, and neatly, Prince George was the same age when William and Kate took him to Australia in 2014. Harry, meanwhile, made his first appearance during a royal tour in Venice with Diana, Charles, and William when he was six months old in 1985.

According to a source who spoke out at the time, Harry and Meghan planned to "do some serious work on the ground, particularly at a community level." This motif of relaxed informality coursed through the trip, which included South Africa and Botswana. Harry also made a poignant trip to Huambo, Angola, where his mother had famously campaigned for landmines to be outlawed during her final African visit in 1997.

Harry and Meghan aimed to "meet as many South Africans as possible and make a difference where they can." The insider added, "This isn't a holiday and they don't want it to look like one."

GOING ROGUE

Harry felt himself in need of his spiritual homeland, Africa. It was here that the major rupture started that would change the shape of the family forever.

On October 1, 2019, while touring the continent, Harry released the following statement:

> As a couple, we believe in media freedom and objective, truthful reporting. We regard it as a cornerstone of democracy and in the current state of the world—on every level—we have never needed responsible media more. Unfortunately, my wife has become one of the latest victims of a British tabloid press that wages campaigns against individuals with no thought to the consequences—a ruthless campaign that has escalated over the past year, throughout her pregnancy and while raising our new-born son. There is a human cost to this relentless propaganda, specifically when it is knowingly false and malicious, and though we have continued to put on a brave face—as so many of you can relate to—I cannot begin to describe how painful it has been. Because in today's digital age, press fabrications are repurposed as truth across the globe. One day's coverage is no longer tomorrow's chip-paper.
>
> Up to now, we have been unable to correct the continual misrepresentations—something that these select media outlets have been aware of and have therefore exploited on a daily and sometimes hourly basis. It is for this reason we are taking legal action, a process that has been many months in the making. The positive coverage of the past week from these same publications exposes the double standards of this

specific press pack that has vilified her almost daily for the past nine months; they have been able to create lie after lie at her expense simply because she has not been visible while on maternity leave. She is the same woman she was a year ago on our wedding day, just as she is the same woman you've seen on this Africa tour.

For these select media this is a game, and one that we have been unwilling to play from the start. I have been a silent witness to her private suffering for too long. To stand back and do nothing would be contrary to everything we believe in.

This particular legal action hinges on one incident in a long and disturbing pattern of behavior by British tabloid media. The contents of a private letter were published unlawfully in an intentionally destructive manner to manipulate you, the reader, and further the divisive agenda of the media group in question. In addition to their unlawful publication of this private document, they purposely misled you by strategically omitting select paragraphs, specific sentences, and even singular words to mask the lies they had perpetuated for over a year.

There comes a point when the only thing to do is to stand up to this behavior, because it destroys people and destroys lives. Put simply, it is bullying, which scares and silences people. We all know this isn't acceptable, at any level. We won't and can't believe in a world where there is no accountability for this.

Though this action may not be the safe one, it is the right one. Because my deepest fear is history repeating itself. I've seen what happens when someone I love is commoditised to the point that they are no longer treated or seen as a real person. I lost my mother and now I watch my wife falling victim to the same powerful forces.

We thank you, the public, for your continued support. It is hugely appreciated. Although it may not seem like it, we really need it.

The sweet sign-off preceded the news that Harry and Meghan were suing the

Mail on Sunday and had also issued legal proceedings against the owners of *The Sun* and the *Daily Mirror.*

The global reaction, as well as that within the Palace, was not long in coming. "It just feeds the media machine, and that is the one thing Harry really hates," said Penny Junor in *The Guardian*, issuing a warning sign of what was inevitably to come. "In a way it is the very reverse of what he has said he wants for him and his family, namely, privacy."

The statement was a bombshell.

It was almost unheard for a senior Royal to react to media gossip in such a way. Meghan's ongoing refusal to deal with that situation had only made a delicate situation incalculably worse and left the door open for seemingly anyone related to the Markles to helpfully fan the flames. The British tabloids were a known quantity—venal, vicious, and unforgiving. Meghan had known this better than most, having absorbed the details of her idol Diana's death, long before she knew Harry.

Tom Bradby, the former Royal correspondent at the ITV network's "News At Ten" flagship bulletin, was about the only media correspondent Harry and William trusted. A long-term observer and pal of the pair, he was drawn especially to Harry and now, on the occasion of their trip across the African continent, was commissioned by ITV to make a documentary about the couple's charity work with their full blessing and cooperation.

What Bradby didn't expect is that rather than focusing on the myriad charity causes and endeavors that had so long been close to Harry's heart, the documentary became a personal profile of the pair, presenting them as hapless victims in a sea of hostility and strife. While many could legitimately sympathize with the awful headlines Meghan was receiving on an almost daily basis, the documentary sent shockwaves through the establishment and began the process that would lead to the couple exiling themselves from the family and the UK. The British press was furious that Harry and Meghan had legally challenged them—and specifically, the *Mail on Sunday*, for reprinting Thomas Sr.'s private letter from Meghan, claiming misuse of private information, breach of data protection rights, and infringement of copyright. Tradition dictated the couple should put up and shut up with the press, as it was considered all part of the job. "Never explain, never complain," as the Royals would tell one another. But that era was over.

Now, in a major documentary, Harry and Meghan ignored all advice and seemingly contradicted their fierce injunctions for privacy by airing their grievances about being globally famous and about having to deal with critical coverage. The move paralleled Diana's astonishing BBC appearance in 1995, during which she unburdened to the world about her dysfunctional marriage and her husband Charles's infidelities.

The ITV documentary *Harry & Meghan: An African Journey* was supposed to focus on the couple's important causes. Instead, their candid revelations hijacked the show's narrative and stirred up a hornet's nest of controversy within and outside of the family.

A doe-eyed Meghan revealed to Bradby that before her marriage, British friends warned her that the UK tabloids would "destroy her life." "When I first met my now-husband, my friends were really happy because I was so happy," she recounted. "But my British friends said to me, 'I'm sure he's great, but you shouldn't do it because the British tabloids will destroy your life.' And I very naively thought—I'm American, we don't have that there—what are you talking about? That doesn't make any sense . . . I didn't get it. So, it's been . . . complicated."

This was an amazing claim coming from the woman who had already endured press attention ever since her days on *Suits* and who made regular appearances promoting her lifestyle brand on NBC's *TODAY Show*. Furthermore, it again called into question just how much she was willing to admit she knew of the Royals before getting caught up with them—former pal Ninaki Priddy had explicitly stated that Meghan was obsessed with Diana and had Andrew Morton's bestselling biography of her on her bedroom shelves. Meghan's professions of surprise at the media attention caused a huge collective gasp of disbelief when the documentary was aired. But more was to come.

"I've really tried to adopt this British sensibility of a stiff upper lip," Meghan said. "I've tried, I've really tried. [And] I've said for a long time to H—that's what I call him—it's not enough to just survive something, right? That's not the point of life. You've got to thrive, you've got to feel happy."

At this, the Queen's phone no doubt started buzzing in alarm. The senior officials at the Palace weren't alone in decoding Meghan's words as being a steely ultimatum. The fact she was publicly stating that her life was so unbearable that she was just "surviving" was regarded as a serious and grave insult to the Royals, who had been working nonstop to try and accommodate her continuous behind-the-scenes demands to courtiers and aides and Harry's blustering support of them. But it was becoming now abundantly clear that despite everything that had been done for the couple to make them happy and content, against all advice, flying in the face of tradition, duty and loyalty—this was a declaration of war.

"Look, any woman—especially when they're pregnant, you're really vulnerable, and so that was made really challenging . . . and then when you have a newborn," Meghan added in the documentary. "Especially as a woman, it's really, it's a lot. So, you add this on top of just trying to be a new mom or trying to be a newlywed. And also thank you for asking because not many people have asked if I'm okay, but it's a very real thing to be going through behind the scenes."

The key takeaway was that Meghan was saying she was upset. This was greeted by bafflement at the Palace, especially with her two biggest fans in the family outside Harry, the Queen and Prince Charles, both of whom had made strenuous efforts to welcome Meghan into the family as much as possible.

One senior courtier said: "I know the Prince of Wales has several times reached out to Meghan. They get on and share a love of music. I know he invited her to a preview of an exhibition at the Palace. The Queen has been a source of strength too and invited them both to Balmoral, where family problems are usually aired." There was further disappointment at Meghan's comments from the teams that had been working around the clock to come up with suitable roles and challenges for the couple in the future, at great inconvenience to everyone.

But Meghan's gripes were merely the lead-up to Harry's sensational, if somewhat less polished, interview.

Here, Bradby sympathetically asked him about his relationship with William being under strain.

"Umm . . . part, part of this role and part of this job and part of this family being under the pressure that it's under, inevitably, stuff happens," Harry said awkwardly, shuffling his feet and looking like he fervently wished he was anywhere else. "But look. We're brothers, we'll always be brothers—and we're certainly on different paths at the moment, but I'll certainly always be there for him as I know he'll always be there for me. We don't see each other as much as we used to because we're so busy. But I love him dearly and the majority of the stuff is created out of nothing. But as brothers, you have good days, you have bad days."

No one had expected such a revelation of pain, of hurt and upset. Somehow, in comparison to Meghan's performance, Harry's painful shyness and agonizing discomfort at discussing his most personal and intimate familial relationships—which he simply hadn't been brought up to do under Royal rules and protocol—was heartbreaking to watch.

The news flashed around the world in seconds. Social media was ablaze, with the couple's fans and detractors equally vociferous and impassioned. Within the Palace, tensions were immediately running high.

"The Duke and Duchess have much to offer and could be a formidable asset for the Royal Family," retorted one royal aide stiffly, the day after the documentary was aired. "But they need to work as a team with the rest of the royal household and, rightly or wrongly, there is a lot of distrust right now." The aide was seemingly articulating the view of many, which had been previously left diplomatically unsaid within Palace walls, that there was a "startling lack of self-awareness" over problems Meghan and Harry created for themselves—including the row over their private jet use over the summer. One sensed that the ITV documentary was a signal for many in senior positions to finally break, with exasperation, the code of silence around the family and go public.

A source described as being "close" to the Sussexes quickly came forth to defend them, telling CNN that the newlyweds had "single-handedly" modernized the British monarchy. The source then amazingly claimed that the Royal Family "was not doing enough to protect the star couple from negative media attention or to appreciate the value they bring to the 1,000-year-old monarchy."

Furious Palace staff shot back with an incognito advisor of their own, responding to the CNN claims to the *Daily Mail*: "[That]'s akin to saying that [Harry and Meghan] are too good for the Royal Family—which is extremely disrespectful to everyone who works for, and on behalf of, the Queen and other senior members of the Royal Family. The truth is that no-one is 'anti' Harry and Meghan, and no-one is briefing against them. And it is also just plain wrong to say they have 'single-handedly modernized the monarchy.' Modernization is an ongoing process led by the Queen."

A source close to the brothers said Harry's behavior, including attacks on the media and weeping in public as he spoke of son Archie's birth, showed all was not well.

"Harry is not in great shape," they told these authors. "I'd say he's not well, declaring war on everyone, crying in public. These are not the actions of a well-balanced man. He and William are badly split over his mother's legacy and add to that, William is clearly in training to be King and recognizes that, while Harry has little purpose, he doesn't really have a job of any description and stews on perceived wrongs."

Royal biographer Penny Junor also felt that Harry was in a bad place.

"In the past when we have seen Harry on TV, we have come away with a smile on our face because he is a character who is funny, and is so positive," she told *The Sun*, in a conversation about the documentary. "I felt sorry because he was not behaving as he would in the past. Something's wrong. He looked burdened and playing the victim, which does not sit comfortably with him."

William himself made his feelings known, with characteristic tact and obliqueness, about the situation. He and Kate were on an official tour of Pakistan, which was going splendidly. The couple had conducted themselves impeccably. William reflected sagely on the country's precarious political, security, and social problems and offered strong friendship and encouragement to the reformist prime minister, former cricketer Imran Khan. He managed to look statesmanlike, dignified, and serious, while Kate was solid, reliable, and drama-free, playing games with children and being feted for her happy demeanor everywhere she went.

In the days after the film was aired, it was made known by Kensington Palace that William was "genuinely worried" for Harry and Meghan after their emotional television tell-all and hoped "they are all right."

"William is going to be King and acts like that," a source continued. "The Pakistan trip brings that into sharp focus. They are doing what's expected of senior Royals. At the same time, you've got Harry and Meghan pouring their hearts out and on the verge of tears."

But his laconic leaked comments belied the fact that William's concern was very real. Ever since their troubles had begun, dating back to when he tried to advise Harry to take things slowly with Meghan, he had been fretting over his wayward younger brother. William knew, more than anyone, how much unresolved anger and anxiety lay in Harry's psyche from childhood, as those who know him have described. He also knew how vulnerable and softhearted his little brother was. He understood how hard it had always been for Harry to be always second, behind him, the spare to William's heir. He loved his brother's warmth, his laughter, his determination, and his innate sweetness and kindness. He cherished Harry's sense of justice, his empathy with the underdog and those who had been subject to misfortune and pain. Deep down, in the place where William had taken to hiding his feelings way back in his teens, where only he could find his true self, he was mourning their relationship.

In the aftermath of Harry and Meghan's dramatic revelations to Bradby, any lingering doubts that Meghan's entry to the Firm had been a success were violently shattered. The sense of betrayal and disbelief must have been mind-boggling as the couple mused openly on their desire to leave the United Kingdom and live in Africa.

"I don't know where we could live in Africa at the moment," Harry had pondered in his interview with Bradby. "We've just come from Cape Town, that would be an amazing place for us to be able to base ourselves, of course it would. But with all the problems that are going on there, I just don't see how we would be able to really make as much difference as we'd want to."

"None of this is remotely helpful to the monarchy as an institution," noted a Palace insider. "It is promoting discord and taking attention away from the good work senior Royals do across the board."

Meghan was especially frustrated by the reaction from eminent writers on postcolonialism, such as Kehinde Andrews, associate professor in sociology at Birmingham City University. He wrote an op-ed for CNN titled "Harry and Meghan, Africa Doesn't Want You":

> *Presumably, whichever country Harry and Meghan choose is supposed*
> *to be grateful for their presence. But charitable donations and being*

pictured with elephants cannot overturn the historical nature of the monarchy's relationship to Africa. Plenty of the privileged well-meaning elite during colonial times moved to the colonies; they just did not have the royal public relations machine to spin their visits in positive terms.

Harry and Meghan living in a gated community, surrounded by the largely white elite and locked away from extreme poverty, would be the most appropriate symbol of royal privilege in the 21st century. It is the height of British colonial arrogance for the royal couple to be cherry-picking their dream destination at a time when African migrants have never been less welcome in Britain.

Bradby himself spoke to the media in the torrid wake of the revelations.

"I went intending to make a documentary that was always going to be about their work in Africa and then a little about where they are at in life," he told *Good Morning America* a few days after the film was broadcast. "I knew that everything wasn't entirely rosy behind the scenes. I found a couple that seemed a bit bruised and vulnerable. That was the story I found, and it seemed the right journalistic thing to do to try and tell that story as empathetically as I could. The thing about Harry is, whether in private or in public, if you ask him an honest question, he'll give you an honest answer, for better or worse."

Commenting on the tensions between William and Harry, Bradby speculated that this too would take time to settle. "It's quite interesting," he said, diplomatically. "William is taking a more traditional approach. He has to—he's going to be King, he can't afford to alienate any constituency. Harry and Meghan have just decided to play things very differently." Bradby concluded by expressing his hope that everyone would now "take a deep breath." He was to be sorely disappointed.

Britain at the end of 2019 was riven with the grisly aftermath of Brexit, years of political uncertainty, underfunded public services, neglect, and austerity. The Royals, who once were seen as a calming, stabilizing influence on the nation in times of trouble, seemed to be contributing nothing but more chaos and misery.

Prince Andrew, a man of overweening pomposity and arrogance, gave a calamitous television interview with the BBC's *Newsnight* program, in which he firmly denied any impropriety with a girl alleging abuse by his rapist friend, Jeffrey

Epstein. A denial of involvement would have sufficed, but Andrew left the viewing public seriously questioning his mental health. Virginia Roberts, a young victim of Epstein's, claimed the portly, perspiring Prince had been dancing with her the night the Prince is alleged to have assaulted her in London. Andrew claimed that due to his heroic war service (flying helicopters in the Falklands conflict of 1982) he had a medical condition that meant he couldn't sweat. Furthermore, he couldn't have been with Epstein that night because he had been at his daughter's birthday at Pizza Express, in the nondescript suburban town of Woking. "I've only been to Woking a couple of times and I remember it weirdly distinctly," he added, helpfully.

As the country held its hands and groaned at the sight of what the Royals had become, their newest recruit was equally unimpressed with the unedifying spectacle of her boorish uncle-in-law dissembling in a manner that would make even Thomas Markle, Jr., himself a match to the Markles' headline-grabbing antics, wince.

"Meghan doesn't view Andrew as one of the family's great assets," a source told *The Sun*. "She views him as the ultimate embarrassing uncle. Not just because of his questionable attitude to women and how he referred to them in that awful *Newsnight* interview, in which he was talking in an almost alien language, as if all women were conquests."

Meghan's disapproval of her uncle only roiled ferment inside the Palace. No one, with the exception of the Queen, his ex-wife, and daughters perhaps, had much sympathy left for the boorish Andrew. But for Meghan to be heard and vocal about a long-standing Royal was regarded by many as being wildly inappropriate. Meanwhile, it emerged that William was the prime mover behind having Andrew "step back" from his royal duties in the wake of the scandal and the BBC interview.

"William is becoming more and more involved in decisions about the institution [monarchy] and he's not a huge fan of his uncle Andrew," said a source.

"William thinks the right thing happened," added another aide.

The Duke withdrew from all his 230 patronages and royal duties, with the blessing of his mother, the Queen. The loss of this senior member of the Royal Family, under such unhappy circumstances, was shocking and would have been unthinkable just a few years back.

Just when the Queen and the Palace felt the Andrew situation was being resolved, with a grim sense of inevitability, a new announcement was made from Frogmore Cottage.

"The Duke and Duchess have a full schedule of engagements and commitments until mid-November, after which they will be taking some much-needed family time." In effect, Harry and Meghan were going off the grid for almost two months, at least.

The couple insisted that a six-week sabbatical from onerous royal duties was essential, to spend some valuable time as a family with Doria and Archie over Thanksgiving. There was no plan to make contact with Thomas Sr. or the rest of the Markle clan.

The dilemma faced by Harry—as to his position as a Royal—celebrating the traditional American holiday historically conflicted with Britain, would have taxed the most agile of brains in the Palace press office. In any event, Thanksgiving with Doria evolved into an extended private holiday, free of royal or any other obligations, for the young family, to be spent in the United States and then in Toronto.

But there was more to this trip than a chance to eat turkey and pumpkin pie with the family and show off Archie to friends back in Canada. Meghan had been patient, but this whole Princess thing didn't seem to many to be working out the way she wanted. The gossip was that the pair was scoping out possible new homes in Los Angeles, ahead of a move Stateside, or at the very least, a permanent base in California.

There was some relief in London at this idea, as the Palace continued to struggle with the wishes and dreams of the couple. "There's an acceptance that things haven't worked out with the Sussexes full-time in Windsor," a royal insider commented. "Theoretically, they could have a second base in America."

The six-week break began after Harry and Meghan joined other Royals at the the Field of Remembrance, as part of the annual Royal British Legion Festival of Remembrance on November 9 and the Remembrance Day Service on November 10. They then flew to Los Angeles to join Doria for Thanksgiving, an intimate feast reportedly cooked solely by Meghan "without any servants."

Thanksgiving is traditionally a time for family, so it wouldn't have been complete without a special contribution from the Markle side of the clan, and into the breach stepped eighty-year-old Michael Markle, Meghan's uncle. Weighing in with his thoughts on his niece's relationship with her sister-in-law, he ensured that Meghan be reminded that at this special time of the year, her family was still keeping a close eye on her.

Talking to *The Sun* in the United Kingdom, Michael accused her of acting immaturely "towards family members" since she became a member of the Royals. Mr. Markle admitted that Meghan had left the family behind despite support from them. "It could be that that's part of the problem she's having with her sister-in-law," he confided. "Meghan is immature in some ways. I feel that because of the way she acts—not only towards family members, but other people."

Also weighing in was the figure of Paul Burrell, Diana's former butler. In the wake of her death, he had notoriously caused mayhem with his bizarre and shrill assertions that he had been Diana's "rock." He had been peeved with William and Harry ever since they had begged him to be quiet after hurtful revelations and betrayals of their mother's final years, back in their teens. Now, Burrell echoed Mike Markle's comments about Meghan.

"What comes with maturity is a set of beliefs and they don't sit well with the Royal Family," he pontificated. "She has to tow the party line."

Ironically, this was in complete contrast to Palace musings about Kate before her wedding, when the Queen expressed her concern that Kate didn't have any charities associated with her—an essential part of the gig. She was asked to step up her charity work and individual identity, whereas Meghan, who had charity coming out of her ears, was told to get in line and be less outspoken.

But meanwhile, what of Meghan's sister-in-law? Kate had reacted to the news that the Sussexes were leaving town for a prolonged period of time with mixed feelings, according to a source. On the one hand, with the removal of the constant stream of drama and chaos, their absence meant her own standing in the Palace would be golden. Kate, who seemingly never caused a fuss or behaved in an unseemly manner, was regarded by everyone now with even more appreciation and fondness for her stability and calm, as she busied herself with her photography, her royal duties, and her growing family. She now held the upper hand, observers would note.

Kate had made visible attempts at getting along with Harry and Meghan over the preceding year, after Charles had warned them all to make an effort. But now things had changed. "Kate's standing in the palace has never been so high, so she feels no obligation to make nice with Meghan and Harry," an insider said. The source added that Kate would "not be apologizing or attempting to mend fences until they reciprocate the effort she and William have been making with them for well over a year now."

In a move clearly designed to show Meghan who's who, Kate planned a series of cool social events for her BFFs in January 2020; regardless of whether the dynamic duo would be back in town from their sabbatical, she made sure that Meghan would not be invited. "Kate's decided she needs to be cruel to be kind and it's time her sister-in-law learned a harsh lesson," said the source. "Needless to say, it hasn't been well received at all."

After the dramatic revelations of Harry and Meghan's documentary, Kate and William lightened the mood somewhat as they got competitive over Christmas roulades, with celebrity chefs Mary Berry and Nadiya Hussain on the BBC special, "A Berry Royal Christmas."

It couldn't have come as a greater contrast to the intensity of the ITV documentary, much to everyone's relief. William played the jokily inept dad messing about in the kitchen while Kate shook her head fondly and knocked the baking out of the park. The kids acted cute and adorable while the regal Mary Berry and engaging Nadiya Hussain brought the festive mirth. The message was one of cheery knockabout family fun.

When he saw the show and read the rave reviews and fond comments that came in its wake, Harry was upset. "He felt cut off and excluded," said an insider. "He wished he had been there with them all, laughing, fooling around, having fun before everyone gathered at the table for a lovely family feast."

On top of that, there was the question of their own disappearing portrait. During the Queen's Christmas speech, curious viewers always note the monarch's surroundings, especially the family photos carefully placed in shot. This year, much comment was aroused by the fact that among the massed banks of framed family snapshots on the desk, one particular branch of the family was missing, even though they had produced a cute baby that year and come up with a family Christmas card featuring him nosing at the camera adorably. Social media went into a ferment, with people debating whether the Queen was throwing sly regal shade at Harry and Meghan for deserting her at Yuletide along with the rest of the family at Sandringham. There were also reports that despite some Royals asking Harry and Meghan to return, to spend Christmas in the United Kingdom following the sudden and unexpected hospitalization of Prince Philip over the holiday, he refused to do so.

Wearily, the Buckingham Palace press team rose to the occasion to deny anything untoward was going on. "As has been reported," a slightly testy statement read, "Their Royal Highnesses The Duke and Duchess of Sussex are spending private family time in Canada. The decision to base themselves in Canada reflects the importance of this Commonwealth country to them both. They are enjoying sharing the warmth of the Canadian people and the beauty of the landscape with their young son."

At that moment, the couple and Archie were indeed somewhere in the Great White North. The following month, they would publicly thank the Canadians "for the warm Canadian hospitality and support they received during their recent stay in Canada."

As it turned out, the Sussexes spent their first Christmas with Archie in a $14.1 million waterfront mansion owned by a mystery multimillionaire on Vancouver Island. With eight bedrooms, the gated estate had two private beaches and stunning views across the peninsula, from the four-acre property.

"Locals in the island's rural community of North Saanich noticed cameras and fences erected at the property as early as December 19, and the mansion is now swarming with security guards," reported the *Daily Mail*. "One officer from the couple's royal protection team was spotted patrolling the roads dressed in a Barbour jacket and driving a black Range Rover, and two other British guards were seen flying out from nearby Victoria International Airport, swapping in for new officers."

Unfortunately, once the family's location was leaked, a local restaurant, the Deep Cove Chalet in North Saanich, became the target of a demented hate campaign by Meghan fans. Bored over the holidays and deprived of hourly updates about their hero, numerous emissaries of "Team Meghan" somehow got the idea that owners Pierre and Bev Koffer had turned the Sussexes' entourage away, due to the size of their security detail, and decided to make their feelings plain. There was no support or apology to the couple from the Sussexes.

"We've been getting hundreds of emails," reported a harassed Koffer. "Nothing but s**t, saying what terrible people we are, and we didn't even meet the people or see them. It just took on a life of its own. It's f***ing p****d me off. They came to have a look and then they left," he said. "I didn't turn them down. I've got no idea where that came from, things take a life of their own. I wish I was never involved in it, it's getting worse and worse."

Meanwhile, Prime Minister Justin Trudeau sent out his own personal greetings to Harry and Meghan. "Prince Harry, Meghan, and Archie, we're all wishing you a quiet and blessed stay in Canada," he tweeted. 'You're among friends, and always welcome here."

A COSTLY WITHDRAWAL

The Firm knew that in 2020, something would have to give.

The situation with Harry and Meghan had become unsustainable and matters were at a boiling point. The ITV documentary, the ongoing internal discussions about their future roles, the desperation of the Queen and Charles to keep Harry happy and Meghan satisfied—all of this was on the top of everyone's agendas, as the new year dawned.

So, it was nothing less than a body blow to the establishment, when, on the morning of January 8, 2020, Harry and Meghan's @sussexroyal media channels issued a statement, without any prior warning or alert to the rest of the family:

> After many months of reflection and internal discussions, we have chosen to make a transition this year in starting to carve out a progressive new role within this institution.
>
> We intend to step back as "senior" members of the Royal Family and work to become financially independent, while continuing to fully support Her Majesty the Queen. We now plan to balance our time between the United Kingdom and North America, continuing to honor our duty to the Queen, the Commonwealth, and our patronages. This geographic balance will enable us to raise our son with an appreciation for the royal tradition into which he was born, while also providing our family with the space to focus on the next chapter, including the launch of our new charitable entity.

The statement, couched in bland Hollywood PR speak, caused shockwaves around the country—and the world. For all intents and purposes, this was Harry and Meghan *quitting*. Not since the abdication crisis of the early 1930s had a senior Royal willingly relinquished their role for the sake of love.

The immediate uproar in the media was akin to a hurricane of outrage and shock. As developments unfolded over the course of that gray January day, it became known that the news was as much a shock to Buckingham Palace as it was to everyone else. With that ingrained British sense of solidarity with the Queen and her family, there was a great deal of upset at the young couple's decision and the astonishing snub to the monarchy. This was not the Harry—the loving, respectful, and kind soul—that his family knew.

Rushing out a statement, the Palace scrambled to respond to the news with clear shock and surprise. Officials admitted the Queen was "disappointed"— Royal speak for "hopping mad"—and other senior Royals were understood to be "hurt."

One exasperated Palace insider told the *Daily Mail*: "People had bent over backwards for them. They were given the wedding they wanted, the house they wanted, the office they wanted, the money they wanted, the staff they wanted, the tours they wanted and had the backing of their family. What more did they want?"

Another royal source told us: "It's deeply unfair to the Queen, who doesn't deserve to be treated this way. It is a shoddy way to treat her. The family understands that they want to do something different and is perfectly willing to help them. People are just devastated."

"I think it indicates a real strength of feeling in the palace—maybe not so much about what has been done but about how it has been done—and the lack of consultation I think will sting," observed the BBC's Royal reporter, Jonny Dymond. "This is clearly a major rift between Harry and Meghan on one part, and the rest of the Royal Family on the other."

From positioning themselves as the messiah of the Royal Family, to throwing their toys out of their pram and running away when they got bored with it, the announcement made clear just how committed Meghan really was to the royal role she had held for just 20 months. The fun parts—getting to gallivant around the world in private jets, the fame, the HRH title, and the status—were cool. The less fun parts—not being able to say whatever she wanted whenever she wanted, having to open a dreary leisure center on wet Tuesday afternoons in front of hordes of little people, having to endure Uncle Andrew's ghastly jokes and William and Kate's constant, beady judging—not so much.

It had all apparently finally broken Harry. He had been making public statements about his ongoing struggles with his mental health and for months supporting excellent and much-needed initiatives designed to address mental health issues among young men such as himself. He wanted to reconcile his mother's death and shining legacy with his own life and emerge as his own man, the strong, brave, and true Harry everyone knew lay beneath the troubled and often inarticulate exterior.

But instead, he had been caught between his family and the relentless ambition of his wife, alternately comforted and worried by her, loving her dearly while going against his better judgment. Despite his lifetime experience growing up royal, he had complained constantly about the press madness, ignoring that the overwhelming tone of the media's reporting had been vividly pro-Meghan for about as long as possible, until stories of her demanding demeanor became so pervasive they were, to the tabloids, too hard to ignore.

He had avowed he would no more be "silent witness" to Meghan's "private suffering," adding for good measure that his "deepest fear is history repeating itself."

Not for the first time, Harry's words were carefully digested by friends, many of whom couldn't recognize their old pal behind them at all. The uniform texture of all the statements that were now emanating from the couple's own PR representatives and social media bore the indelible imprint of self-importance that had seemed foreign to Harry prior to Meghan.

This sour sense of entitled disdain for their family inspired some lively reactions in the media. Trisha Goddard, a British television presenter and actress best known for her morning talk show *Trisha*, didn't mince words. "He's, if I can use that term, he's pussy-whipped. That's the term [Americans] use."

Not that she saw the Prince as an unwitting victim. "I think a lot of the push would have come from Harry," she added. "In fact, I wonder if he didn't choose a bride from another country because it gave him an out, because it gave him some security."

Feminist and intellectual Germaine Greer had seen this writing on the wall even before Harry and Meghan's nuptials. In 2018, she told *60 Minutes Australia*,

"I think the pressure to escape from the firm is crushing. I think she'll bolt. I hope, in a way, that she'll bolt, but maybe she'll take Harry with her."

After her prediction became a reality, she said in a follow-up interview: "That's possibly why Harry fell for her. He was looking for a way out."

Hugo Vickers, a royal biographer, likened Harry and Meghan's circumstances to those faced by Edward VIII and Wallis Simpson: "If they're not careful to end up as sort of slightly tarnished celebrities. If you set up an alternative court, it's not going to work. It's very sad actually."

"It's almost as though nothing matters to this couple apart from their own immediate happiness and gratification," wrote the *Daily Mail*'s Sarah Vine. "It's as though they are incapable of seeing beyond their own little bubble of privilege. It has often been speculated as to whether they might end up walking away from Britain. But the timing of this announcement could hardly be more insensitive, or more indicative of how little either seems to understand the true nature of their roles as royals."

London's *Daily Mirror*, on the opposite end of the political spectrum, for once was in accord with its right-wing counterpart. "Harry has selfishly turned his back on the institution the Queen has fought to modernize and secure for him and his children. The Sussexes strutted back from their extended holiday gushing about how keen they were to get back to work. Well, good riddance. I for one have had a bellyful of Harry's eco-warrior hypocrisy." Not to be gagged, Thomas Markle weighed in from Rosarita, Mexico, still seeming blithely unaware of how big a part his actions had been in motivating the couple's news.

"I'll just simply say I'm disappointed," he said.

Harry had inherited millions of pounds from his relatives' estates, including that of his late mother. Prior to her marriage, Meghan was a highly successful actor with an income to match. The Queen also gave them a home to live in, and the taxpayer had footed the colossal bill for its renovation. Of all the young Royals, Meghan had spent the most on her wardrobe, endless accessories, lifestyle accoutrements, and private jet travel. Aware of this, the couple's "withdrawal" statement had kindly offered to continue to fulfill whichever aspects of their current duties they felt like, which would ensure that they continue to get funding from the Palace.

At this suggestion, the monarch decided enough was enough. For some time now, according to aides, she had been privately wondering who exactly the head of the Royal Family was and, as such, who should be making key decisions and shaping the course of the monarchy. After a great deal of thought and deliberation, she had concluded it was in fact still her, not Meghan—or for that matter, anyone else in the family. So, the pushback from the top began to muster, with senior courtiers, advisors, and the family gathering around their boss. It was crisis time.

Immediately, questions were aired. The pair had said they intended to become financially independent. But that would present challenges. As Andrew, Edward, and Sarah Ferguson had all found, to varying degrees, no senior member of the Royals had been able to successfully and ethically survive outside the family, without running into sticky constitutional conflicts over how they made their money and what proportion of their income and lifestyle would still be covered by the taxpayer.

"The level of deceit has been staggering and everyone from the top of the royal household to the bottom feels like they have been stabbed in the back," one source said.

"It's a masterclass in wanting to have your cake and eat it," another royal insider raged. "Even their own staff cautioned against them making this public until they actually sat down and discussed it with the family properly. But they are in this weird bubble and have this strange siege mentality. They feel like it's them against the world and are painting a very unfair picture of how this is a family that supposedly doesn't understand or support them, which is complete and utter rubbish."

One insider mused: "The family is perfectly willing to help them but this was a discussion better had discreetly and quietly. Why on earth they have put it out in the public domain is a decision only they can justify. They have no idea where they are going to live, have no idea how they are going to make their money. The feeling is one of deep disappointment that they have chosen to do this unilaterally and without prior warning or consultation."

The anger and shock soon mutated into a very profound sadness, and no one was more sorrowful than the man who had been beside Harry every step of the way since birth, his brother, his closest ally and most loving friend, William.

"I've put my arm around my brother all our lives and I can't do that, we're separate entities," William was quoted as telling a friend. "I'm sad about that. All we can do, and all I can do, is try and support them and hope that the time comes when we're all singing from the same page."

It's not surprising that William would "want everyone to play on the same team," as he went on to say. After all, his wife is particularly affected by Megxit. As it so happened, Harry and Meghan made their bombshell announcement just a day before Kate's thirty-eighth birthday. If we're to believe Meghan's sister, Samantha, the timing wasn't a coincidence. "Sad she would do that on Kate's birthday," she told the *Daily Star*. "I believe she was jealous of beautiful Kate. She could never compare—Kate is iconic! Perfect Queen material and lovely as a family member, especially as a mother."

Since Harry and Meghan's departure from the Royal Family, Kate and William have had to take on extra work. An insider said: "Meghan leaving the fold has put a tremendous amount of pressure on Kate's shoulders. Although she is willing to do the heavy lifting and take on extra work in their absence, Kate does feel that she was doing an awful lot already. Kate has found herself trying to do it all—console her husband, look after her children, take on more work, and try to smooth things over."

"She's been absolutely put under pressure with it all," the insider concluded, "but has been putting a brave face on as always."

Clearly, the Firm was learning, in the harshest of ways, that there is no *i* in *team*—and not in Meghan, either.

PART TWO

THE MAKING OF MEGHAN

Just as black and white, when mixed, make grey, in many ways that's what it did to my self-identity: it created a murky area of who I was, a haze around how people connected with me. . . . So you make a choice: continue living your life feeling muddled in this abyss of self-misunderstanding, or you find your identity—independent of it.

—MEGHAN MARKLE

Sometime in the first half of the eighteenth century, an adventurous Methodist from the Cornish village of Falmouth, on the Southwest coast of the United Kingdom, set sail to make his fortune in the New World. Upon arriving, William Ragland moved between Virginia, North Carolina, and Georgia, where he finally settled in Jonesboro. He managed a cotton plantation, run by a cohort of slaves of African origin, who labored, rain and shine, through endless backbreaking days, picking cotton and enriching their owners. The mid-1800s was boomtime in cotton exports, with the South producing over one million tons of cotton annually, mainly exported to British textile mills. Cotton demanded intensive manpower, and so by the time the Civil War began, there were an estimated three million slaves in the South alone.

One of the slaves working on Ragland's cotton plantation was Richard "Dick" Ragland, who was born in 1830, taking, as was customary, his owner's surname. In 1848, Richard and his wife, Mary, produced a son, Stephen, who lived long enough to see the ending of slavery and emancipation by President Abraham Lincoln when he defeated the Confederates in June 1865. Now a free man, Stephen married the superbly named Mattie Turnipseed, and they became parents to a baby daughter, Claudie, on February 20, 1885, in Jonesboro, Georgia.

But any hopes former slaves and their children had held that postemancipation life was about to get better were quickly dashed as it became clear that racial discrimination, hatred, and prejudice remained firmly a way of life in the South, due to the fearsome "Jim Crow Laws," segregation, the rise of the Ku Klux Klan, and lynching. Black children weren't allowed to be educated with whites, and there were two heavily enforced lanes in public places such as stores, diners, and so on. Slavery might have been abolished, but apartheid, a South African policy of segregation or discrimination on grounds of race, took its place, and life that had been hard on the black population stayed hard and looked unlikely to change anytime soon. Meanwhile, post-Civil War America was booming in the North, as cities flourished. A new industrial era brought thousands of country dwellers into the expanding metropolises, abandoning the dead-end drudgery of the cotton fields for work in the new factories, offices, and service industries. By the time Claudie married fellow Georgian Jeremiah Ragland in 1905, the pair was faced with a choice—start afresh in the city and give their own children the best opportunities possible, or endure a lifetime of backbreaking, following literally in their parents footsteps as sharecroppers.

Jeremiah and Claudie moved to Chattanooga, Tennessee, in 1910. Jeremiah became a tailor, ultimately founding a successful business, while Claudie worked at one of those new-fangled department stores that were mushrooming up across the United States, catering to a newly affluent, urban white middle class. While it was better than tilling someone else's soil for upward of twelve hours a day, life wasn't easy. The best a young black person could hope for was a job as a maid, janitor, tailor, or factory hand.

Yet Claudie and Jeremiah were sure of one thing: their kids were not going to be menial workers, if they could help it. They were going to college and they were going to make something of themselves. A colossal ambition for a young black family to hold in 1910s Tennessee, but then Claudie and Jeremiah knew they had to think big or fail.

That fierce determination and burning desire to succeed paid off. Two of their five children, sisters Dora and Lillie, blazed through their "Blacks Only" schools and achieved what would have been unthinkable just a generation previously: they went to college. By 1930, Dora was the first member of the family to be a professional, when she qualified as a teacher. Her sister Lillie studied at the University of California and became director of an estate agency and was ultimately featured in the *Who's Who Among African Americans*.

While not reaching the heights his sisters attained, Dora and Lillie's elder brother Steve had also found a job, pressing clothes in a Chattanooga cleaners. He had married Lois Russell, the daughter of a hotel porter, and together, the pair moved to Los Angeles to seek their fortunes. In 1930, their son Alvin was born. He was a bright kid, known for the characteristic Ragland work ethic. After his schooling, he went to work for his Aunt Lillie's realtor business before marrying and moving out to Los Angeles.

In fact, Alvin Ragland married twice. His first wife, nurse Jeanette Arnold, bore him a daughter named Doria Loyce, in September 1956. Doria and her parents moved to Los Angeles shortly after her birth, along with innumerable families, seeking a new life on the Pacific coast, where mile after mile of housing tracts were being quickly constructed, new suburbs created and a new era of bright prosperity predicted. However, shortly after the family arrived, Alvin left Jeanette. He served a brief stint in the military and opened his own antiques business called 'Twas New, starting out huckstering at local flea markets and steadily expanding, until he had a fine business and a collection of rare automobiles. Yet, although he was in regular contact with his daughter, he was an absentee father, rarely getting involved to any serious degree with her life during her childhood and teenage years.

Despite the trauma of her father's desertion, Doria sailed through high school, known for her kindness, serenity, and deepening interest in Far Eastern philosophies and spirituality. After graduating from Fairfax High, she worked briefly as a travel agent (to get flight tickets on the cheap), before setting up small businesses designing clothes ("A Change Of Address") and a company importing incense from India and Nepal. When that folded, she found a new career as a makeup artist. Since Los Angeles was home to hundreds of television and movie studios, Doria quickly found herself in demand and joined one such studio as a trainee.

Working on the set of the soap opera *General Hospital*, Doria discovered a new world. Amidst the stars, directors, producers, sound guys, wardrobe artists, and general mayhem of a daily Hollywood television show, she kept catching the eye of a tall, slightly balding bearded man. He was in charge of the lighting and people treated him with profound respect. He was clearly some kind of big shot in the studio, but then every time Doria passed him on the set, in a corridor, on the lot—she noticed, he couldn't take his eyes off of her. Finally, they went on a date.

It was one of those whirlwind romances that baffle everyone except the lovers themselves. At barely 5'3", twenty-three-year-old Doria Ragland was gentle yet focused and ambitious, obsessed with yoga, Eastern mysticism, and meditation. Thomas Markle was a thirty-three-year-old divorcé with two small children and a demanding, successful job as an Emmy Award-winning lighting director. But the pair was in love, so much so that within six months of meeting, Doria Ragland became Doria Markle. They were married on December 23, 1979, at a faux Indian temple festooned with gold orb-topped turrets, stone elephants, and plastic Buddhas—"the Self-Realization Fellowship Temple"—on the famed Sunset Boulevard.

The fact that Markle was white scarcely bothered the Raglands. Many years later, her brother Joseph told a newspaper: "We would have accepted pink, black, brown, or red as long as Doria loved him. All that mattered to us was he treated her well."

Unlike Doria Ragland's ancestors, Thomas Markle's forebears were raised in comfort, privilege, and security. The Markles were European in origin, their ancestors originating from Alsace, Germany, where one Abraham Merckel (1630–1698) was considered sufficiently aristocratic to warrant a family coat of arms, a gold feather set between two gold fleur-de-lis on a blue background. His son, Johann Martin Merckel, married Juliana Safftler, and the pair emigrated to the New World sometime in the mid 1700s, where Johann altered the spelling of his name, settled in Pennsylvania, and died in 1777, in York County.

Ironically, compared to Doria Ragland's, Thomas's ancestry is harder to trace.

What is known is that generations of Markles lived and thrived in Pennsylvania in relative affluence. Yet, in the wake of Harry and Meghan's engagement, as genealogists around the world went into overdrive researching the new princess's family, it emerged that not only was Meghan's ancestry German, like her new husband's, but their families may have shared a rather less savory link.

The story goes that, during the reign of the infamous Henry VIII (1491–1547), a plot was hatched by wealthy landowner Lord Hussey, 1st Baron Hussey of Sleaford, to overthrow the well-upholstered monarch, who found out and beheaded him. Hussey is alleged to be an ancestor of the Markle clan, along with the nineteenth-century land (and slave) owner, Mary Hussey Smith.

Fast-forward ten or so generations, and a boy named Thomas Wayne Markle was born on July 18, 1944, in Newport, Pennsylvania, the son of Doris May Rita and Gordon Arnold Markle. Doris and Gordon were a blue-collar couple; he worked in the local post office, while Doris looked after Thomas and his two older brothers, Fred and Michael. Despite the family's low income, childhood was idyllic for Tommy and his brothers. The five Markles lived in a small clapboard house, from where young Tommy would venture out to fish in the Juniata River, swing from monkey vines in the surrounding forests, or pick blackberries for their mom. After spending his teen years picking up holiday work such as stacking bowling pins at the local bowling alley or helping out at the sorting office with his dad, Thomas's life diverged from that of his brothers'. Unlike Fred, who today is a bishop in Florida, or Michael, who joined the US Air Force and became a diplomat, Thomas craved a future of creativity, drama, and art. Leaving the small town of Newport, he chanced his luck in the Poconos, a mountain resort in the north of the state, where he fell in with a local theater group. Soon, he was manning the stage lights.

It was an education and an inspiration for the small-town boy. Here was everything he had dreamed of—the glamour and excitement of the stage, a creative outlet for his artistic eye, and the chance to excel and, literally, to shine. Once he had learned everything he could from the small Poconos setup, he decided to take the next step in his burgeoning career. Moving to Chicago, he secured a job as a lighting technician at WTTW, a public broadcasting service. On the side, he also worked at the Harper Theater as a lighting director as well as the long-running kids' show *Sesame Street*.

Thomas was also, when not working at all hours to further his career, a convivial and handsome young man with a wandering eye for the ladies. The nearby

University of Chicago provided Thomas with a steady stream of dates as well as buddies to hang out with, and it was at one of their parties in 1963 that Thomas met a sunny, tall, and vivacious eighteen-year-old student and part-time secretary, Roslyn Loveless. The pair hit it off immediately, bonding over a shared absurd sense of humor, their red hair, and similar heights. It was a quirky, laugh-filled partnership that soon solidified into marriage when the couple exchanged vows the following year. Seduced by Thomas's playful nature and "light air," Roslyn and he made a great team. Shortly after the wedding, along came daughter Yvonne, followed by Thomas Junior in 1966.

Initially, Thomas took to family life with gusto. He was a prankster and a joker and always up for a laugh and a good time. Thomas Jr. has happy memories of visiting sets where his dad was directing the lighting, including *Sesame Street*, an especially cool experience that afforded him much-envied bragging rights at school. Likewise, Thomas Jr. shared his old man's passion for baseball, the two making frequent trips to Wrigley Field to watch the Cubs. It was a fun-filled childhood, but as Thomas's career flourished—it was around this time he began receiving Emmy nominations for his lighting work, with commensurately generous paychecks—he and Roslyn began quarreling during his increasingly rare spells of downtime. He was spending more and more time at work, something that would become a lifelong habit. He no longer seemed to have enough time for Roslyn and the kids. Those parties he still managed to find the time to attend—he seemed to be too fond of them—and the sight of a hungover, grumpy, bear-like dad came to become a sadly familiar sight to the growing children.

Finally, in 1970, Roslyn and Thomas went their separate ways. It seemed Thomas's easygoing personality and jokey disposition had vanished, and they both felt young enough to start over. Initially, the break seemed to work out. Thomas was living nearby and had the children on weekends. But by 1975, the lure of glittering new opportunities for a talented lighting director in Hollywood finally proved too much to resist, and Thomas moved to Santa Monica. Roslyn and the kids moved to Albuquerque, New Mexico, to live with her brother, Richard. Things didn't go well, despite the stability provided by Richard's reassuring presence. Among other problems, Thomas and Yvonne had developed an especially hostile sibling relationship, and they were both bullied at school. As a final straw, Thomas Jr. witnessed an armed robbery that went horribly wrong, severely injuring Roslyn's new partner and traumatizing the young boy.

It was decided that in light of all these issues, it would be better all around if the children moved to Santa Monica to live with their father, despite his punishing work schedule. Thomas had barely seen his kids for the past few years, and this would mean that the pair, now approaching their teenage years, would again get to bask in the limelight of their father's rocketing career.

But, despite moving to a large new home on Providencia Street, Thomas and Yvonne's sibling rivalry only deepened with the onset of adolescence. Tensions ran high. The seeds of a family estrangement were being sown, with Yvonne's bratty behavior and Thomas Jr.'s frustration at his sister causing bad blood all around.

It was perhaps unsurprising that yet again, Thomas Sr.'s prolonged absences from the house grew longer and longer. To the kids, however, something seemed different about their dad, when they did see him. Against the backdrop of his warring offspring and his heavy workload, he somehow seemed to have become—lighter, more joyful and easygoing. He had, in short, essentially reverted to the father they remembered from their early childhood. It was not long before they found out why. Thomas was in love—and his new girlfriend's name was Doria Ragland.

A TALE OF TWO COMMONERS

When Prince William and Kate Middleton married, much was made of the fact that she was a "commoner," one of the minuscule number of nonaristocrats to marry a senior Royal since the 1700s. To detractors, it was another nail in the coffin of dignified British tradition. To fans of the Royals 2.0, it was another welcome sign of a slowly modernizing Royal Family, who preferred love marriages over strategically planned alliances and were taking a more pragmatic approach to the inner circle's private lives in light of a generation of divorces, mismatches, and heartbreaks.

Amazingly, until 2013, the Queen had to grant permission for all members of the Royal Family to marry, from her firstborn son all the way down the hierarchy. This was due to the Royal Marriages Act of 1772, which was brought into place to avoid any unpleasantness over spouses who may "diminish the status of the royal house." Although, arguably, some of the principal members of the family seem to have needed no help in that particular regard over the years, there were sighs of relief throughout the upper echelons of the Firm when the Queen finally repealed the Act. However, the Queen's approval is still mandatory for the immediate six in line to the throne: Prince Charles, Prince William, Prince George, Princess Charlotte, Prince Harry, and Prince Andrew.

It's also worth noting, according to my palace insiders, that the reigning monarch is pleased with all her grandchildren's matches, including working-class rugby player Mike Tindall, who is happily married to Zara Phillips; and son Prince Edward's wife Sophie, Countess of Wessex, a self-made woman from a business background.

Of course, by the time Queen Elizabeth's children had reached marriageable age, the marital protocol had already been profoundly disturbed by the antics of the wayward Princess Margaret in the 1950s, who had caused chaos first by trying to secure permission to marry the divorced Group Captain Peter Townsend, then actually marrying the louche, decadent society photographer Anthony Armstrong-Jones. Princes Edward and Andrew went on to marry posh commoners, albeit of upper middle-class stock. And famously, by 1981, Lady Diana Spencer, from an aristocratic background, was considered suitable for the heir to the throne, Charles, Prince of Wales (who also carries the royal titles Duke of Cornwall and Duke of Rothesay.)

But what constitutes a commoner? In order to understand the royal dilemma, we need to travel back in time, to the sixteenth century, when dark intrigues that beset the Royal Court would have the modern-day Royal Family's teacups rattling in shock. King Henry VIII had never had a reputation for moral rectitude and restraint; the burly monarch was, after all, a literal lady-killer. But one particular liaison—a four-year affair with his second wife Anne Boleyn's sister Mary—ended up reverberating down the centuries. Such that he eventually came to be great-great-great-great-great-great-great-great-great-great-great-great-great-grandfather to one Catherine Middleton, born in Berkshire in 1982.

But let's rewind back to 1524, when Henry's mistress, Mary, gave birth to another Catherine, who had a daughter of her own, Elizabeth Knollys. In 1578, Elizabeth, then courtier and Maid of Honor to Queen Elizabeth I, married a noble Elizabethan soldier and aristocrat, Sir Thomas Leighton. Their offspring went forth and multiplied across the country. Their fortunes waxed and waned over the centuries, mostly waning. It wasn't until 1914 and a wedding in the northern city of Leeds that the dynasty that would lead directly to the Duchess of Cambridge came into place, with the wedding of Olive Lupton to a solicitor, Noel Middleton.

The Luptons, though not aristocrats, have been established in Yorkshire since the fifteenth century—the earliest-recorded member being Roger Lupton, who became Canon of Windsor in 1500. They were a powerful presence in the county, as wool manufacturers and merchants, and as civic and cultural figures of some importance—indeed, Michael Middleton's great-great-great-great-grandfather, Arthur Lupton, was a friend of the German writer Goethe.

Hugh Lupton, the brother of Michael Middleton's great-grandfather, meanwhile, was Lord Mayor of Leeds, and with his wife, Isabella, the Lady Mayoress, hosted visits by Princess Mary during the 1920s. Hugh Lupton's brother-in-law, Viscount Bryce, served as British ambassador to the United States, where his social circle included Prince Arthur, governor general of Canada. Plainly, Olive was quite a catch for the status-conscious Middleton family.

Noel Middleton himself came from a long line of wealthy attorneys. Once married, the young couple wanted for nothing, other than to raise their family in peace and security. They had four children, Christopher, Anthony, Peter, and Margaret, who enjoyed a life of genteel upper middle-class comfort. A secure, happy unit, the Middletons lived in a sprawling house, in the city's Roundhay Park district, the children enjoying a fine education and frequent holidays. However, tragedy struck in 1936, when Olive suddenly died of peritonitis at fifty-five, while on a walking holiday in the scenic Lake District.

The family's youngest son, Peter, was only sixteen when Olive died. Three years later, war was declared, and he and his brothers joined the military. Peter entered the Royal Air Force and flew Mosquito fighter jets as part of the Kent-based 605 Squadron. (He trained at RAF Cranwell, where, over seventy years later, a certain cadet known as William Wales would also gain his flying wings.) His father, who had suffered the loss of his own siblings during World War I, stayed in Leeds, where the manufacturing industries remained luckily unscathed by German bombs—probably due to the fact that the belching black smoke from the factories had obscured the terrain so effectively, German bomber pilots shrugged and went off to batter Coventry or Liverpool instead.

Noel was mightily relieved when his family reunited back in Leeds after the war. On December 7, 1946, his son Peter, by now a commercial pilot, married Valerie Glassborow, the daughter of a prominent local banker. A few years later in 1951, Noel died, leaving a fortune estimated to have been somewhere in the ballpark of £1.5m, divided between his four children.

The Middletons' increasing wealth over the generations owed much to the foresight of Olive Lupton's father, Francis, who had wisely set up a trust expressly for the education of his descendants. As the decades passed, the amounts flourished across a wide range of holdings, from the family business, various property holdings across Leeds, and a broad portfolio of stock market investments.

Cushioned with this wealth and celebrated as a wartime flying ace, Peter Middleton and Valerie had four children, the eldest of whom, Michael, was born in 1949 in Moortown, Leeds. One of eventually four children, Michael grew up in privileged surroundings, as had his immediate forebears. Like his father and grandfather, he attended the prestigious Clifton College in Bristol, where he excelled at sports as well as in his studies.

But for young Michael, there was no need to go on to university like his peers. Like his father, flying was in his blood. In 1962, Peter had been chosen to accompany the Duke of Edinburgh as copilot on a two-month tour of South America—forging a bond with the Royal Family that was to echo decades in the future in the most unimaginable way.

Naturally then, upon leaving school, there was only one thing Michael wanted to do—fly. Accordingly, he enrolled at flight school at British European Airways (the forerunner to British Airways). Following six months training as a pilot, he switched to ground staff training, where he graduated as a flight dispatcher, a senior position equivalent to captain.

With his tall, military bearing, smart uniform, movie-star looks, and quiet, self-possessed character, Michael was never short of admirers. One of them, an equally glamorous and popular new recruit, managed to catch the young flight despatcher's eye. Her name was Carole Goldsmith.

CAROLE MEETS HER CAPTAIN

In 1974, the British government unveiled the country's new flagship airline, British Airways. A merger between the UK's two state-run airlines BOAC and BEA, as well as two smaller domestic airlines, the move was designed to remove rivalry between the airlines and solidify into one flagship brand a new entity to compete in a world of rapidly expanding global travel. As a result, thousands of staff from both existing corporations, as well as new hires, had to be redeployed and reassigned within the new hierarchy.

Travel was still glamorous, far from the depressing cattle class ordeal it is today. Cabin crew had to be elegant and gracious and embody the magic of long-distance travel. For a young man or woman looking to travel the world in style, being part of a cabin crew was a real dream job. The kind of job that would attract someone ambitious, smart, focused, and beautiful.

Among those finding new opportunities in the restructured company was a teenage typist from the former BEA typing pool. Carole Goldsmith, a tall brunette with striking features and a figure that was the envy of her colleagues, had left school at sixteen and worked temporarily at a low-budget clothing store before joining the airline in 1974 on the strength of her Pitman professional qualifications. The life of a typist may have suited someone happy with stability and regularity in their career, but within a couple of drudgery-filled years, Carole was deeply and profoundly bored. Peering into the future, she saw a future in which she might end up being a personal assistant or a company secretary, a role that had no place in her long-term plans to see the world, elevate her social standing, and meet a man worthy of her and her ambitions.

Fortunately for Carole, the new British Airways company was restructuring. Having brushed up on her schoolgirl French—a second language was mandatory for ground staff—Carole secured herself a coveted role as a dispatcher. The job was based out of London's Heathrow Airport, just a few miles from Southall, the down-at-the-heels suburb where she was born in January 1955, in Perivale Hospital, to a lower middle-class couple, Ronald and Dorothy Goldsmith.

As one of the most striking young recruits in the new company, she quickly made a name for herself as a face to watch. "In those days, British Airways was very exciting," said a former colleague of Carole's. "It was a good job with lots of good-looking people and it felt like you belonged to a large club. It had a feeling of being glamorous."

The life was glamorous indeed, while also being hectic and high-pressure. And yet Carole's professionalism soon resulted in her progressing from flight dispatch to a coveted position as cabin crew, sailing around the planet with quiet elegance in her Baccarat Weatherall uniform. Carole's new job brought her into daily contact with a wide range of situations and people from all sorts of backgrounds. They presented no problem for the seemingly unflappable young woman, colleagues recalled. Her equally ambitious mother, Dorothy, had instilled confidence and self-possession in her daughter, gifts that were invaluable in beginning an ascent up the ladders of British society. The next step was to find the right man.

Flight dispatcher Michael Middleton couldn't help but notice the tall, leggy woman who worked alongside him as ground staff at the airport. To be honest, not many of his male colleagues had been able to ignore her, either. Offers of drinks, dates, and no doubt more—the airline industry is renowned for colorful after-hours shenanigans—rained down on Goldsmith. But she was impervious. She had the quiet, courtly Middleton firmly in her sights. They began dating, to the delight of friends, who appreciated the dynamic between the pair. Carole's energetic drive matched Michael's quiet steadfastness and solidity. He came from a comfortable, cushioned background but wasn't snobby about it, which drew in this working-class girl with big ideas. His calm and pleasant demeanor and especially his uniform, complete with brass buttons and the four gold stripes of a Captain, gave him a distinctly military bearing. Carole's rangy physique and classically English Rose features—modest, natural beauty—made him light up whenever she came near. The pair was deeply in love. At just twenty-four years of age, Carole knew she had met her lifelong soul mate.

After dating for some months, in 1979, the couple moved into a small, nondescript apartment overlooking the M4 motorway near Heathrow Airport, in an equally bland suburb of Slough. It was certainly an inauspicious start for a couple who would one day own luxury properties around the world. Shortly afterward—Michael having proposed—they moved to a small village, Bradfield Southend, where they found a pretty red brick house more in line with their plans for a big, happy family.

Michael and Carole married on June 21, 1980, at the Parish Church of St James the Less, in the historic village of Dorney, Buckinghamshire. It was a momentous affair, with the twenty-five-year-old bride arriving in a horse-drawn carriage. The church was a chocolate-box, traditional British country building, dating back to medieval times, set in blissfully bucolic surroundings. On that hot summer's day, it echoed with laughter, prayers, and the hubbub of friendly chatter as the Middleton and Goldsmith families joined together to celebrate the union. Michael's parents, Valerie (then fifty-six) and Peter (fifty-nine) sat across from Carole's parents, Ronald (forty-nine) and Dorothy (forty-four) before all celebrating long into the night at a nearby manor house, where a lavish banquet heralded a night of dancing, drinking, and celebrating in style. As she ate, danced, and gazed fondly through teary eyes at her pretty, happy daughter, Carole's mother, Dorothy, would have sat and thought back to her own nuptials, all those years ago when she and Ronald had celebrated the humble church ceremony with a reception in a local pub. She had had to borrow a suitably special outfit to wear from a friend. If Dorothy had asked anything of her daughter, it was to better and elevate herself as far as she could. Now, as she swung around in the arms of her dashing new husband on the dance floor, watched by generations of comfortably affluent Middletons—she was ecstatic.

For Carole, an upwardly mobile girl from a nondescript neighborhood and undistinguished family, her relationship with Michael was actually her first serious romance. Drawn by his saturnine good looks, Carole's mother, Dorothy, was especially excited by her daughter's new love. Said to be obsessed with status and class, she couldn't have helped but beam with pride as her daughter grew ever closer to her handsome man, never imagining that one day he would walk their daughter down the aisle of Westminster Abbey to wed the second in line to the British throne.

POOR LITTLE CHAP

The baby who would grow up to be His Royal Highness Prince Charles Philip Arthur George, Prince of Wales, K.G., K.T., G.C.B., O.M., A.K., Q.S.O., P.C., A.D.C., Earl of Chester, Duke of Cornwall, Duke of Rothesay, Earl of Carrick, Baron of Renfrew, and Lord of the Isles was greeted with national euphoria when he arrived on the evening of November 19, 1948. Within hours, the first-born son of Princess Elizabeth and the Duke of Edinburgh was cleaned, swaddled, and on display for the courtiers of his grandfather, King George VI.

"Just a Plasticine head," observed Major Thomas Harvey, the Queen's private secretary. "Poor little chap, two and a half hours after being born, he was being looked at by outsiders—but with great affection and good will."

Meanwhile, the newborn's father also generously made time to visit his wife and first-born son and heir. After being notified of the birth, during an energetic game of squash, Philip went for a refreshing swim before popping by his wife's rooms to inspect the newcomer, whereupon he brusquely blurted that his new son looked like a "plum pudding."

The Duke of Edinburgh aside, the public's goodwill reverberated across the land, only amplifying when, at the age of three, Charles became heir to the throne following his mother's coronation. The cherubic toddler represented a fresh new era in the Royal timeline, a symbol upon which the postwar nation could focus their hopes that he would lead them out of an age of hardship. But in truth, there was precious little happiness at home for young Charles. His mother attended to her punishing program of global travel around the Commonwealth, while her husband was also often posted abroad on naval business.

In the meantime, Charles would be left in the care of nannies and Palace staff, with brief visits from his mother, when she was at home. And when his stentorian father did return home, he was not pleased to discover his firstborn seemed ill-suited for the robust huntin', shootin', fishin' lifestyle Prince Philip wanted for the boy. Charles grew into an unhappy, nervous, timid boy, prone to illness and noticeably sensitive. "Never, not even as a baby, did he have his mother entirely to himself for any length of time," writes British author Penny Junor in her biography, *Charles*. "His mother saw him regularly for half an hour after breakfast, looked in on him briefly at lunchtime, and spent another half hour with him at the end of the day before he went to bed."

In a 2017 profile for the *New Yorker*, writer Zoë Heller argued that the Prince of Wales has made himself most unpopular when he tries hardest to be a worthy heir to the throne.

She recanted how the Queen, whom Charles later recalled as being "not indifferent so much as detached," oblivious to the effects of her distance-mothering technique, wondered if he was a "slow developer." He also remembered Prince Philip snorting that Charles was simply "weedy, effete and spoiled." Poor Charles, courtiers thought. Hopeless at team sports, shamefully scared of horses and even more humiliatingly homesick when, at the age of eight, he was sent away to boarding school, he was happiest spending time with his grandmother, the Queen Mother, Elizabeth Angela Marguerite Bowes-Lyon—the wife of King George VI. She indulged him and nurtured his artistic side, cosseted and pampered him, much to the frustration of the Duke of Edinburgh.

Alarmed at Charles and the Queen Mother's trips to the ballet and galleries, Philip determined to toughen the boy up by wasting no more time in sending him to the school he himself attended, Gordonstoun, in rural North East Scotland. Founded by a strict, yet not wholly unsympathetic pedagogue, Dr. Kurt Hahn, a Jewish émigré from Nazi Germany, Gordonstoun took in the shy Prince Philip as a boy and turned out a lean, mean, highly disciplined athletic machine a few years later. Philip always spoke fondly of his time at the spartan and brutal school, so it was a nervous Prince Charles who arrived in the autumn of 1962, aged thirteen, having been flown up by his annoyingly athletic pa in a private plane.

The boys (and then, it was just boys) were subjected to harsh military-grade routines and discipline. The academic curriculum took second place to sporting and physical prowess. From the cold showers first thing in the morning to the endless cross-country runs, assault courses to sailing and PT classes, the young Prince endured what he later referred to as "hell in kilts" with lip-wobbling ineptitude. Charles also had to endure the merciless teasing and bullying of the other boys, who would either mock his stammering shyness, delicate manners, and big ears or make life unbearable for anyone who would show the young Royal friendship, thus being guilty of "sucking up." "Bullying was virtually institutionalized and very rough," recalled John Stonborough, a classmate of Charles's.

Inevitably, Charles was miserable at Gordonstoun, and he begged to be allowed to leave. Philip wouldn't hear of it. But it was clear something had to be done to avert a total calamity, so it was only after some special privileges had been afforded the Prince that he resigned himself to staying. He was allowed to spend weekends at the nearby home of family friends (where he would "cry his eyes out") and even mysteriously became Head Boy of the school in his last year, enjoying the private room that came with the position. He took up the cello and was invited to perform recitals in the homes of neighboring aristocracy ("I was," said Charles with characteristic gloom, "utterly hopeless"). What's more, it was not only the school that was grinding down any tendencies to the artistic and aesthetic the young Prince had.

Two years after Charles joined, a new English master, Eric Anderson, recognized Charles's deep love of drama and literature and encouraged the Prince to act in school productions. In November 1965, Charles played the lead in *Macbeth* leading to Anderson admiringly noting that Charles's performance showed "a sensitive soul who is behaving in a way that is really uncharacteristic of him because of other forces." Charles, for his part, was thrilled, as his parents would be present for the opening night and he could finally show he had found something in which he could excel and dazzle.

But, as he later wrote sadly in a letter, all he could hear as he emoted and writhed onstage was a particularly loud and depressingly familiar guffaw. It was Prince Philip, doubled over with laughter at his son's amateur theatrics. "It sounded like *The Goons!*" cackled Philip to his crestfallen son afterward. Charles was devastated. It seemed that, yet again, in the face of his hopelessness on the sports fields, Charles just couldn't get that fatherly approval he craved. Ridiculed by his family, abandoned by his mother for long periods of time throughout his early years, mocked by his peers, alienated by his privileged position, and weighed down by the expectations heaped upon his shoulders, Charles was becoming adept at hiding his feelings behind a carapace of duty and traditional stiff upper lip.

Speaking many years later, Charles described his growing horror as he realized what destiny had in store for him in adulthood: "I think it's something that dawns on you with the most ghastly inexorable sense—the idea that you have a certain duty and responsibility."

Breaking with Royal precedent, Charles headed straight to Cambridge University immediately following school, rather than ambling around the world preparing for a career shaking hands and asking people what they did. At Cambridge, where he read anthropology, archaeology, and history, Charles found intellectual sanctuary and comfort. In another life, he would have loved to have stayed at the university indefinitely, subsiding into a comfortably anonymous life in academia, surrounded by books, friends, culture, and country pursuits. As if to remind him of the impossibility of this path in life, it was also while at Cambridge that his mother invested him with the title Prince of Wales and Earl of Chester in a grand ceremony in the historic Welsh town of Caernarfon.

So, instead of punting leisurely through his twenties, Charles had to follow family tradition and join the military. On June 23, 1970, he graduated from Cambridge, a Bachelor of Arts in his hand and a daunting future as the professional heir to the throne lying in wait ahead of him.

"I PUSHED HER DOWN THE STAIRS"

One would have imagined the childhood of Diana Spencer as an idyllic upbringing in the bosom of one of Britain's oldest, most aristocratic families. Yet, from an early age, Diana was witness to the painful disintegration of her parents' marriage, emotional and physical neglect, and a nagging sense of inferiority, something that had already traumatized her elder sister Sarah.

Diana Frances Spencer was born into genteel nobility on July 1, 1961, at Sandringham in Norfolk, near the Royal Family's country residence, to John, Lord Althorp, the eighth Earl of Spencer, and Frances Shand Kydd. She was one of five children alongside Sarah, Jane, and younger brother Charles. Another brother, John, sadly passed away while he was still an infant. Her mother, Lady Althorp, was born Frances Ruth Roche in 1936 at Sandringham, the daughter of Ruth Roche, who was a close friend, confidante, and lady-in-waiting to Queen Elizabeth, the Queen Mother.

Diana's childhood was turbulent. Cursed with parents who seemed barely able to tolerate each other, the terrible marriage collapsed with Diana's mother, Frances, Lady Althrop, being committed to a mental home and subsequently divorced by her husband in 1967, when Diana was six. A root cause was Frances's inability—or unwillingness—to have more children. This was something Diana's irascible father, Johnnie Spencer, could not countenance. A certain degree of what today we would call "gaslighting" of the unfortunate Frances ensued. Yet, contrary to what Diana herself would later refer to as her mother "legging it" for London, Frances made every effort to retain custody of her four remaining children. Despite the fact Diana had precious few fond memories of the marriage, the split stunned the child profoundly.

To her school friends, the preteen Diana was a cheeky character, a girl who would eat numerous platefuls of food at a sitting for a bet, enjoyed joking and pranking, and was obsessed with ballet and sports while being an academic washout. In an era where divorce was still something of a stigma among the aristocracy, both parents sought to assuage their split and lack of emotional nurturing by indulging the children with limitless amounts of toys, gifts, and cash.

As a result, the Spencer children gained a reputation for wildness, lack of discipline, and, as a result of being spoiled by their parents, arrogance and selfishness.

"They never said they loved me," Diana, in September 1992, told close confidant, Peter Settelen, her voice coach who recorded a series of explosive interviews with her. "I was always told by my family that I was the thick one, I was stupid, and my brother was the clever one."

Growing up in the family's Park House home on the Royal Family's Sandringham estate also meant she knew the Queen's younger children, Princes Andrew and Edward, well, establishing herself on familiar terms with the Royals from an early age. From their late teens, Diana's family, led by her socially ambitious mother, had Prince Andrew in their sights as a match for their youngest daughter. In fact, so confident were the Spencers that Diana would marry the Queen's middle son that they nicknamed Diana "Duch," or "Duchess," in anticipation of the role that would eventually fall to the hearty country gal and Diana chum, Sarah Ferguson.

Meanwhile, at home, matters failed to improve when in 1976, her father remarried a frou-frou socialite, the Countess of Dartmouth, Raine McCorquodale, whom Diana and her siblings loathed on sight. Dubbing her "Acid Raine," Diana's hatred of her stepmother peaked on her brother Charles's wedding day, when she apparently—by her own admission—set out to hurt Raine.

"I pushed her down the stairs, which gave me enormous satisfaction," Diana told Settelen. "I wanted to throttle that stepmother of mine. She brought me such grief."

Bearing hardly any formal qualifications, Diana had little idea what the future held in store for her when she moved to London in 1978, ostensibly to work with children, but more in hope of bagging a wealthy husband who worked in finance. In those days, it was expected that young upper-class girls should occupy a more decorative, subservient role to their typically oafish buffers of boyfriends. Diana was unworldly, naive, and innocent. In other words, she was perfect prey for the soft-spoken men surrounding the Royal Family, now seeking a pliable, unquestioning girl to marry the Prince of Wales.

CHARLES AND THE
SWEET-CHARACTERED GIRL

London, 1980. Matters had reached breaking point. Something simply had to be done. Throughout the 1970s, the Prince of Wales's colorful love life had kept the media titillated and his family irritated, in equal measure. For much of the decade, the heir to the throne had been squiring a stream of lovelies around town, much to the dismay of his family. His one true love of the decade—indeed, of his life—Camilla Shand had ended their brief, passionate two-year affair in 1973, when Charles was sent abroad with the Navy, and in his absence, she married an old flame, Anthony Parker Bowles. Charles, devastated, tried to blot out his feelings for Camilla with other women, polo, a deeply unfashionable fascination with spirituality, his military career, and a hectic social life—centered around the infamous Mayfair nightclub, Annabel's.

One of those doyennes of Park Lane, where fruity posh girls fell over themselves to catch the eye of a Prince, was Lady Sarah Spencer, the eldest daughter of an old friend of the Royal Family, the eighth Earl Spencer. Although barely in her twenties, Sarah was already plagued with severe anxiety and eating disorders as well as a discreet alcohol problem. She and Charles dated for around three years until 1977, when one night, during a particularly fragile period, she met two newspaper reporters in a London restaurant and gleefully spilled the beans on their clandestine love affair. Dismissing the idea that she would one day marry the heir to the throne ("I wouldn't marry him if he was a dustbin man," she reportedly scoffed), the escapade firmly terminated any prospect of her becoming queen in waiting. Charles, notoriously sensitive to publicity and even more to criticism, swiftly ended the relationship.

But the Prince's roving eye, never missing a trick, remembered Sarah's young-est sister, a gangly collection of gawky limbs, huge blue eyes, and shaggy blonde hair, which more often than not tended to obscure her pretty, blushing features. This was eighteen-year-old Diana, a nursery school assistant and the polar oppo-site of Charles's typical companions. Shy and unsure of herself, she had been working for her sister Sarah as her cleaner, earning a lowly $1.60 an hour to do the dusting, dishes, vacuuming, and laundry.

To Charles, she had made a fleeting impression, and he began to notice her out and about during the late 1970s. But it wasn't until they were formally reintro-duced at a BBQ party in 1979 that Charles began to seriously contemplate Diana as a wife capable of surviving in the House of Windsor. Pressure was mounting on him to find a suitable girl, befitting the heir to the throne, and that meant an innocent yet pliable girl without a past. In fact, months before his untimely death at the hands of the IRA in 1979, Lord Mountbatten had recently told his adoring great-nephew Charles in no uncertain terms to get cracking and find a "sweet-charactered [sic] girl."

The trouble was, Charles didn't know any such girls, his lady friends tending toward the more outgoing and confident. And so, when Diana meekly tiptoed from the wings onto the confused carnival stage of Charles's life, a gigantic spot-light suddenly flashed between those famous ears.

She was young—very young—and painfully shy. She adored children, was suf-ficiently sporty, agreeably sensitive, happy with informality, and, crucially for the Royals, entirely at home in the countryside. But on the flip side, the twelve-year age gap was stuffed with problems—they had no intellectual connection, barely any close mutual friends, and precious few interests in common. Charles, the thinker who would become a controversial public figure in the 1980s with strongly held opinions on everything from contemporary architecture to medicine, reli-gion to literature, found himself with a disapproval of Diana's love of cheesy pop music, fashion, and soap operas, hobnobbing with her fellow "Sloane Ranger" (a British reference to young women from rich upper-class backgrounds) society pals and behaving more or less like a typical, rather giggly, upper-class nineteen-year-old girl.

Nevertheless, by the time Charles attended a Sussex house party weekend in

July 1980, thrown by one of Diana's friends, he and Diana tentatively bonded at a postmatch barbecue, after she had watched him playing polo at the nearby Cowdray Park. It was reportedly during this conversation that Diana pointed out how sad she thought he had looked at the recent funeral of Lord Mountbatten. Charles melted. Meanwhile, hovering suspiciously nearby was one of Charles's exes, the strident Sabrina Guinness, who observed the couple's first real conversation. "She was giggling," recalled Sabrina. "She was looking up at him . . . furiously trying to make an impression."

Whether by coincidence or design, shortly after this meeting, Diana went to stay at a small cottage at the Queen's Balmoral estate in rural Scotland, to help her sister Jane, who had just given birth. Charles, vacationing—as was traditional at the main house with his family—began to hang around the cottage and started making a point of spending time with Diana. Thus began, according to a close relative of Diana's who was visiting at the time, the romance that kick-started the chain of events that would lead to one of the most dramatic, tragic episodes in royal history.

The next month, Charles invited Diana to join him on the royal yacht, the Britannia, during the annual Cowes regatta. His valet, Stephen Barry, watched as Diana "went after the prince with single-minded determination." "She wanted him and she got him," he recalled. During the regatta, Charles confessed to one of his surprised closest friends that he wanted to get married—to Diana.

The final and most important affirmation of the romance took place when the Queen invited Diana to Balmoral in early September during the weekend of the traditional Braemar Gathering, an ancient Highlands celebration of medieval games, from tug-of-war to caber tossing, bagpiping and burly kilted men dancing jigs and reels. The Royals were known for their patronage of these games, attending in full Scottish garb, and despite the sight of the men of the family in their kilts and tartans, Diana acquitted herself wonderfully—no mean feat when it was plain the event was an audition for the family, in all but name. Adding to the pressure was the watchful presence of the Parker Bowleses and another close family, the Palmer-Tomkinsons, who were quietly assessing the potential bride.

Once mummy had given her royal thumbs-up, Charles moved like a hesitant man in a hurry. Meanwhile, the tabloid frenzy about the Prince's bashful girlfriend bubbled and boiled, creating severe problems for Diana as she now attempted to go about her London life, trailed by dozens of shouting paparazzi. Seeing the degree to which the press was hounding her, surprisingly, it was Prince Philip, not widely known for his tact and diplomacy, who urged his dithering son to put a ring on her finger or end the relationship before Diana went mad. Charles, no stranger to his father's imperious ways, grumbled and moaned to friends about the old man's interference (he took to carrying the Duke's letter around with him, reportedly showing it, plaintively, to friends and complaining bitterly), but clearly it was time for action.

On February 3, 1981, at a private dinner at Buckingham Palace, Charles proposed in what must have been an epic speech. The pair, who had only been on a handful of dates together since Balmoral, would see each other barely a dozen or so times before the date they had set to wed—Wednesday July 29, 1981. So, it was Prince Philip who had fired the starting pistol of a new, extraordinary era in the Royal Family's lives that would climax horribly in August 1997—and change the monarchy forever.

***

The wedding date had been fixed. Charles was resigned to marriage, while Diana had started to wonder what she had gotten herself into. She would lose six inches from her waistline in the following three months, from stress. Once the wedding was formalized, the bride-to-be moved into the palace awaiting instruction and guidance on her future role as consort to the first in line to the throne and primarily, from the Royal's point of view, the vessel for the second and maybe third in line.

The media was salivating like a pack of hungry dogs, confronted with a particularly juicy bone when finally summoned to the Palace for Charles and Di to explain themselves and their wedding plans on February 24, 1981. To look at, the couple was bashful, blushful, and tense. "Are you in love?" shouted the assembled media throng. "Of course" answered nineteen-year-old Diana, flashing her thirty-thousand-pound engagement ring and looking bashful. "Whatever love means," mumbled Charles, looking like a man silently trying to pass a kidney stone. "Put your own interpretation on it."

Clearly, this was a marriage borne amidst convenience, opportunity, and necessity. Had Charles been less in thrall to the memory of his beloved Uncle Dickie, or had the pressures of life in the Firm been less pressing, the engagement might never have happened. But as worldwide excitement reached fever pitch and Royal wedding mania swept the country, Charles was said to have become increasingly aware of the fact that not only did he profess not to know what love was—but he was, in no way, in love with his fragile, naive bride-to-be. He was still secretly seeing the strapping country girl who had captured his heart back in 1971, then deemed unsuitable by Palace officials for matrimony and now unhappily married herself—Camilla Parker Bowles. The night before the wedding, he wept with anguish, telling a friend later in a letter that going ahead with the marriage was "the right thing for this Country and for my family."

Hoping for the best, looking at preceding Royal marriages of convenience that had "worked out"—all was futile. In the depths of his tormented, confused heart, Charles knew he was about to commit the biggest mistake of his life.

For her part, Diana admitted she knew even before her wedding that Charles was still seeing Camilla. But she was young and naive enough back then to believe her love was strong enough to change things.

"We always had discussions about Camilla. I once heard him on the telephone in his bath on his hand-held set saying, 'Whatever happens, I will always love you.' I told him afterward that I had listened at the door and we had a filthy row."

To add to Diana's angst, she found a bracelet Charles bought for Camilla engraved with the initials "GF" for the nicknames they had for each other, Gladys and Fred. "I was devastated. This was about two weeks before we got married." The Monday before her Wednesday wedding, the immensity of the hole she dug herself into overwhelmed Diana, who recalled "sobbing my eyes out."

WASTING AWAY

January 8, 1981, was just another day for fashion designers David and Elizabeth Emanuel, a young couple who had recently graduated from the Royal College of Fashion and had set up a small atelier in London's high-class Mayfair district, painstakingly creating gorgeous outfits for young preppies, Bianca Jagger, and the Duchess of Kent alike.

On that day, Elizabeth was doing a fitting with a customer, hands full, on her knees, when the phone rang. Shouting to an assistant through a mouthful of pins to get the phone, she was quickly told it was a new customer asking Elizabeth if she would make her a dress for a friend's upcoming twenty-first birthday party. If that would be possible, a "Debra" would come over at 2:30 p.m. that afternoon? It was.

At the appointed hour, Elizabeth answered the door to Debra and did a double take. Although the engagement had yet to be announced, she immediately recognized the shy young girl from the blanket coverage the royal romance had been getting in the newspapers. "I recognized her immediately," Elizabeth told the *Daily Mail*. "She'd been in the papers since she and Charles had started dating the previous year—but photographs didn't do her justice. I was immediately struck by her height, her beautiful blue eyes, and that flawless complexion."

The result was a gorgeous taffeta gown, which thrilled Diana so much, she returned to the Emanuels on a number of occasions to commission new designs, each gaining more and more attention as her public profile skyrocketed after the engagement. In March 1981, when every British designer was holding their breath to find out who would win the coveted commission to design Diana's wedding dress, the Emanuels were stunned to discover they'd landed the gig.

"From the minute she asked us, we knew nothing was going to be the same," said Elizabeth. Diana, making her first steps in the world of haute couture, had given the duo no direction or specific requests, other than stressing a deadly need for secrecy.

"I tracked down every book I could find on royal weddings from history," she recalled. "Queen Victoria, her daughter, Princess Beatrice, Queen Mary. And I watched all my favorite old films—*The Leopard, Gone With The Wind, Barry Lyndon*. Inspiration came to me from everywhere."

The pair had to bring in military-grade security while the dress was being made, given the virtual round-the-clock surveillance by the media. A heavy safe was installed to store designs in, thick window blinds were acquired and kept pulled down, and Diana herself was referred to by everyone as "Debra" or "Dorothy Cornwall."

Having secured their premises, outsourced the shoes and bouquet, and commissioned silk weavers and lace manufacturers—all British family-run companies, naturally—the Emanuels were left to concentrate on fittings with Diana.

Once Diana and her mother, Frances, had selected a design from the dozens of ideas the Emanuels came up with, a mock-up was created in calico. Unfortunately, the measurements for the dress were shrinking practically each week. Diana, a healthy teenage girl, had decided to starve herself, despite having witnessed her elder sister Sarah's battle with bulimia to the point of being hospitalized. According to Diana, her own eating disorders were triggered by her fiancé's insensitive comments after the engagement.

"The bulimia started the week after we got engaged," she confided to biographer Andrew Morton in 1992. "My husband put his hand on my waistline and said, 'Oh, bit chubby here, aren't we?' and that triggered off something in me." Yet, according to another biographer, Lady Colin Campbell, Charles said nothing of the sort. Diana was simply fishing for sympathy. Campbell, a former close friend of the princess, defended Charles to the hilt. She claimed that far from being the cold-hearted emotional abuser Diana depicted him to be in her traumatic interviews of the early 1990s, he was a sensitive and mature adult who had been pushed into marriage by his own belief in duty, his eager family, and—with admirable guile and cunning—Diana herself.

"I've discovered a marvelous new diet," Diana confided to a shocked Palace flunky shortly after her unofficial move into Kensington Palace. "I eat all I want and then—[mimes sticking a finger down her throat]—blllleeeuuuggghhhhhhh."

At her first fitting in January 1981, Diana's waist measured twenty-nine inches. By the big day, it was down to 23.5 inches. "Every time she turned up for a fitting, she had lost more weight," Elizabeth said. "We put it down to nerves. But it did make it incredibly difficult for us to get on with making the dress. We had to keep taking the bodice in and changing the pattern. The last thing we wanted was to make it up in silk, then have to play around with that. Silk soon looks worn if you work it too much." Finally, fifteen fittings later, the final tryout took place two weeks before the wedding, with Elizabeth Emanuel making the final adjustments. "She was incredibly tiny by the end," recalled Emanuel. "It was suddenly very real. She was just so excited—you could see it in her eyes."

The Emanuels' team of seven seamstresses spent weeks on the dress, working flat out to have it ready by July. The silk came from Stephen Walters & Sons, a family firm of Suffolk weavers dating back to the 1700s. Having been instructed to keep it as British as possible, they used up all the raw silk they could get from busy silkworms at Lullingstone silk farm in Kent. Still, there wasn't enough. Some eleven thousand strands of raw silk were used, so they had to make up the difference with imported silk. The silkworms briefly became global celebrities during the wedding celebrations when it was revealed that they had been gifted to the royal couple in an ornate box. Unfortunately, utterly worn out from their exertions, they all died within hours of the marriage.

The dress's bodice and skirt were made of gleaming ivory silk taffeta, and the trim on the bodice, sleeves, and edges was lace. The creation was festooned with ten thousand pearls and tiny mother-of-pearl sequins. Underneath, a petticoat, made of 295 feet of tulle, was fluffed into shape. And, in accordance with one of the very few directions from the future Princess, the train was designed to be longer than any previous royal wedding dress. The colossal, twenty-six-foot trailing confection was fashioned from antique lace and ivory taffeta, just like the dress, and would need six young bridesmaids to carry it.

Finally, just in time, after numerous fittings, panics, last-minute dashes, and frantic preparations, all was ready. For Elizabeth and David Emanuel, a life-changing day was just around the corner.

The whole country was ablaze with excitement that week. Crowds began converging on St Paul's Cathedral in London, camping on the streets and creating a party atmosphere in the usually staid narrow streets around the historic monument in the heart of London's financial district. As excitement reached fever pitch the night before the wedding, the BBC evening news sent reporter Angela Rippon to interview the couple. Speaking years later to London's *Daily Express* newspaper, Ms. Rippon recalled the interview as being an excruciatingly awkward affair, claiming Diana's body language clearly boded ill: "At the end of the interview, he looks at her and she just looks away, down at the floor. Goodness, maybe we should have read so much more into that. Those five seconds at the end of the interview might have told us so much more about what was to come."

After filming the BBC interview, the couple went their separate ways, with Diana heading home to Clarence House for her last night as a single woman. That night, beset with nerves, she began stuffing herself with food, before inducing severe vomiting. "I had a very bad fit of bulimia the night before [the wedding]," she confessed years later. "I was sick as a parrot that night. It was such an indication of what was going on."

THE FURIOUS BRIDE

If I'd had the courage I would have hitched up my dress and bolted out the church.

—Diana, Princess of Wales

At dawn on the morning of July 29, 1981, Elizabeth and David Emanuel drove carefully past the guards, past the already substantial crowds, police on horseback, paparazzi, and barricades into the grounds of Clarence House, in central London. Inside sat the world's most famous woman, in a t-shirt and sneakers, giggling with her girlfriends and makeup artists. She was watching herself on television, eating cookies, and drinking orange juice.

"Diana had her own enormous dressing room, full of the hustle and bustle of people coming and going, flowers being delivered, and all the rest of it," remembered bridesmaid India Hicks, in Rosalind Coward's book *Diana The Portrait: Anniversary Edition*. Describing the scene hours before Diana walked down the aisle, Hicks said: "I distinctly remember there was a small television on the side of this dressing table, and Diana was seated in front of it, again, dressed in her jeans, and the tiara was being put on her head. She started to shoo anyone who got in the way of the television screen out of the way, because, obviously, she was very excited to see herself on television . . . and then the commercials came on, and there was the 'Just One Cornetto' ice-cream commercial.

"Diana started to sing, and we all started to sing along, too . . . It sort of indicated, I think, the sort of mixture of feelings around getting dressed—she was obviously intrigued to see herself on television, and relaxed enough to be able to sing, but yet sort of nervous enough that we're all laughing and joking along."

The dress itself had been carefully delivered the night before in an unmarked van that had been hired and driven personally by David Emanuel, so nervous was he of any mishaps en route. Now, as the morning wore on, more and more anxious Palace officials ran around, fussing over the Princess-to-be and generally making everyone nervous.

The Emanuels were ushered into a bedroom to dress Diana, mindful of her freshly applied makeup and hair. Despite the high tension in the room, the trio managed to find enough laughter in the chaos to lighten the mood. As David crawled under Diana's petticoats to affix a final button, the Queen Mother decided to pop in to wish Diana luck. David emerged to find the redoubtable dowager peering at him in astonishment.

While David was burrowing through Diana's petticoats, outside, the preparations were well under way. By daybreak, tons of sand, for the procession's horses, were spread along the two-mile route through the historic heart of London, already lined by hundreds of policemen, who were joined by 2,228 members of Britain's armed services. Behind them were tens of thousands of spectators, many having camped out for several days. Meanwhile, four thousand police officers were busy preparing for a massive security operation to ensure the safety not only of the Royals, but also of visiting dignitaries and guests for any threats or suspicious activities.

Then there were the technicians for a hundred television companies from fifty countries, setting up several hundred cameras, 750 miles of cable, and 330 control circuits to broadcast the procession and wedding ceremony to more than 750 million viewers across the globe, helped by several thousand reporters, photographers, and radio and television technicians. In any event, it became the most-watched Royal wedding in history. "A great ceremonial occasion that assumed the gaiety of a carnival rather than the gravity of state," observed London's *The Times* newspaper at the time. "In a grey world, for a troubled nation smarting from a crown of social and political thorns, it was a day of unbridled romance, color and celebration, shared with half the globe."

The wedding day was declared a national holiday. The center of London was closed down to traffic, and a holiday spirit pervaded much of the rest of the city and country, as thousands prepared to watch the hours of pageantry on television before moving outside for a jubilant afternoon and evening of neighborhood street parties.

Surrounded by cheering crowds, Diana arrived at the Cathedral that sunny morning with hope in her heart that Charles's reticence and emotional distance would melt in the sunshine of this tremendous global outpouring of love and goodwill for the couple. Her father, Earl Spencer, heaved himself out of the open carriage (he had recently suffered a stroke and had battled to prepare himself for the big day). Standing near the entrance were Elizabeth and David Emanuel. As they watched Diana climb the steps, the Emanuels' hearts sank—the dress was noticeably crumpled.

"I remember whispering to David: 'Oh my God, it's creased,'" Elizabeth later said. "I thought: 'We've got to straighten out that dress.' But, when she came out of that carriage, it was the most wonderful vision I'd ever seen. She looked like a butterfly emerging from her chrysalis, unfurling her wings and about to fly. It was so romantic. Oddly, the imperfections seemed to make her even more beautiful."

While the world watched on television, Elizabeth and David, with the help of the bridesmaids, smoothed out Diana's dress, adjusted her veil, and spread out that astonishing train. Then Diana, to roars from the crowds, on her father's frail arm, entered the Cathedral in front of millions of people, worldwide, to marry her Prince.

But as she walked down the aisle with her father, the organ playing the "Prince of Denmark's March" and the eyes of the world upon her, Diana drew in her breath in horror. Standing in a pale gray dress with a veiled pillbox hat, Camilla stood to one side of the congregation, right in the sightline of the bride, rendering Diana stunned moments before she shared her vows with the waiting Prince.

This was Diana's most "vivid" memory of the wedding day, she later confided to biographer Andrew Morton. "I was furious," Diana would say later of her emotions after learning too late that Camilla was on the wedding guest list. "I wanted to turn and run. If I'd had the courage I would have hitched up my dress and bolted out the church."

Nevertheless, at 11:20 a.m., the couple exchanged vows. Diana, in a state of high anxiety only compounded by Camilla's neutral gaze, botched Charles's name. Charles, also distracted, messed up his lines too. The press beamed at the "ordinariness" of the couple in fudging their words. The real reason would not be publicly known for many years hence.

The parties, receptions, balls, and celebrations carried on far into the night, accompanied by nationwide firework displays and a network of flaming beacons. In a moment of posthuptial euphoria, Diana described Charles to a relative later, writing: "There were several times when I was perilously close to crying from the sheer joy of it all." For her part, Diana enthused, "It was heaven, amazing, wonderful, though I was so nervous when I was walking up the aisle that I swore my knees would knock and make a noise!"

"It was the worst day of my life," she had also said of her wedding, a decade later. "If I could write my own script I would have my husband go away with his woman and never come back."

Within days, the Princess was facing the harsh reality of her predicament as the bride of convenience to a man who expected her to stay silent as he carried on his life exactly as he wanted, with his much older mistress most definitely in tow.

Departing a London still bathed in postwedding fever, the newlyweds went by train to Broadlands, the Hampshire estate where the Queen and Prince Philip spent time as a young couple. This was followed by a fortnight's cruise through the Mediterranean. Diana was so bored, she attempted to engage with the ship's young crew members in friendly banter and cheeky chat, it was reported. At one point, she even appeared unannounced in the shower rooms, much to their discomfort.

Diana recalled how, on arriving at Broadlands on their first day as a married couple, Charles immediately unpacked seven novels by his favorite author, the South African philosopher Laurens van der Post, and settled down to start reading them.

"I thought, you know, it was just grim," said Diana. "I just had tremendous hope in me, which was slashed by day two."

To cap off the disappointing trip, she was taken up to Balmoral, the Scottish estate where the Royals traditionally retire for the summer. She continued her honeymoon in the company of the Queen, Prince Philip, the Queen Mother, and Charles's three siblings, Anne, Andrew, and Edward. It was nothing like the romantic escape Diana had dreamed of her whole life. When she begged Charles to return to London, he quickly shot her down.

Initially, the couple went on public engagements together, but Charles became increasingly agitated by the attention his wife received. As "a proud man," the Prince became so put out at being left in the shade that he demanded they work separately. Inevitably, more cracks began to show, and Diana's eating disorder intensified. Diana had dreamed of a loving father figure as a husband, a man who would nurture and encourage her. She got none of it.

"He [Charles] ignored me everywhere," she told biographer Morton. It didn't help that while Charles was portrayed as a great thinker and a man with many interests, Diana claimed she was treated like she was "stupid."

Diana said she made the grave mistake once of saying to a child she was "thick as a plank" in order to ease the child's nervousness, which it did. But that headline went all around the world, and she lived to regret it.

"Charles was in awe of his Mama, intimidated by his father, and I was always the third person in the room. It was never, 'Darling, would you like a drink?' It was always, 'Mommy, would you like a drink?' 'Granny, would you like a drink?' 'Diana, would you like a drink?' Fine, no problem. But I had to be told that was normal because I always thought it was the wife first—stupid thought!"

Nobody told Diana what was expected of her as the future Queen of England. As she spiraled out of emotional control, struggling with bulimia and so despondent, she tried to kill herself up to five times, according to the British tabloids. Remarkably, there was no sympathy from Charles—and certainly none from the Firm. In recounting the toll, the *Los Angeles Times* noted, "Diana was said to have flung herself down stairs, cut her wrists with a razor, cut her chest and thighs with a knife, thrown herself at a glass cabinet and cut herself with a lemon slicer in tormented cries for help."

"Well, maybe I was the first person ever to be in this family who ever had depression or was ever openly tearful," Diana later told Morton. "I couldn't believe how cold everyone was."

Over the years, Diana changed from a shy, self-effacing young woman afraid of putting a foot out of place to a force to be reckoned with. So much so that a year before her divorce from Charles became official on August 28, 1996, she refused to be intimidated by Prince Philip when he warned: "If you don't behave, my girl, we'll take your title away."

"My title (The Lady Diana Frances Spencer) is a lot older than yours, Philip," she shot back, noting that the Spencer family was older and more aristocratic than the House of Windsor.

Speaking later to Martin Bashir in her 1995 BBC interview, Diana said the royal household saw her "as a threat of some kind": "I think every strong woman in history has had to walk down a similar path, and I think it's the strength that causes the confusion and the fear. Why is she strong? Where does she get it from? Where is she taking it? Where is she going to use it? Why do the public still support her?"

As it turned out, it was the Royals who should have taken their cues from Diana if they were to adapt to the kind of monarchy the public wanted in the twenty-first century. But they certainly put her through the wringer first.

She noted, "I do things differently, because I don't go by a rule book, because I lead from the heart, not the head, and albeit that's got me into trouble in my work, I understand that. But someone's got to go out there and love people and show it."

Although she was seen by the senior Royals as a rebel intent on making them look bad and refusing to kowtow to convention, Diana said she always did her very best to conform and do what was expected of her, even after her marriage turned sour: "They can't find fault with me when I'm in their presence. I do as I'm expected. What they say behind my back is none of their business."

But the die had been cast. Charles continued to see Camilla, despite Diana's full awareness of the situation. The couple found each other's company trying, yet the pressure for a fairy-tale romance meant that in public, all was well. Meanwhile, each evening at home, Charles would retire to his study, his beloved books, and classical music. Or he would discreetly slip into the night to meet Camilla. Diana, isolated from her old friends, spent days alone, apart from royal flunkeys and courtiers, wandering the endless corridors of Kensington Palace. Wary of her new in-laws and aware of their increasingly chilly view of her emotional temperament, she would stay in, watch soap operas, and binge and purge, binge and purge, binge and purge. Charles and she spent very little private time together, but the pressure was on for her to produce an heir to the throne.

THE HEIR AND THE SPARE

Just after 9 p.m., on the evening of June 21, 1982, Diana gave birth at St Mary's Hospital, Paddington, to William Arthur Philip Louis—a prince from birth and immediately second in the rank of succession. Prince Charles, who broke royal precedent by being present at the birth, later wrote: "I have never seen such scenes as there were outside the hospital when I left that night—everyone had gone berserk with excitement."

The nation came as close to collective celebration as a country could, that day. The blushing Princess, who had charmed the patrician editors of the British tabloid media from day one, handled her public appearances throughout her pregnancy with aplomb, prompting grannies around the world to send scores of knitted bootees and jackets to Buckingham Palace for the impending arrival. But behind the scenes, the marriage was unraveling at an alarming speed. On one occasion, when Diana was pregnant with William, she claimed to have attempted suicide. "I warned [Charles] I'd take my own life. He just sneered and said I would never do it. So I stood at the top of the stairs and threw myself down."

A shocked Queen Mother discovered her, in a crumpled heap at the bottom of the stairs. This was not the Royal way of doing things, naturally, so the matter was quickly hushed up before it could reach the ears of the press.

But Diana was determined. She cut her wrists with a razor, slashed at her chest and thighs with a knife, threw herself at a glass cabinet, and even hacked at herself with a lemon slicer in frustrated, frantic bids to get her husband to take some notice of her. And her violent behavior wasn't confined just to self-harm. In *Diana: The Intimate Portrait*, Judy Wade describes another battle royale some years later, in the parking lot of Smith's Lawn polo field in Windsor. It began when Charles playfully and ill-advisedly tapped Diana on the head after she gave the Duchess of York's father, Major Ronald Ferguson, a warm good-bye kiss.

"Diana was not about to let him get away with that and kicked out at her protesting husband, then gave him a hefty push," wrote Wade. "In return, he shoved her back against her car. Diana then ducked for cover but, as she jumped into the driving seat, he brought one hand down on the back of her neck. Realizing that people were staring in amazement, the couple laughed, but no one was in any doubt that the pushing and shoving looked too forceful to be funny. The rows that were regularly taking place inside their home were now spilling out into public view."

Things seemed to improve immediately following their son's birth. Charles was genuinely keen to be a hands-on, modern dad, albeit a modern dad who had his toothpaste squeezed out for him each morning (as Diana's former butler Paul Burrell claimed) and carried a white leather toilet seat with him for exclusive use when he was on the road. And once Diana had given birth, everyone in the Royal Family was thrilled. "It was all peaceful again," remembered Diana, "and I was well for a time."

This period was perhaps the most tranquil and happy era of the Waleses' marriage. Charles was genuinely thrilled with his little son and, remembering the isolation and emotional repression of his own childhood, made every effort to plan his engagements and commitments around his baby boy. For his part, William was a lively, indulged child and the center of attention of a delighted nation. The apple of his mother's eye, he forged an intense and increasingly codependent bond with her as he grew up. Across the Royal court there was a sense of relief that the emotionally volatile and unpredictable Diana had managed to fulfill her role as wife to the heir to the throne and produce the second in line. After a year or so with the "heir" in place, Diana announced she was pregnant with the "spare."

ROYAL AFFAIRS

Suddenly, as Harry was born, it just went bang, our marriage. The whole thing went down the drain.

—DIANA, PRINCESS OF WALES

Charles wanted a baby girl. Contrary as ever, against traditional male roles in the Royals, he desperately hoped his second-born would be female. In September 1983, with William just over a year old, Diana had suffered a miscarriage while at Balmoral. Charles was sure it had been a girl. He girded his loins and did his duty again, and sure enough, in 1984, it was announced that the Princess of Wales was expecting again.

It was a difficult pregnancy, beset by sickness—Diana was now deep in the throes of bulimia—but ameliorated by the constant hovering fretfulness of her husband, with whom Diana had been enjoying an unprecedented closeness and tenderness. It was "the closest we've ever, ever been and ever will be," she told biographer Andrew Morton of the weeks leading up to Harry's birth, after a grueling nine-hour labor, on September 15, 1984.

"Oh God, it's a boy—and he's even got red hair!" exclaimed the Prince of Wales as his wife gave birth to a yowling Henry Charles Albert David Mountbatten-Windsor. Later, a flustered Prince claimed his startled reaction had been a "joke," but his exhausted wife didn't see it that way, feeling the comment was a snub to the Spencer family trait of ginger-haired children. Later, at Harry's christening in December, Charles reportedly told Diana's mother, Frances: "We were so disappointed—we thought it would be a girl!" "Mummy snapped his head off, saying, 'You should realize how lucky you are to have a child that's normal!'" Diana recounted. "Ever since that day the shutters have come down, and that's what he [Charles] does when he gets somebody answering back at him."

The press had been speculating on the Royal baby's name for weeks, with George tipped as the front-runner (one bookmaker was offering 500-1 odds on the child being named Elvis). According to the *Evening News*, Harold Brooks-Baker, the director of Burke's Peerage, said, "It is known in Royal circles that Charles plans to call one child George." In any event, the baby was called Harry.

But despite witnessing Charles's distress over the boy child, Diana had a little secret that she'd been keeping to herself during the pregnancy. She had known the child's gender ever since they'd had a scan in the early stages—and she'd simply not told her husband. Perhaps it was because they were enjoying such rare intimacy and tenderness, perhaps she needed that power over the Royals. Whatever the reason, Diana later pinpointed Harry's birth as being the moment her marriage hit the rocks for good.

Speaking to Morton, Diana confessed: "Suddenly, as Harry was born, it [their marriage] just went bang. The whole thing went down the drain. Something inside me closed off. By then, I knew Charles had gone back to his lady."

Far from saving the royal marriage, Harry's birth had the opposite effect. Now that the novelty of children had worn off, the painful divisions between the couple had solidified beyond all hope of repair. Charles, abstracted, seeking higher truths and deeper meanings, simply had nothing left to say to the young Princess, who wanted to have fun, giggle, and gossip. She robustly resented the strictures of royal life. Their mutual interests and pursuits drew them further apart, and the Prince and Princess increasingly avoided each other by spending time alone either at Kensington Palace or Highgrove.

Despite having tried to understand and treat Diana's depressions and bulimia, Charles's entire family was starting to grow restive. There was another problem, too. Though the pair enjoyed a very physical attraction in their premarital courtship, by the time William was a few months old and Diana knew what Mama really needed, she had had enough of Charles's unwillingness to get busy in the bedroom. "He's dead below the waist!" she complained to friends, including her confidante, Lady Colin Campbell. Lady Campbell in fact claims that Diana, desperate for some love action after William's birth, set her sights on the dashing, older seventeenth Earl of Pembroke, Henry Herbert. The Earl, whose family line was one of the grandest in the kingdom, managed to boost and reassure the perpetually insecure Diana's self-confidence. When the fling ended, she happily returned to her husband to prepare for Harry's birth, believing she was succeeding in "training" the Prince of Wales into becoming a model dad and husband.

But Charles saw things differently. Having coped with Diana's worsening bulimia during her pregnancy with Harry, he had become trapped in a nightmarish situation. A man who valued, above all, a peaceful life, he had dealt with Diana's demands, tempers, and symptoms of depression by trying to accommodate her as far as possible. As a result, Diana thought she had placed him under her thumb. In fact, Charles was, as had been his wont since childhood, retreating into a shell from where he could wring his hands helplessly and grimace impotently at his wife's bonkers behavior. He took solace in ever-longer spells alone at his country retreat or, increasingly, on the sympathetic shoulder of Camilla Parker Bowles.

One close friend of the couple at the time observed that "Diana had become too domineering. She'd gone and become anti-everything he liked. You can't make a success of your marriage if you're anti-everything your husband stands for."

Diana was permanently on edge. She knew her erratic behavior was pushing Charles away, yet she couldn't seem to help herself. And the more she acted up, the more convinced she was that Charles was seeing someone. Maybe that person was Camilla, that eternal presence hovering on the margins of the marriage, as she confided to Lady Colin Campbell: "I didn't particularly suspect the Rottweiler [Diana's code word for Camilla], but I just knew he had to be having an affair. My instincts told me he was."

"Diana's problem was that she had no sense of control over her own situation," said astrologer Penny Thornton, to whom the Princess had turned for advice in the mid-1980s. "I used to see her in 1986 and 1987 especially when things were really very bad. Things got better in 1989 and 1990 was all right, but by 1991 they were not very good again."

The marriage had also suffered from a number of infidelities on both sides. From around 1986, a lonely and exasperated Charles began discreetly fooling around with a number of aristocratic women, including old friends such as the elegant Eva O'Neill and the Italian stunner Marchesa Bona di Frescabaldi. Meanwhile, Diana also sought excitement from within and outside the palace walls. A handsome personal protection officer, Barry Mannakee, was "one of the biggest crushes of my life," according to the Princess herself. "I don't find it easy to discuss, [but] when was I was twenty-four, twenty-five, I fell deeply in love with somebody who worked in this environment. And he was the greatest fellow I have ever had."

Diana believed that Mannakee may have paid the ultimate price for falling for the Princess. The dashing Royal Protection Squad officer was transferred from his duties at Kensington Palace in 1986 amid suspicions he was getting too close to Diana after Charles's bodyguard, Colin Trimming, allegedly caught him being overly affectionate with his boss's wife.

"I should never have played with fire. But I did—and I got burned." Nine months later, Mannakee—who was married with two young children—was killed when his Suzuki motorbike collided with a teenager's car. Despite a verdict of accidental death, it was revealed at the inquest that a mystery car with dazzling headlights played a part in the crash.

Said Diana, "It was all found out and he was chucked out—and then he was killed. I think he was bumped off. But, um, there we are. I don't . . . we'll never know."

Other than her well-honed instincts, Diana had no proof of foul play behind Mannakee's death. But in secret tapes she made with her former voice coach and confidant, Peter Settelen, between September 1992 and December 1993, one of the most turbulent periods of her marriage, she made no attempt to hide her feelings for her former protector. She didn't use his name but described his death as "the biggest blow of my life."

"I was always waiting around trying to see him. Um, I just, you know, wore my heart on my sleeve. I was only happy when he was around. I was like a little girl in front of him the whole time, desperate for praise, desperate."

So enamored was she with the handsome cop that she was "quite willing to give all this up" and said she had talked of running away with him. "Can you believe it? And he kept saying he thought it was a good idea too."

There was also the romance with hunky rugby captain Will Carling, and in

1987, the sleazy James Hewitt, long rumored to be Harry's father (he's not; it's chronologically impossible). In Hewitt, Diana thought she'd found her shining white knight riding to her rescue on horseback. As it turned out, British Army Major Hewitt was a rat who betrayed his secret lover by cashing in on their relationship with a tell-all memoir.

Hewitt and Diana first met at a party. He offered to teach William and Harry how to ride—and to help Diana overcome her fear of horses. It wasn't long before the couple were regularly meeting in secret at Combermere Barracks in Windsor. A skilled and apparently well-endowed lover, Hewitt's lessons went way beyond horseback riding. According to Hewitt, the couple also had trysts at Althorp, her ancestral home; in the bathroom at Highgrove, Charles's country estate; and even in his mother's Ebford, Devon, home. When he reported to duty as a tank commander in the first Gulf War in 1991, Diana was said to be frantic about his safety.

In her love letters, she used her nickname for him, "Dibbs." "Every minute we're apart, I count the seconds till we meet again. You are my man, my moon, my stars, my everything."

But when Hewitt returned from war, their passion began to wane, and Diana worried their affair would mean she would be blamed for the collapse of her marriage. She stopped accepting his calls. It wasn't until 1994 that the relationship would come back to bite her. By then their fling was history, and Hewitt decided to risk Diana's wrath by selling her out. His book, *Princess in Love*, contained shocking details about their five-year romance.

"He was a great friend of mine at a very difficult, yet another difficult time, and he was always there to support me. And I was absolutely devastated when this book appeared, because I trusted him, and because, again, I worried about the reaction on my children. And, yes, there was factual evidence in the book, but a lot of it was . . . comes from another world . . . didn't equate to what happened."

Diana told friends she was "heartbroken" that the money-grabbing former soldier had sold her down the river.

She also had to explain what happened to William and Harry before they read it splashed across the front pages of all the newspapers.

"Well, there was a lot of fantasy in that book, and it was very distressing for me that a friend of mine, who I trusted, made money out of me," Diana said. "I really minded that—and he'd rung me up ten days before it arrived in the bookshops to tell me that there was nothing to worry about, and I believed him, stupidly. Then when it did arrive, the first thing I did was rush down to talk to my children. William produced a box of chocolates and said, 'Mummy, I think you've been hurt. These are to make you smile again.'"

Then there was the semipublic romance with the strapping Old Etonian merchant banker and scion of an old British family, Philip Dunne. By now, Charles was so blasé about his wife's public cuckolding that he even encouraged it, by inviting Dunne on skiing holidays to Klosters and, astonishingly, to the Royals' private box at the Ascot races. There was even a liaison with King Juan Carlos of Spain, ignited on a family holiday with Charles, William, and Harry.

There was a dalliance with dashing art dealer Oliver Hoare and a brief affair with James Gilbey, details of which were embarrassingly brought to light when a recording of an intimate phone conversation between the pair was leaked to the media in 1992. Dubbed "Squidgygate," after Gilbey's lascivious nickname for the Princess, the tape, which was recorded on New Year's Eve 1989, embarrassed and upset Diana incredibly.

Speaking to the BBC's Martin Bashir in 1995, Diana reflected ruefully on the affair: "I felt very protective about James because he was a very good friend to me, and I couldn't bear that his life was going to be messed up because he had the connection with me. And that worried me. I'm very protective about my friends. I mean he is a very affectionate person. But the implications of that conversation were that we'd had an adulterous relationship, which was not true."

Asked if she had made the call, she answered: "Yes, we did. Absolutely, we did."

Excerpts of the tape included Diana giggling as she told the heir to a gin fortune: "I don't want to get pregnant."

"Squidgy, kiss me," he demanded.

"Oh God, it's so wonderful, isn't it? This sort of feeling? Don't you like it?"

"I love it, I love it," Diana told him, getting friskier when she asked him: "Playing with yourself?"

He let her know: "I haven't played with myself actually—not for a full 48 hours."

Diana burst into laughter and made kissing noises, telling Gilbey he was "the nicest person in the world."

"[Leaking the tape] was done to harm me in a serious manner, and that was the first time I'd experienced what it was like to be outside the net, so to speak, and not be in the family," Diana remembered. "It was to make the public change their attitude toward me. It was, you know, if we are going to divorce, my husband would hold more cards than I would—it was very much a poker game, chess game."

Diana never knew exactly how the recording got out, but she was fairly certain that her husband's establishment friends were responsible. Charles was losing the popularity war that was being played out between the couple in the media. By revealing the contents of the tape, it was clear the Princess

wasn't quite the innocent angel people believed. Needless to say, the whole episode "mortified" the Princess and the Firm.

There were no such revelations from the man she would later describe as being the "love of her life," Pakistani heart surgeon Hasnat Khan, with whom she separated in June 1997, a year after her divorce from Charles was finalized. Diana's closest friends say the soft-spoken, dedicated surgeon was very different from the other men she had turned to in an attempt to escape the misery of her marriage. He shunned the spotlight and had little interest in the razzle-dazzle glamour of a royal lifestyle. He was also a devout Muslim. But when Diana first met him in 1995 during the final throes of her marriage, she told pals it was love at first sight. She'd gone to London's Royal Brompton Hospital, where Khan worked as a lung and heart surgeon, to visit a friend recovering from surgery.

It was the beginning of a discreet two-year relationship that ended shortly before her death. Diana's aide, Paul Burrell, claimed the Princess begged the doctor to marry her—and Khan's parents said she even talked at one time about converting to Islam and moving with him to Pakistan to start another family.

Close friend Rosa Monckton said Diana was "very much in love with" the shy and quiet physician. She was so smitten, she once turned up at the hospital where he worked completely naked except for a long fur coat, said Burrell, who claimed his boss even asked him to speak to a priest about the possibility of organizing a secret marriage to Khan. "I found my peace," Diana said of Khan. "He has given me all the things I need."

But for Diana, the affair would turn out to be yet another bitter disappointment. For all her urging to make their relationship official following her July 1996 divorce, Khan decided the cultural divide between them was too wide and they would be doomed to failure.

"If I married her, our marriage would not last for more than a year. We are culturally so different from each other. She is from Venus and I am from Mars. If it ever happened, it would be like a marriage from two different planets," he told his family. At the inquest into Diana's death, Rosa testified that her friend was still infatuated with Khan at the time of her death. She said Diana was "deeply upset and hurt" when he broke off with her in the summer of 1997. "She hoped that they would be able to have a future together. She wanted to marry him," she said.

That romance gave way to a dalliance—her last one—with the man who would ultimately die by her side, Dodi Fayed.

***

On the rebound from her Good Samaritan surgeon Hasnat Khan, Diana ended up in the arms of Egyptian playboy Fayed, the son of Mohamed Al-Fayed, the multimillionaire owner of London's exclusive Harrods department store.

Other friends—and much of the world—were doubtful about Dodi's intentions. He had, after all, romanced a series of famous women, including Julia Roberts and Brooke Shields. But unlike Khan, he cared little about the round-the-clock media exposure. Some thought he relished it. He also offered Diana a tender understanding and unlimited funds to hire private yachts and planes to try to ensure her privacy.

The couple first went public with their relationship when they showed up together at Lucas Carlton restaurant in Paris on July 25, 1997. Two weeks later, the pair was spotted cuddling on a $32 million yacht off Sardinia. Their families had known each other for years, but now, it seemed, Diana and Dodi were taking it one step further. She was thirty-six at the time, and he was forty-two. It was Dodi's softer side that attracted the Princess. "He was so romantic and thoughtful," said Suzanne Gregard, who was amicably divorced from him in 1987 after a lightning eight-month marriage.

After the couple was snapped together off the coast of St. Tropez in the South of France, Diana zoomed over to the paparazzi in a motorboat and shouted out that she was planning to catch everybody off guard. What did she mean? We would never find out, as she was killed a few weeks later with Dodi in the infamous Paris car crash. There was talk after the accident that Dodi had bought an engagement ring days earlier and his father was convinced a marriage was in the works. But Diana's friend, Rosa Monckton, told the crash inquest that the Princess had no plans to marry Dodi. We will never *really* know.

MISERABLY EVER AFTER

The words "Happily Ever After" were never in Diana's stars—quite literally, as the People's Princess was fixated on astrology, the pseudoscience that claims to divine information about human affairs and terrestrial events by studying the movements and relative positions of celestial objects. Perhaps it's no coincidence then that romantic happiness was fleeting, at best, in her life . . . despite a long string of lovers.

Like Meghan, Diana was somewhat of a rebel in the royal ranks. She didn't fit into the Windsor's way of doing things. History will define that she was often mocked, scorned, and resented by her in-laws—and her own husband, Charles, considered her little more than an irritation. She, too, would go on to despise him.

But it didn't start like that.

Charles was the man initially idolized, then despised, by Diana.

Diana was an introverted virgin who thought she was unfit to become a Princess when they met, even though she was said to have had posters of Charles on her wall at both her divorced parents' homes, seeing him as some sort of James Bond character. Though he was not the sporting type, Charles viewed himself as some kind of a Renaissance Man—a swashbuckling eligible bachelor with a fierce intellect, to boot.

A year before he proposed to Diana, the Prince of Wales was on the rebound from his affair with Anna "Whiplash" Wallace, whose ferocious temper earned her that nickname. Wallace was a dangerous version of Lady Diana—tall, blonde, and a reckless horsewoman.

Charles was sexually obsessed with her and would probably have married her if she hadn't dumped him—because of his love for Camilla Parker Bowles. It was that enduring love that drove Diana to tears a week before her wedding to Charles, who, according to folklore, famously once told Diana he refused to be the only British prince without a mistress.

Instead of spending their honeymoon sleeping with Diana—a trip aboard the Royal Yacht Britannia for a fourteen-day cruise of the Mediterranean before ending their getaway at Balmoral Castle, the Queen's estate in Scotland—he was said to have lain in bed reading the books of Laurens van der Post, about the author's mystical and religious experiences in Africa.

While Charles was steeped in his newfound interest of horticulture and indulged his passion for fishing at Balmoral, Diana had two words for the place: "Rainy/Boring."

His cruelties continued throughout the marriage—Diana spent every day crying during their month-long stay at the Queen's rain-lashed Balmoral estate in Scotland when she found out he had been wearing a pair of cufflinks given to him by Camilla.

***

To understand Diana, we must understand the deep loneliness of Diana's time as an official Royal, from her isolation from Charles to the icy royal snobbery served up to her as an outsider. We must also appreciate her bouts of depression, bulimia, and self-harming, and how after she produced the required "heir and a spare" sons, William and Harry, her usefulness was effectively over.

As Charles and Camilla Parker Bowles resumed their affair, Diana also sought comfort in the arms of other men . . . with sometimes tragic consequences, as in the case of bodyguard-lover Barry Mannakee, who, in 1987, shortly after their affair was discovered, died in a mysterious car crash.

She also admitted to a five-year affair with James Hewitt in a television interview. There was former car salesman James Gilbey, the other half of "Squidgygate," the tabloid scandal when a newspaper got ahold of their intimate conversations in 1992. Others included art dealer Oliver Hoare, billionaire Theodore Forstmann, rugby star Will Carling, musician Bryan Adams, heart surgeon Hasnat Khan—and most scandalous, John Kennedy Jr., the son of former President John F. Kennedy.

According to Diana's former "energy healer" Simone Simmons, Diana once told her: "We started talking, one thing led to another—and we ended up in bed together." The rumor was never confirmed.

Outside the palace walls, however, the press provided the attention she so desperately craved, and soon Diana's every move became front-page news. The rogue Princess was born—and as the paparazzi grew more insatiable, Charles's resentment of her popularity increased.

***

The woman they called the "queen of hearts" was lauded with extraordinary affection. But the final year of Diana's life was far more complicated; behind the headlines and photos, the Princess had cultivated enemies who could have cost her her life. Yet, for most of the public, these enemies were invisible and unknown. The legions of admirers knew only Diana and could not fathom that anyone would or could want to harm such a loving and dedicated woman.

As Diana's biographer, Tina Brown, put it in an interview: "Diana had charisma . . . She had this great accessibility in which she always made everyone she spoke to feel as if she were only connecting with them."

Put another way, people took Diana personally.

She meant something to them.

It went beyond being relatable; there was empathy and sympathy. She was painfully shy and had been thrust into the limelight of the world's stage. There had been Royals before—and would be Royals after—but Diana was the first true superstar. What must this burden have been like? Many shuddered to imagine the burden on the poor girl's shoulders. They felt protective of her.

And Diana touched millions in this way. Her adoring public hung on every word that she said, every item that she wore, and every time she changed her hairstyle. Even her facial expressions in newsreels were powerfully meaningful to many.

Explains Tina Brown:

> You could tell what she thought from the flush of her face and her big, huge, luminous blue eyes that welled with emotion when she looked at you, and made you feel completely connected. She had this great

accessibility in which she always meant everybody she spoke to feel as if she was connecting only to them. That was who she was. That combination of her stature, her incredibly refined beauty, that wonderful peachy skin that was just flawless. Then, this great accessibility and kindness where she was able to connect with people in this very human way. In a rope line, she would get down on her knees and bend down and talk to the children as if she was their mom, and she would have great personal conversations with people and made them feel very special.

Indeed, it didn't take a rocket scientist to understand that Diana's beauty far surpassed those of other Royals.

She was literally stunning, sometimes rendering those who met her utterly speechless. Her grin could disarm the powerful and make people forget themselves utterly. On television it was one thing; but in person and up close, it was truly a kind of magic.

Yet the magic died forever in the early hours of August 31, 1997. Diana's light was snuffed out forever, and in highly suspicious circumstances.

***

Among many other things, Diana's death had the effect of freezing her in time. She would never grow wrinkled or old or suffer any of the indignities that come with age. Her failings and foibles would be, mostly, concealed. She would not make a slip of the tongue or rash statement in anger that might betray a secret. She would stay as she was—as she had been in people's minds—forever.

As Ingrid Seward, royal expert and editor of *Majesty* magazine, said: "It was like a Greek tragedy, the whole of her life . . . Diana was so many different people whirled into one that she was endlessly fascinating. She was one thing to me, and she would've been one thing to somebody else, and it depended on her mood of the day. Because her life ended in such a terrible tragedy, she will be like Marilyn Monroe. She will be an icon forever . . . Because certain people in certain parts of the world are determined to believe that there was a conspiracy theory, the rumblings will always go on."

But to tell the story in this book, we are forced to tell the story of another

Diana. The one behind closed doors. The one whose life was—to put it indelicately—a complete mess. Diana doubted herself. She was self-conscious about her own body and feared that those who admired her were insincere. Further, she believed she had alienated herself from the very people she desired to be closest to, including husband Charles, Prince of Wales (the heir apparent to the British throne), whose wandering eye—and hands—would stab Diana in the heart.

Interviewed for one of my previous books, *Diana: Case Solved*, her butler of many years, Paul Burrell, expounded on the alienation Diana felt:

> I think the Royal Family takes the view that things happen. The queen knows. She's never interfered in any of her children's relationships. Her attitude is they make their beds, they lie on them, and they have to get on with it. These things aren't spoken about. They happen but they happen in private and very quietly. I stood beside the queen for a long time. I know how she performs, and I know what her attitude would be. The queen would say to Diana, "It's your husband. You have to sort out this situation. It's nothing to do with me." She does not interfere until it upsets the apple cart, until it comes to a situation where it involves the constitution of the monarchy—or the country.

The one area where Diana really came into her own was in her tireless devotion to charity work. Millions benefited in real, tangible ways from her crusades against land mines and the spread of AIDS/HIV. What's more, Diana always insisted that she should not be a figurehead only. She insisted on being in the trenches, sometimes literally.

As Burrell noted, "I remember the Red Cross once said to her, 'We would like you to become an executive member of the board,' and she said, 'No, that's not what I want. I want to be on the factory floor. I don't want to be in the boardroom.'"

Put bluntly, Diana's charity work—the most rewarding and straightforward part of her life—eventually became yet another place where she ruffled feathers and made enemies. But none would ever be as fierce as Charles.

When her marital feud spilled from the private to the public arena, Diana became an embarrassment . . . and a liability. For example, in a letter written ten months before the accident in the tunnel—and divulged years later by former butler Burrell—the Princess wrote that "this particular phase of my life is the most dangerous."

"Immediately, there was Team Prince of Wales and Team Diana," Paul Burrell said. "I was happily—by now—on Team Diana, and I thought I was on the winning side. I thought I was on the side that mattered most, but a lady-in-waiting whispered in my ear, 'Oh, don't you realize? Diana will be gone and forgotten within a couple of years, so you're backing the loser. Remember who pays your wages. Remember where the money comes from. Remember who's going to be king.' All of that was being drilled into me as I gave my allegiance to Diana. Soon Diana was being undermined, seriously undermined, by Charles's people. There was a movement."

For any person in a Royal Family, going through marital difficulties would come with the added strains of being in the public eye.

But to say Diana was merely "in the public eye" would be a gross understatement. She was the most photographed woman in the world, probably the most photographed in all of human history. Media outlets were building an empire on her. She had created an entirely new level of interest in and adulation for the Royal Family. Even the most hardened journalists and photographers realized that something uncannily special was going on.

Darryn Lyons owned one of the largest international photo agencies in the world and photographed Diana personally many times. He told me: "Really, the hairs on the back of your neck stood up when the Princess of Wales was in your presence . . . It was just an extraordinary experience . . . She was truly hypnotic for a photographer, and truly an extraordinary experience to photograph. It was a penny for her thoughts, the world around her. Although, the penny turned into a multimillion-dollar business of photographing her every movement, of every minute of every day. I think she was the first of the great royal supermodels as well."

Yet crucial to understanding her life and death is to understand that Diana was not only under the surveillance of photographers looking to get the next great cover shot. She was under almost constant surveillance by the Firm.

***

Diana was many things to many people. For many members of her adoring public, she was a naive waif who'd been cast into dangerous waters. She was a victim. She was beset on all sides.

This was true.

It was also just what Diana wanted people to think.

For, you see, Diana truly was a woman in great peril. She was mistreated by her powerful husband and had in-laws who did not particularly like her (and the way she stole the spotlight). She was acutely, and correctly, aware of the powerful forces she had angered through her targeted charity work. And she knew that her own romantic liaisons were transgressive in a way that would not be long tolerated.

But Diana had learned something. As the woman arguably subject to more press attention than anyone else in the world, Diana had come to understand the power of the printed word. (And the photograph. And the video clip.) Diana's manipulation of the press started gently but quickly grew in intensity.

Diana had seen what kind of a weapon the press could be. What a powerful force it could create. And—in a move that further angered those who disliked Diana—she began using it to protect herself from her enemies.

There were the stories. At one point during the marriage, the frustration of an unfruitful union grew into rage and poisonous exchanges—Charles at one point telling Diana she was moronic and mocking her bulimia by telling her it was a "waste" for her to eat if food was going to be brought up again. There was the time she blamed Charles for sparking her self-harm and suicide attempt when pregnant with Prince William.

In retribution, the Royals circulated stories that Di was delusional and had developed a mental illness.

"Charles, Philip, and senior bureaucrats spread stories that she was crazy," said one media insider. "They were always pushing the line that Diana had a screw loose and no one should listen to her."

But Diana still hadn't played the king in her deck of cards. She'd begun keeping diaries and recordings of both her personal experiences and the Royal Family's secrets. She was perfectly positioned to access the innermost privacies. And when she saw that it would help insulate her from harm—or dissuade someone else from coming after her—she was only too willing to leak this material herself.

By the time Andrew Morton's sensational, tell-all book *Diana: Her True Story* was published in 1992, the Windsors were already embittered against Diana—forever, in perpetuity, no takebacks—with Prince Philip especially furious. Diana had spoken to Morton about her marriage, about her bulimia, about her frustrations with the Royal Family, and about Camilla.

No other Royal Family member had ever done such a thing. There had been royal transgressions, certainly. There had been abdications. There had been forbidden romances. But no Royal had ever told tales out of school to the press itself.

This was a deep and profound shock.

As the marriage between Diana and Charles very publicly unraveled, Diana also gave a sensational tell-all interview with BBC journalist Martin Bashir.

Observed Tina Brown:

> She elected to do go on television, on BBC of all channels, which has always been big supporters of the Royal Family, and give this wildly explosive interview to Martin Bashir where she really did look tragic with makeup that she'd applied very skillfully, with a pebble face and dark eyes and looking like a haunted woman, talked about the agony of being in love with a man who wasn't in love with you, and who had always been unfaithful with Camilla. She said, of course, there are three of us in this marriage, which became a hugely quoted phrase all over the world. How she thought that Charles wasn't appropriate to be king and how the Royal Family were out of touch. This was explosive stuff. In another century, she would've been sent to the Tower of London, and then executed for talking like that about the monarch.

This proved to be the final straw. It was more than manipulation of the press; it was a declaration of war. Charles would not have it, and the couple divorced in 1996.

Refusing to simply disappear (as the Windsors fervently hoped she would do),

Diana instead chose to use her fame to "double down" on her charity work, most especially her work with AIDS awareness and campaigning against land mines.

And now the paparazzi were insatiable. Despite the royal divorce—or perhaps because of it—photos of Diana could be worth a fortune, and they had photographers hounding Diana day and night, watching her every move in the hopes of securing a bumper payday.

The ensuing chaos was unsafe—as we would come to learn on August 31, 1997. A more ominous date in Diana's life there never was.

"YOU'LL BE KING, I WON'T!"

While the fissures were deepening in their parents' marriage, the two young Princes were flourishing. Secure in their toy-stuffed nursery, on the top floor of Highgrove, and watched over by nanny Barbara Barnes, they thrived under their mother's doting watch. Diana was like a lioness, protecting her cubs, even shooing Charles away when he attempted to spend time with Wills and Harry. Eventually, she alienated the loyal Barbara herself; she quit, unable to cope with Diana's fluctuating moods and whims.

The two young Princes, meanwhile, were already emerging as distinctive characters. William was a naughty, tempestuous toddler and, from an early age, displayed a regal attitude. During playground brawls (always discreetly monitored by his security team), he would threaten opponents with his grandmother's soldiers. He was also known to disrupt parties by throwing his weight around and on more than one occasion was sent home from a birthday celebration for throwing a tantrum when he couldn't cut the birthday cake himself. William had been reared from birth for the role that was to one day be his—King. Just a year old when he went on his first overseas trip, to Australia and New Zealand with his parents in the spring of 1983, he quickly learned to respond to the constant presence of cameras and reporters, although his status as the coddled firstborn often led to naughty, rebellious behavior.

Harry, much shyer, was more prone to hiding behind his mother in public. He had quickly understood that his place in the pecking order was below his brother's. He remembers from an early age William being favored by some senior members of the family, including the Queen Mother, who would often ask William to sit with her, or invite him to her home at Clarence House, without his younger brother in tow. "Harry has always known he was number two," Royal authority and writer Ingrid Seward explained. "Obviously Diana was very anxious that he shouldn't feel that."

But rather than complaining, Harry soon realized the advantages of his position. Family lore has it that at the age of just six, Harry taunted his older brother with the words: "You'll be King, I won't. So I can do what I want!"

Harry lived up to his promise. As he grew older, he reveled in his privileged position of relative freedom, until he managed to enrage even his most staunch supporter, his mother. Diana's bodyguard, Inspector Ken Wharfe, who frequently looked after the boys, once saw Diana hit the roof when Harry walloped his older brother with a pool cue, when they were staying on Richard Branson's Caribbean island, Necker. "Harry was always pushing the boundaries," remembered Wharfe. "That was never the case with William."

Unlike his brother, Harry was not academic. Again, Diana had eschewed private tutoring in the royal tradition, by sending her second son to a Mrs. Mynors' nursery school in London's trendy Notting Hill in 1987, before he went to the Wetherby School in 1989. He began boarding at Ludgrove Prep in 1992. William had preceded him there, enjoying the privileges and protection afforded by an old-fashioned British school. Aged eight, Wills was sent to board at the one-hundred-year-old school, a favorite choice of the aristocracy. For the first time, he experienced life outside the Palace bubble. He slept in a communal dorm, had a strict timetable for classes, sports, meals, and recreation, and despite the constant discreet presence of his security detail, he was treated like any other pupil. As Diana wished, her sons were receiving a solid grounding outside the bubble of the Royal Family. As it would turn out in the coming years, the two young Princes would need the security and safety of their schools more than anyone could have anticipated.

The boys being at school ended the last tenuous thread between Charles and Diana. He endured her constant sneering at his stuffiness and fuddy-duddy interests.

"You look like a stiff!" she yelled at him, according to Lady Colin Campbell. "You embarrass me in front of my friends!" He had tried to arrange psychiatric help for her, to address her fragile mental health and worsening bulimia. Yet the very public narrative offered by Diana meant that for years after the eventual divorce, Charles was painted as a scheming cold-hearted fish, suckering in a naive innocent English rose.

Talking to her friend Princess Margaret of Hesse and the Rhine, Diana claimed that "he [Charles] tried to lay a head-trip on me, saying that my behavior drove him away. My behavior had nothing to do with it. He was having an affair with that woman all along. That was the problem, that's what caused my behavior . . . No wonder he couldn't give me the love I needed. He was giving it all to Camilla fucking Parker Bowles."

Despite both being sequestered at boarding school, it was impossible for the young Princes not to be aware of the problems facing their parents, especially as Diana would frequently cry on William's shoulder, according to former royal protection officer Ken Wharfe. They were also often confronted with another "friend" of their mother's, with whom they would have to politely acknowledge as being at least a fleeting source of happiness to her. This—combined with their own impending adolescences and the public scrutiny of their lives—ratcheted up the pressure on them to barely tolerable levels.

***

Located twenty-five miles from central London, sprawling across twenty acres of English countryside, Eton school was founded in 1440 by King Henry VI, ironically to provide a launch pad for poorer boys who wanted to go to Cambridge University. With annual fees today in excess of $52,000 per year, those days are clearly long gone. Today, Eton is known worldwide as Britain's premier educational establishment, having produced nineteen prime ministers (including David Cameron and Boris Johnson), assorted actors (including Eddie Redmayne, Tom Hiddleston, and Damien Lewis), as well as, of course, most sons of the aristocracy, including, not so long ago, Princes William and Harry.

A world of tradition, privilege, arcane rituals, and rugged British values, Eton's reputation as a breeding ground for gentlemen stands alone. The uniform of tailcoat, stiff collar, white tie, waistcoat, striped trousers, and top hat (worn only on special occasions) in the nineteenth century was originally designed to wipe out any foppish tendencies the aristocratic youngsters may have had. The anachronistic get-up today denotes the British devotion to history.

Eton had been described in the past as "the nursery of England's gentlemen" and "the chief nurse of England's statesmen." When it came to decide a school for their sons, both Charles and Diana favored it, the former so they could be spared the horrors of Gordonstoun, the latter so that her sons could follow in the Spencer family tradition. William, having thrived at the small elite Ludgrove Prep school, graduated to Eton in 1995 at the age of thirteen. The world's media showed up to see the young Prince, blushing bashfully under his thick blond fringe and dressed up like a particularly dashing penguin. Both his parents, in a rare show of unity, showed up to escort him to school on his first day.

"That period when Harry and William went there, it was kind of a major transition from when Eton had gone from being kind of a preserve of the landed gentry, where you have a lot of real idiots there, to be a proper academic powerhouse," one former pupil said. "William was very integrated. I think Harry probably had it harder finding his way. The attitude towards them was very matter of fact and every now and again the Queen would turn up for something, and we thought, 'Oh, the Queen's here, that's pretty neat,' we all got to stand and wave our little flags and shout three cheers for the Queen."

Less academically inclined than his brother, Harry, who followed William to Eton in 1998, was also popular among his fellow pupils, not least for his daring exploits on the athletic field (he scored an exceedingly rare rugby goal in the infamously grueling Eton-Wall game), but in later life would play down his time at the school.

"I didn't enjoy school at all," he told a group of South African students on a trip to Cape Town in 2015. "When I was at school I wanted to be the bad boy." Arriving at the school in the immediate aftermath of his mother's death and struggling to manage the myriad emotions the trauma sparked, Harry's turbulent adolescence meant he had a far bumpier ride through his teens.

Nevertheless, despite enjoying accolades such as House Captain of Games, representing his school at rugby, cricket, and polo, and excelling in the Combined Cadet Force, Harry was, by his own admission, marking time at Eton before he could fulfill his dream of joining the military proper.

"Harry was a couple of years above me, I think," recalled another pupil. "The school and all the people there wanted to make him feel included. He had normal friends; he used to go to people's birthday parties. He used to go out with people in London and go to clubs."

Like his younger brother, William had immediately made his mark as an excellent sportsman. He captained his house football team and took up water polo. In addition to this responsibility, he was also joint Captain (at Eton known as "keeper") of Swimming, House Captain of Games, and (in his final year) House Captain.

Unlike his brother, though, William achieved the ultimate Eton honor of becoming one of the twenty-one school prefects, or, as Eton terminology had it, in "Pop." He acted on stage, including taking a part in Shakespeare's *The Tempest*, which was watched in 1998 by the Queen and her husband Prince Philip, presumably with more sensitivity than when they had watched his father's *Macbeth* at Gordonstoun.

However, William also revealed a canny knack of knowing when to retreat and avoid hogging the limelight. The family often recalls how at the age of fourteen, he instructed his parents not to attend the most important day of the school's calendar—the Fourth of June celebrations—because he believed that their presence, and that of their bodyguards (and possibly the invited press), would spoil this "parents' day" for his peers. William's parents accepted his request, and his unofficial nanny, Tiggy Legge-Bourke, attended in their place. At the same time, it amplified Diana's paranoia about Tiggy usurping her position. (She was already wrongly convinced that Charles and Tiggy were having an affair, as was widely known among the palace.)

William became secretary of the Agricultural Club and, after joining the school's Army cadet force, received Eton's Sword of Honor, the school's highest award for a first-year army cadet. As if this weren't enough, he achieved the accolade of being fastest junior swimmer at Eton in ten years, something that especially thrilled his water-loving mother.

William gained a total of twelve GCSE passes (three taken a year early), including top marks in English, History, and Languages before going on to study Geography, English, and History of Art at A Level, when he achieved A, C, and B grades. In 1998, Harry left Eton with B and D grades in Art and Geography. There was an unseemly postscript to Harry's Eton career, when a sacked teacher accused Prince Harry of cheating on his A-Level exams in order to gain entry to his dream school, Sandhurst Military Academy. Sarah Forsyth claimed she ghost-wrote his A-level Art coursework. She was subsequently awarded £45,000 in damages, without any undue blame being attached to Harry or the school.

It was during William's time at Eton, and Harry's at Ludgrove Prep, that the event occurred that would change their world—and the world around them—forever.

THE DEATH OF DIANA

If I had known that was the last time I was going to speak to her the conversation would have gone in a very different direction.

—PRINCE HARRY

On the night of August 30, 1997, Princes William and Harry were staying, as was traditional, with their father and grandparents at Balmoral, the Royals' summer retreat in the Scottish Highlands. Speaking some years later, William recalled how, despite a tiring day romping around the hills and fells, he found it unusually hard to fall sleep that night and woke up frequently.

That evening, his mother had been enjoying a romantic break in Paris, with Dodi Fayed, the playboy son of Harrods boss and Egyptian-born tycoon, Mohamed Al-Fayed. After a summer's fun with Dodi cruising around the Aegean and Mediterranean seas on the Al-Fayed yacht *Jonikal* and zipping around Europe's most chic resorts, Diana had been looking forward to getting back to London and spending some quality time with her sons, before they returned to their respective schools in September. That evening, she had placed a call to Balmoral to say hello to her two boys, aged twelve and fifteen. Speaking on a BBC documentary marking the twentieth anniversary of her death, William recalled that moment.

"I remember getting a phone call at the time [that evening] and you think it's just a parent ringing up to have a chat and I think both Harry and I spoke to her and said we were missing her, and we wish you were back and lots of stuff," William detailed.

"I think it was probably about teatime for us," added Harry. "I was a typical young kid running around playing games with my brother and cousins and being told 'Mummy's on the phone, mummy's on the phone' and was like, 'Right, I just really want to play.' And if I had known that was the last time I was going to speak to her the conversation would have gone in a very different direction."

At 7:15 a.m. on the morning of August 31, Charles woke his sons up and broke the news that had been confirmed barely three hours earlier and had already spread across the world. Their mother had been killed in a horrible car accident in Paris, alongside her lover Dodi Fayed and driver Henri Paul. Their bodyguard, Trevor Rees-Jones, was the sole survivor.

It was at 12:23 a.m. when Henri Paul had lost control of the Mercedes, following a dramatic, high-speed chase through Paris, pursued by paparazzi on scooters and motorbikes. As I detailed in my 2019 book, *Diana: Case Solved*, Diana's car collided with a white Fiat Uno being driven by Le Van Thanh. Before entering the Pont de l'Alma tunnel, Henri Paul clipped Van Thanh, spun around, and smashed into the thirteenth supporting pillar. According to Vincent Messina, a racing and ABS brake expert, Paul was clearly going over the speed limit at the time of the crash. Dodi and Henri Paul were killed immediately. Although he suffered terrible facial injuries, Trevor Rees-Jones survived—his life saved by the airbag and the fact he, unlike the others, was wearing a seatbelt.

When paramedics arrived, they had to clear the crash site of paparazzi, frantically taking pictures of the dying Princess. In the back-right side, Diana was still alive and crouched on the floor with her back to the road and her legs up on the seat. Her face and body appeared remarkably untouched by the carnage. There was little sign of serious injury other than a trickle of blood from her mouth and nose. But that face, known by people the world over, was blank, her eyes blinking.

Shocked eyewitnesses said she repeatedly murmured, "Oh, my God!" and then "Leave me alone." *Those were her last words.*

A French doctor driving through the tunnel, Dr. Frederic Mailliez, was the first to try to help moments before police arrived at 12:28 a.m. It wasn't until 1 a.m. that Diana was removed from the car into an ambulance. Shortly after, she suffered a massive heart attack, and although her breathing was restarted she was found to have extensive internal injuries. Her heart had been pushed to the right side of her chest, tearing her pulmonary vein and causing internal bleeding.

At 1:25 a.m., the ambulance carrying Diana left for the Pitié-Salpêtrière Hospital, 3.7 miles away, arriving there at 2:06 a.m. Despite intense and prolonged efforts there to resuscitate her, French doctors pronounced the Princess dead at 3 a.m., local time.

William recalled the shock of the news making him "disoriented, dizzy . . . and very confused. I remember just feeling completely numb. And you keep asking yourself 'Why me?' all the time. 'What have I done?'"

Harry, meanwhile, recalled their father's gentle stoicism in breaking the news. "One of the hardest things for a parent to do is to tell your children that your other parent has died. But he was there for us." Floored with grief, self-pity, and regret, meanwhile, Charles turned to his courtiers. "They're all going to blame me, aren't they?" he groaned, presciently, according to author Tom Bower in *Rebel Prince: The Power, Passion and Defiance of Prince Charles.*

The news shattered Britain. Speaking that morning, Prime Minister Tony Blair described Diana as "the People's Princess." With the utterance of that now-legendary phrase, he unleashed a veritable tsunami of grief across the country—and the world. Britain collectively wept, grieved, raged, and emoted like never before.

Up at Balmoral, William, Harry, and the Royals were receiving frantic briefings from Buckingham Palace describing the escalating crisis in the capital. It had been naively assumed in the immediate aftermath of the tragedy that Diana's funeral would be a simple Spencer family affair, despite her still being technically a member of the Royal Family. But it was almost immediately apparent that this would be woefully insufficient. Returning Diana's body home from Paris, Charles's team prepared to take her to a mortuary in Chelsea, central London. Charles angrily instructed them to take her body to lie at St James's Palace, as befitting a royal. It was clear that Diana's funeral would be a historic event.

The morning of Diana's death, the Queen and Princes Philip and Charles quickly formed a protective shield around the stunned William and Harry. Also present, by sheer luck, was their much-loved nanny, Tiggy Legge-Bourke, who had planned to escort them back to London that day, to be reunited with their mother, who had planned to return from Paris that evening.

That morning, the young Princes asked specifically to be taken to the tiny local church at Craithie, where the usual service took place with no mention of

Diana. Later, William took the first of a number of long solitary walks across the Highlands, with his black Labrador, Widgeon. The Queen and Prince Philip, he later recalled, provided a close, sympathetic, and loving support network, the latter especially belying his gruff public reputation.

Down in London and across the world, shock was turning to anger, as the circumstances around Diana's death became known. Whipped up by the media, smarting from the blame for Diana's death, and seeking to deflect some of the blame—the public began calling for the Queen to make an appearance. The Royal policy of closing ranks and mourning in private was being portrayed as a cold, out-of-touch callousness, quite erroneously. Fanning the flames of public emotion, speaking from his home in South Africa, Diana's brother, Charles, angrily announced that the media had Diana's "blood on their hands."

Having pursued a not-always-uncooperative Diana for years, it was in the global media's interests to find a common target for the anger. After days of unprecedented headlines in the papers, condemning the Royals for their silence, the monarch cut short her holiday and, along with Princes Charles and Philip, returned to London with the grieving Princes. William and Harry both have recalled the excruciating public walkabout with their father, in a sea of ugly weeping and wailing by strangers reaching for them, pawing at them, sobbing, and displaying a grief that shocked and greatly upset the two boys, who had barely begun to process their bereavement themselves. On the urging of her advisors and the prime minister's office, that evening, the monarch made an extraordinary television address, for only the second time in her reign [the first time was the Gulf War in 1990] in which she publicly paid tribute to Diana and to the British people.

Deciding to mourn in public had been "a very hard decision for my grandmother to make," said William. "She felt very torn between being our grandmother and her Queen role. And I think she—everyone—was surprised and taken aback by the scale of what happened and the nature of how quickly it all happened."

"A TIDAL WAVE OF GRIEF"

The reappearance of the Royals and the sight of the two heartbroken boys undertaking the brief walkabout seemed to quell the public furor. A date was set for the funeral, September 6, at Westminster Abbey. It was not technically a State funeral, but at the urging of Prince Charles, it came about as close as it could possibly be without completely shredding royal protocol.

By convention, Diana, as a former Royal, would normally only qualify for a quiet interment at St George's Chapel and burial at the small royal cemetery at Frogmore, London (near the home of Harry and Meghan, Duke and Duchess of Sussex, before their self-imposed exile). The Spencer family and the Queen also favored a small, dignified affair. But having seen the public fervor for commemorating Diana, the Prince of Wales quickly realized anything less than a major production would be a calamity. Therefore, it was an unprecedented show of pageantry and informality, pomp and populism, charity, celebrity, and aristocracy.

The event was pulled together at top speed. Extreme shuttle diplomacy between Tony Blair's team, the Royals at Balmoral, and the Spencer family was needed to assuage the heightened emotional and constitutional demands being placed on the principals, while the needs and wishes of Princes Harry and William were respected by all concerned. Observers at the time noted young Harry's very apparent grief and shock—in contrast with William's almost frightening levels of self-possession and emotional control. Only his repeatedly chilly loathing of the media belied his roiling emotions within, yet it was that very media that was now clamoring for Diana's eldest son to make himself prominent during the service and especially in the preceding procession.

It had been suggested that William and Harry walk behind Diana's coffin. Charles Spencer proposed that he alone should follow the coffin. Tony Blair wanted a "People's Procession" whereby members of the public could form the funeral cortege. Prince Charles wanted to walk behind the coffin. Everyone wanted the two young Princes to walk behind the coffin, but all felt uncomfortable pushing the request, as William had refused point-blank, feeling it was a sop to the loathed media. Harry immediately followed his brother's lead. Rumor had it at the time that Charles had urged the young Princes to walk with him to deflect any spontaneous outbursts of anger. "There was genuine concern as to what reaction the public might have to the Prince of Wales," explained Charles's press secretary, Sandy Henney, to royal biographer Penny Junor. "[But] at no time was there ever a question of using the boys as a barrier against possible reaction from the public towards my boss."

As was so often the case with the Royal Family, the impasse was solved by an irate Duke of Edinburgh. Philip had been vociferously defending and protecting his young grandsons throughout that whole nightmarish week. Unsurprisingly, he told them to get out in the fresh air of the remote bleak beauty of the Highlands, trek, ride, hunt, and walk. Surprisingly to some, he also gently encouraged them to talk, express their grief, and share their emotions.

Away from the boys, he wasn't afraid to stand up for them, at one point slamming his fist on the table and roaring down the speakerphone to the prime minister's office in London, arguing that William and Harry were not to be treated as "commodities" at the funeral, according to ex-Prime Minister Tony Blair's "gatekeeper," Anji Hunter, who spoke of it in a BBC film about Diana's funeral. He also emphatically put an end to the dithering over who would walk in line behind the coffin by assuring the boys that if they wanted to, he would walk with them, and if they didn't want to, they didn't have to.

The day of the funeral dawned. Over a million people lined the route through London, in a poignant echo of that sunny summer's day, almost sixteen years ago to the month, when cheering crowds had gathered along a similar route to celebrate a shy young bride and her dashing Prince, as they made their way to Westminster Abbey for the wedding of the decade.

The night before the funeral, Diana's mother, Frances Shand Kydd, quietly and anonymously picked her way through the people camping along the Mall and in the surrounding royal parks, which had been specially opened for the purpose. Candles flickered and guttered in the soft August evening breeze, fresh after a heavy downpour that afternoon. The air was heavy with the scent of the thousands of bouquets massed along the procession route and by the gates of Kensington and Buckingham Palaces. In that very British way, strangers became friends over shared sandwiches and thermoses of tea.

On the morning of the funeral, London ground to a halt as thousands of people lined the route through the city. Eight members of the Queen's Welsh Guards carried Diana's coffin, which was covered with three wreaths of white flowers from her brother and her sons. Five hundred representatives of various charities the Princess had been involved with joined behind them in the funeral cortege. As the coffin passed Buckingham Palace, where members of the Royal Family were waiting outside, the Queen bowed her head.

As the cortege moved slowly from St James's Palace, the world watched the heartbreaking sight of the two young Princes, who, with remarkable dignity, slowly walked alongside their father, grandfather, and uncle, Charles Spencer. Spencer described the feeling of walking behind Diana's coffin as the "worst part of the day by a considerable margin."

He explained, "The feeling, the sort of absolute crashing tidal wave of grief coming at you as you went down this sort of tunnel of deep emotion, it was really harrowing and I still have nightmares about it now. So, there was [my] inner turmoil of thinking, 'My God this is ghastly,' but then the point of thinking these two boys are doing this and it must be a million times worse for them. It was truly horrifying, actually. We would walk a hundred yards and hear people sobbing and then walk around a corner and somebody wailing and shouting out messages of love to Diana or William and Harry, and it was a very, very tricky time."

Unknown to everyone at the time, Charles Spencer was planning a surprise for his address at the funeral.

In paying tribute to his sister, the ninth Earl Spencer angered the Queen with lines like "Someone with a natural nobility who was classless and who proved in the last year that she needed no royal title to continue to generate her particular brand of magic" and "I pledge that we, your blood family, will do all we can to continue the imaginative and loving way in which you were steering these two exceptional young men so that their souls are not simply immersed by duty and tradition, but can sing openly as you planned."

His words created a sensation. Billions of viewers worldwide caught the stony expressions on the face of the Royals as Spencer's incendiary speech reached its climax. Spencer later defended himself, saying he understood the Queen believed he had "every right to say whatever he felt." He saw the eulogy as a chance to "speak for somebody who had no longer got a voice."

"I don't feel I said many pointed things," he told the BBC, twenty years later. "I believe that every word I said was true and it was important for me to be honest. I wasn't looking to make any jabs at anyone, actually. I was trying to celebrate Diana—and if by doing that it showed up particularly the press, I think, in a bad way, well, they had that coming."

He also recalled keeping the speech secret to prevent anyone else having a say in it. Well, almost secret, if you discount Diana's corpse. For Spencer admitted that he read the speech to Diana's body in St James's Palace chapel a couple of days before she was buried. "I know people will think I'm some sort of fruitcake but I do remember hearing almost some sort of approval then, and then I realized I had probably got the thoughts in order."

Four days after his mother's funeral, Prince William returned to Eton College to find six hundred letters waiting for him. Over half the school had written to him, offering their condolences and with the firm instruction that there was no need to reply. A fellow pupil said: "It was simply a show of solidarity." William, then fifteen, also had the support of a good friend who had lost his mother several years earlier.

The reaction that greeted Harry at his Berkshire prep school, Ludgrove, was more wary. Staff and pupils were told not to talk about what had happened. No newspapers were allowed, and television was more closely monitored than usual. If Harry, just coming up to the age of thirteen, saw as much as a glimpse of his mother's face on screen, he would jump up, turn off the television, and leave the room, according to another pupil.

An inquiry in 1999 by the French authorities blamed Paul, concluding that he was incapacitated by a cocktail of alcohol and drugs before losing control of the car while speeding.

However, there has been a continued unwillingness by the public to accept the official version of Diana's death, even after the tragedy was revisited by the authorities in Britain in a belated 2007 inquest. In his book *Diana Inquest: Corruption at Scotland Yard*, John Morgan said Diana's lawyer, Lord Victor Mishcon—who died at age ninety in 2006—told police in 1995 that the Princess expressed her fears to him that she'd be assassinated in a staged car crash.

The British peer allegedly handed his notes about the meeting over to police following his famous client's death, but they were suppressed for years. It was only when Burrell revealed the existence of Diana's compelling letter making similar allegations that the British police reluctantly handed the minutes of Lord Mishcon's meeting over to the French coroner. "I believe Diana cannot rest in peace whilst her killers walk free, and the people who ordered this assassination and the ensuing massive cover-up live in peace," blasted Morgan.

Harrods owner Mohamed Al-Fayed, Dodi's father, has long been convinced that Diana and Dodi were murdered by British security services at the behest of Establishment forces. More specifically, he blames Prince Philip, the Queen's now-ninety-two-year-old husband, and Prince Charles.

Sixteen years after the accident, significant questions still remain unanswered from that fateful night. Incredibly, it took 101 minutes to get Diana to the hospital after the initial emergency call—a delay Al-Fayed claimed British secret service agents instigated to slash her chances of survival. President Reagan, after all, suffered the same pulmonary tear as Diana in the assassination attempt against him in 1981, yet he was saved and lived until the age of ninety-three.

CASE CLOSED

This particular phase in my life is the most dangerous. My husband is planning an "accident" in my car, brake failure and serious head injury, in order to make the path clear for him to marry.

—DIANA, PRINCESS OF WALES

Written with chilling foresight just ten months before her untimely death in a horrific crash in a Paris tunnel, Diana put her fears that she was the target of a sinister death plot down on paper as "insurance" for the future.

While there has never been any definite proof that Charles or the Royal Family was involved in the crash that ended Diana's life, explosive allegations pointed a finger of suspicion at the Queen and shadowy figures behind the crown for ordering an assassination to silence the rebel Princess.

Author John Morgan claimed in *Diana Inquest* that Her Majesty decided that Diana had become too much of a threat to the British monarchy after divorcing Charles. He also accused Scotland Yard of orchestrating an elaborate cover-up to protect the crown.

The truth, however, is far less sinister.

"Voilà, c'est pour ça je les laisse penser ce qu'ils veulent," Le Van Thanh, driver of the mysterious white Fiat Uno, told me in the summer of 2019. ("That's why I let them think what they want.")

Finding the Fiat Uno was clearly the number-one priority for any serious investigation into Diana's death. Initially, the search identified photographer James Andanson as the driver. His charred body was later found locked inside his BMW with a bullet hole to the temple. Curiously, his death was ruled a suicide.

But was he really the driver? A thorough examination of the moments before Andanson's death proved that he had marital problems. The conspiracy theories surrounding his death were also unpicked: the deceased was alone in his car, in the countryside, and tipped petrol over his entire body, then set himself alight and burned to death. The fire was so fierce that his head exploded from the heat. Clearly suicide. Further, former homicide detective Colin McLaren, who has studied the case, was able to prove Andanson was on an aircraft hours after Diana's accident, flying to a photography job. The timelines between takeoff and the Diana accident made it impossible for him to have been at the Pont de l'Alma crash site.

In November 1997, French authorities located another man who had painted his car the color red the day after the crash—the French Vietnamese national, Le Van Thanh—who claimed he was working security at the time of the crash, and as such he was quickly ruled out.

But McLaren tracked down a vital witness, Sabine Dauzonne, who saw a white car emerge from the tunnel that night for the book *Diana: Case Solved*. McLaren put Sabine under a memory recall session. She remembered seeing a white Fiat Uno leaving the tunnel seconds after the accident, and that it was badly damaged along the driver's side doors and rear lights.

The driver looked scared and confused and was looking back into the tunnel. She also remembered a large black-and-tan-colored dog with a big collar around its neck, sitting on the backseat. Armed with this, McLaren presented Sabine with pictures of similar young men, and she identified Le Van Thanh as the driver—who also had a guard dog—identical to the one Sabine observed in his car that night.

So why would he respray his car?

Could he be the key to cracking the case?

And why did the French police ignore this vital information?

After eighteen months of supposed investigation, a French judicial inquiry concluded that the crash was nothing more than an accident caused by the reckless driving of Henri Paul, who was highly intoxicated at the time. It was also determined that paparazzi were not near the car at the time of the crash.

British Police would drag their feet until 2004 before beginning Operation Paget, their own investigation into Diana's death. And still the questions mounted up: an American couple would testify at the inquest but would be dismissed because the French police had combined their statement. The search for the white Fiat Uno was barely mentioned by either the British or French inquiries. What of the ignored evidence, the dismissed witnesses, and, most worrying, the discounting of Le Van Thanh as a person of interest? This seems highly suspicious, so McLaren and I were determined to track down the mysterious Le Van Thanh.

Le Van Thanh has never spoken publicly. The French police had dismissed him as a player in the tragedy owing to an intact taillight (but if he could respray his car, he could surely replace a taillight). Operation Paget barely mentioned the Fiat, and Metropolitan Police Commissioner Lord Stevens claimed the driver would be impossible to track down. In a highly dramatic scene, McLaren and I drove to his home in suburban Paris. Our conversation was an explosive revelation that—in our minds—finally solved the case . . . and indeed fueled demands for a new inquest to be opened.

Here is an abbreviated transcript of the exchange between Le Van Than, McLaren, and me:

> **Translator:** The idea was to exonerate you and show that you are a victim in all this.
> **Le Van Thanh:** But I am exonerated; I don't care, to be honest.
>
> **Translator:** They were just trying to exonerate you in this story. That you didn't do anything; you're really a victim (of circumstances).
> **Le Van Thanh:** Yes, but I know I didn't do anything. That's why I don't need to be exonerated, sir.
>
> **Translator:** You have nothing to say?
> **Le Van Thanh:** Yes, I have nothing to say.
>
> **Translator:** No one is accusing you here, pay attention. That's what I'm telling you.

Le Van Thanh: No, but you don't listen. I know, there's nothing to worry about.

Translator: It was just to exonerate you through new evidence. They just have a question or two to ask you. Don't you want to answer them?
Le Van Thanh: No, no.

Translator: Definitely not?
Le Van Thanh: Definitely not.

Translator: He [Colin] says he has read all the police reports and that you are innocent?
Le Van Thanh: But people say otherwise, but that's okay.

Translator: Yes, he talked to witnesses who you saw that night; and you are completely innocent, and you have nothing to worry about.
Le Van Thanh: I know that, sir. That's why I don't even need to talk to them, if they know. I know that. We're all happy; we all know it. But then again, I don't mind at all. People can think what they want.

Translator: Yes, no, that's right. But . . .
Le Van Thanh: Because you know, you are Vietnamese, I am a Buddhist.

Translator: Yes, I know.
Le Van Thanh: That's why I let them think what they want.

Translator: Oh, yes.
Le Van Thanh: They imagine everything they can imagine, it's not my problem.

Translator: Okay. There's just one thing on his mind, you're completely innocent, but you repainted your car. That's what he doesn't understand. It's the only thing.

Le Van Thanh: Yes, it is. That was mentioned in the newspaper and so on. You can read it everywhere.

Translator: But what was the story then?

Le Van Thanh: I said it from the beginning.

Translator: And why did you repaint it?

Le Van Thanh: I will not repeat the same thing. Everyone knows that. The police report, they know why I repainted it.

Translator: But then, why was that, what was the reason? That's right, actually what messed things up. I don't know if . . .

Le Van Thanh: When you have no money and you have a damaged old car, what do you do?

Translator: Okay. He just has one last thing to say to you. He's a really great cop. It's not a . . .

Translator: No, there is no problem. There were lots of things that were said to me again.

Translator: We are friends, I would like to tell you something. Are you listening? The English police is coming to see you soon. Because he, there is an English policeman who told him, they want to question you. They will come to see you, because when they asked you to come you didn't go.

Le Van Thanh: No, but I know they will come. Several times they told me they would come back.

Because eventually they told me, "Yes, they will come." They wanted me to go to England.

Translator: Yes, that's right.

Le Van Thanh: You know what the French police told me?

Translator: No.

Le Van Thanh: "It's not the same law as in France; don't go there."

Translator: Oh, it was the French cops who suggested that you shouldn't go?

Le Van Thanh: Don't go there. He told me: "Not the same law as in France, don't go there. . .don't go there [to England] it's the police, which means they don't agree with each other. It's the police, which means they don't agree with each other, in other words."

Translator: They will come to you. He says, "If you need him, he can testify that you are innocent. Because he's a former police officer with a proven track record."

Le Van Thanh: Don't worry, I will receive them well.

Translator: Are you going to receive them well? [laughs]

Le Van Thanh: Yes, I will receive them well.

Translator: Yes, yes, they are in France, of course. No, no, they can't do anything anyway.

Le Van Thanh: I will tell them the same thing I told you.

***

"That's why I let them think what they want."

Of all the words spoken by Le Van Thanh during our confrontation with him, these are the ones that most haunt me personally. Van Thanh knows he is a pawn. He knows that there are powerful forces capable of destroying his life—and he is not insane.

In this simple line quoted above, Le Van Thanh is telling us that he cannot do other than what he has done. He must allow the public to believe what they will, because the alternative is unthinkably dangerous.

Will he be killed for speaking the truth?

Will his family?

Will he find himself the victim of an "accident" just like Diana's?

All of these are clear possibilities.

It is also outrageous that a man should be telling us—pleading with us, really—to understand his situation in a certain way . . . and to have the institutions of the world turn a deaf ear. Even if Le Van Thanh wished to tell us the truth, he feels that he cannot. Surely this fuels demands for a new inquest to be opened on the tragic death of Princess Diana.

That is exactly the feelings of Mohamed Al-Fayed, who through his lawyer, Michael Mansfield QC, told me that if it can now be shown Le Van Than was driving the white Fiat Uno, there is a genuine case to be made to reopen the inquest:

> There is a real question mark here because the French authorities were particularly anxious to ensure that it was blamed to the paparazzi. That's why they were all arrested to begin with. He [Le Van Thanh] had the car resprayed. It is very suspicious. If it's him in the tunnel—if it's his Fiat—whether it was an accident or whether he was trying to get in the way, I have no idea. The Mercedes obviously did hit the Fiat. Whether that was an accident by the driver driving too fast into the tunnel or whether the Fiat Uno was in the wrong lane, I can't take it beyond that. I don't know what part the Fiat Uno played other than it obviously had a role as a vehicle that was there. But whether the driver

did this deliberately or not obviously, and what his background is, and why, all the rest of these other questions are in the same league as the [James] Andanson story. Witnesses have said it. It's not contrived. That's the concrete evidence. What I'm more interested in is the sandwiching of the car. There are other drivers out there that have not been traced.

Likewise, former BBC royal correspondent Michael D. Cole (who, after leaving the BBC, worked as director of public affairs for Harrods and thus was also a spokesman for its owner, Mohamed Al-Fayed) suggested our remarkable interview with Le Van Than should be passed to British and French authorities as part of a formal request to reopen the Diana inquest as a cold case inquiry.

He told me: "As a matter of urgency, this information should be conveyed to an officer of the court. If it is reported to the French police or the British police, then there will be the temptation, or the possibility anyway, that somehow the information will be buried. But first of all, Mohamed Al-Fayed needs to know about it, and then the proper authorities need to know about it and then, given the possibility that this gentleman will actually make an affidavit, make a sworn statement, as to what happened to him twenty-one years ago, nearly twenty-two years ago, then other people than me can make a judgment about what to do. But it certainly is prima facie cause for a new thoroughgoing look at what went on, because if this was going on, what else was going on?"

Whatever the truth behind Diana's tragic death, there is no doubt that the Princess was fearful for her own life in the months before her death—and in the years after, the lives of her sons, particularly Harry, would be cruelly effected by that fateful night in Paris.

PART THREE

ROYAL WELCOME FOR THE OTHER WOMAN

The devastating aftermath of Diana's death affected William quite differently from Harry. Unlike the impulsive, emotional younger Prince, William buried his feelings deep down—something he had learned to do at an early age. In the months and years following the tragedy, his schooldays proceeded on a more or less even keel, without any serious bad behavior or scandalous episodes on record.

The calamity precipitated a complete change at the heart of the boys' lives. Gone was Diana's world of fun, traumas, frivolity, and dramas—Charles swept the young, traumatized Princes under the protective shield of the Royal Family. They still had their beloved Tiggy Legge-Bourke, the goofy, lovable family friend who was now a much-needed "big sister" to the teenage Princes. It was Tiggy who, the week after Diana's funeral, shoved William and Harry off on one of their favorite pastimes, following the local Beaufort hunt when it met near their Highgrove home. After a few words of condolence, the huntmaster and the regular participants mounted their horses and took off as usual, accompanied by the stoic Princes.

While their typical laughing and bantering was absent in those dark weeks in 1997, in many ways, the boys' behavior in the wake of Diana's death can be seen to be the making of them. Their bond, already forged during the tumult and pressures of their extraordinary childhoods, became stronger, as they relied on each other for support and understanding. William's natural resilience developed into an inner core of steel, into which he would retreat, protecting himself from the outside world. During one of his earliest interviews, at Eton, he had discussed how knowing there would one day be a crown on his head added an at-times unbearable pressure on his shoulders. That sense of responsibility, which had been instilled into William from an early age, had already emerged before Diana's death. He had, on occasion, expressed his disapproval at his mother's more dramatic public moments and in the aftermath was mindful of his father's embarrassment at publicly grieving for his beloved "Uncle Dicky," Lord Mountbatten, who had been murdered in 1979. William, aware that the eyes of the world were on him, channeled his grandparents' and father's sense of decorum and duty and never would let the mask slip.

At Eton, William's close-knit group of friends and teachers made sure he was well supported and protected from media intrusion, but when he was home from school, the Prince's "Glosse Posse" pals—nicknamed after the county of Gloucester, where the boys stayed at their father's Highgrove estate—haunted the bars and clubs of rural Gloucestershire, behaving like any other group of privileged teens letting off steam. They hung out at the Rattlesnake Bar, where Harry was soon to get spotted allegedly smoking spliffs in a backyard shed, as well as drunkenly making racist comments to a French barman (which was subsequently laughed off by all concerned). William and his mates tended to stick to copious amounts of beer and dad dancing to the bar's cover band, Nobody's Business, who churned out easygoing rock and pop covers for the cheery crowd of local yuppies.

In June 1998, William decided it was time to formally meet the woman he had heard so much about from his mother—most of it decidedly acidic—Camilla Parker Bowles. The Prince of Wales, mindful of the emotional turbulence the boys were coping with in the wake of Diana's death, left it more or less up to William and Harry to decide when they wanted to meet the woman who was the true love of his life and his intended wife. In any family, such meetings are fraught and emotionally terrifying. It was all the more difficult for the heir to the throne to introduce Camilla to his sons and successors as their stepmother-to-be, especially after the horrendous death of their mother, who hated Mrs. Parker Bowles with justifiable passion. But as Charles's fiftieth birthday approached, and the boys got busy planning a surprise party for him, the thorny issue of Camilla loomed ever larger.

Finally, William bit the bullet and asked his father to set up a meeting.

It went well. Despite reports that Camilla emerged from William's rooms ashen-faced, reeling, and demanding a stiff drink, it was apparent that the two young

Princes had reconciled themselves to the fact that not only was Camilla a nonnegotiable part of their father's life, but with their tacit approval would be their stepmother at some point in the not-too-distant future. At his fiftieth birthday, with Camilla and her children guests of honor as stars of the British television and theater world entertained the exclusive gathering, Charles's tears of joy and gratitude for his sons went way beyond their thoughtfulness in arranging the event. He knew that the level-headed William, and by extension Harry, had given his lover the approval she needed to become his wife.

Meanwhile, William's amorous exploits had been gaining attention as he progressed through his late teens. Having been something of a heartthrob for years, with his bashful good looks, the Prince was now a strapping young man with an athletic and rugged physique that only made his admirers melt even more. Even during his schooldays, he had enjoyed the reputation of being something of a heartbreaker, albeit involuntarily, thanks to the near-obsessive coverage by the UK media. And the newspapers went into overdrive when the seventeen-year-old Prince was seen enjoying the company of young aristocrat Davina Duckworth Chad on a cruise through the Aegean Sea in 1999. Typically, the pair were distantly related, as Davina's mother was second cousin to Diana. The pair enjoyed a teenage fling, but it fizzled out of its own accord within months.

Before long, William had found solace in the arms of Arabella Musgrave, the eighteen-year-old daughter of Major Nicholas Musgrave, manager of the local Cirencester Park Polo Club. At a party at the home of mutual family friends, the Van Cutsems, William uncharacteristically made his feelings very clear, by sneaking upstairs with the pretty brunette hours after meeting her. It was the beginning of what friends recall as an extremely passionate affair. During William's last summer at home before heading off to university, Arabella was his main preoccupation. As William packed his bags and prepared to head off on his gap year before college, he and Arabella nevertheless agreed to end things, as they both knew life was pulling them in separate directions. For Arabella, it was a journey that eventually saw her assuming the post of chief of PR at Gucci. Meanwhile, for William, the next stop was . . . a freezing cold beach on the shoreline of Chile.

WILLIAM WEATHERS THE STORM

Belize is a former British colony in Central America, a nation that contains some of the most hostile environments in the world. It's also one of the most awe-inspiring, with the world's second biggest barrier reef. It was the first stop for William on the gap year he embarked on shortly after leaving Eton (where he achieved a very respectable three A-levels, with an "A" in Geography, "B" in the History of Art, and "C" in Biology). The gap year had emerged, in recent decades, as a rite of passage for youngsters wanting to see a bit of the world under their own steam, before heading back to their books at university. For William, who had been sheltered and fiercely protected from the moment he was born, it was the perfect way to prove to the world and himself that he was capable of standing on his own feet and amply suited for his aspirations for a career in the Army.

It was grueling. William, in conference with his father and assorted respected elders, including academics, clergy, and military figures, had stipulated that he wanted to challenge himself. A close and trusted protection officer, Mark Dyer, had done some of his military training in Belize and knew that the tough environment would fit William's needs perfectly. So it happened that William's gap year began deep in the jungle of Belize in late summer 2000, where he engaged in survival exercises with Dyer's old regiment, the Welsh Guards. As William sweated in tropical humidity, lived off the land, slept in hammocks, and dodged snakes, poisonous toads, and an array of unfriendly fauna, his cosseted former life quickly became a distant memory. After a short, intense spell in the heart of Belize, he headed to Chile, where he joined a group of youngsters from all sorts of backgrounds, to participate in an eleven-week program.

According to author Penny Junor, William flew to Santiago knowing hardly any of the people he would be spending the next three months of his life with. Those three months promised to be the hardest of his life.

The expedition was divided into three sections, an environmental project, a community project, and an adventure. These exercises were merciless—the boys were unleashed to fend for themselves after rudimentary crash courses in local orientation, first aid, and cookery.

The following weeks were life-changing for the young Prince as he plunged into sailing, trekking, camping, tracking deer for a conservation project, and coping with working as part of a team of boys from diverse backgrounds. One time, William and the boys were marooned on a stormy beach for five days, in torrential rain, forced to sleep side by side under tarpaulins billowing angrily in gale force winds.

William recalled the traumatic time later on to the press. "That was the lowest point," he remembered. "I don't think I've ever been as low as that. The moment we got there it started raining, and it didn't stop raining for five days. We were stuck on the beach. We couldn't get off because of the weather. There was a howling wind, I think force four or force five, and the waves were too big for the kayaks. It was literally nonstop. You go to bed, you wake up, it's still raining. We were all soaked through. You go to bed with wet clothes."

Another time, when the group was deployed to the tiny village of Tortel deep in the heart of the Chilean countryside, William mucked in and labored on a construction project alongside the other boys. Most of the villagers were unaware that the second in line to the British throne was helping build wooden walkways along the perilous mountainsides or playing with their children in the village school.

Marie Wright, the project manager in the remote village, told London's *The Telegraph*: "If there are any tensions he's the sort of person who will make a joke and it all settles down again. He's a real peacemaker among the group if it's needed. His star quality is that he's just completely human and normal and one of the gang."

Another of the project leaders told the paper, "To me, he's just an example of a good teenager with a good education and a good sense of humor. He's treated the same by me. I told him off within the first ten minutes for being lazy, and after that he got on with it. You can trust him to do a job. Half the time he doesn't need telling."

William was quickly accepted by his peers, despite the fact that many of them came from severely disadvantaged backgrounds, very far from the experiences of the Glosse Posse. One seventeen-year-old boy, a drug user who was homeless in the United Kinddom, said: "Everyone gets on really well and William fits right in. I take the mickey out of him all the time and call him 'Little Princess.' He doesn't mind; he just laughs along with it."

The experience was an outstanding success. William had needed to find himself outside of his royal identity, and the hardcore survival course had given him a golden opportunity to survive under extreme conditions as part of a gang, working together without any of the cosseting usually provided a senior Royal. As he boarded his flight home from Chile, just before Christmas 2000, his head banging from the aftereffects of the group's farewell party the night before, to everyone around him, and probably himself too, William knew that the past three months had transformed him from a shy, bashful teenager into a capable, confident young man.

THE REIGN DOWN IN AFRICA

Between South America and his next foreign destination, William steamed ahead, after a day's chilling with the Glosse Posse and his family. Early in 2001, he was elected to spend a month as a laborer in a Gloucester cattle farm, owned by family friends. Again, William sought anonymity and equality with the rest of the workers, pitching in with the backbreaking daily routine. His days would begin at 4 a.m., with the usual mucking out of the stables, herding and milking cows, and numerous menial tasks that would be handed to any newbie on the farm.

The month on the farm supercharged William's self-confidence and a sense of accomplishment. Here he was, living on the land he would one day rule, knee-deep in cow shit, hoisting hay bales and fixing fences. According to friends, he couldn't have been happier.

"The best bit [of my gap year] was in England," he told journalists a few months later. "I loved working on a farm. It was the best part of my year. I enjoyed the fact that I was put in as a farmhand and was paid and was just another guy on the farm. I got my hands dirty, did all the chores, and had to get up at 4 a.m. I got to see a completely different lifestyle."

William and Harry had been out to Africa with their father's friends the van Cutsems in the wake of their mother's death. William had been enchanted by the continent. In March 2001, he headed back to visit Kenya. He would stay on Lewa Wildlife Conservancy, a 61,000-acre game reserve owned by the aristocratic Craig family since 1922 and famed for its conservation programs for indigenous wildlife.

The Craigs welcomed William to Lewa, Kenya, and their family with an easy-going friendliness that reassured and comforted the young Prince. Always responsive to close-knit, cozy families, William bonded with Ian and Jane Craig and their children, Jecca (Jessica) and Batian. He especially bonded with the glamorous Jecca, the teenage daughter of the family, with many believing she became one of William's first serious girlfriends. Others (including the Craig family) downplayed the relationship, pointing out that the Prince was close to them all.

While in Lewa, William developed an in-depth knowledge of rhino and elephant poaching, a major problem in Kenya and neighboring countries. It was this knowledge that convinced him to become royal patron of Tusk Trust, which remained eternally grateful for it. "You can't exaggerate their [the Royals'] importance in Africa's conservation wars," stated Charlie Mayhew, chief executive of Tusk Trust. "[When William was here] he was in paradise. Lewa's a very dynamic place, there's always something exciting going on."

During his stay in Kenya in the spring of 2001, William again pitched in with the usual crew of laborers and family members in undertaking day-to-day tasks around the reserve, blissfully reveling in the anonymity and indifference to his royal status from those around him. He helped capture and transport a large elephant to another conservation reserve as well as constructing a slide across a particularly treacherous gorge.

And later on, William confirmed his deep love of the continent: "I first fell in love with Africa when I spent time in Kenya, Botswana, and Tanzania as a teenager. I was captivated." As William's gap year came to a triumphant close, with the successful completion of his slide, he returned to Britain confident in the knowledge that he could survive and indeed thrive in some of the world's harshest conditions—and on his own.

"WOW, KATE'S HOT!"

I just want to go to university and have fun. I want to go there and be an ordinary student. I mean, I'm only going to university. It's not like I'm getting married—though that's what it feels like sometimes.

—Prince William

St Andrews is Scotland's oldest university, situated fifty miles north of Edinburgh. William's father, uncle Edward, and great-grandfather King George VI had all attended Cambridge, but the course the young Prince intended to study, History of Art, was regarded as being among the best in the United Kingdom. St Andrews, founded in 1413 and set within the pretty, ancient town of the same name, was secluded and remote, factors that appealed to the privacy-loving Royal. If he needed any further encouragement, the course was four years long, rather than the three that was standard to English universities.

William arrived at the university on the morning of September 23, 2001, a few weeks after the World Trade Center had fallen, reshaping not only the landscape of Manhattan, but the entire world. His father accompanied him during the move into St. Salvator's Hall, his new home. He had spent the previous few days rather unlike most new students, staying at the Palace of Holyroodhouse and touring the region, before giving the world's media some photocalls and interviews. For St Andrews's sixteen thousand or so locals, it was a chance to get accustomed to seeing the Royal and his entourage moving around the small town.

Nevertheless, there were some teething issues. The day after William arrived, nerves frayed to breaking point when one media truck showed up and began filming—furious resistance revealed the embarrassing fact that they were with a production company owned by William's uncle, Prince Edward, making a documentary for US television. The company, Ardent, had even filmed students talking about the Prince, bribing them with restaurant dinners and creating the impression that the freshmen had just finished their first year with William. However, following a turbulent weekend of recrimination and humiliation for Edward, the crew vanished, leaving a rather rattled William to settle into college life.

Nicknamed Sally's, St Salvator's is one of eleven halls of residence, a coed facility. Most mornings, on his way to class, William would notice the same dark-haired girl also making her way to History of Art lectures, amid the throng of students rushing about. He noticed her instantly. There was no shortage of girls anxiously changing their routines to increase the chances of "accidentally" bumping into the Royal, carefully navigating the charming streets and student haunts of the town in hopes of striking up a conversation. But, with his characteristic shyness and near-fanatical obsession with being as low-key as possible, something about the brown-haired girl pinged a chord with William.

He noticed her in class, and in the dining hall, where students typically claimed their spots and kept them over the course of the year, for mealtimes. He noticed she often liked a run before breakfast—another common interest, as well as their choice of course and their natural reticence. One morning, when William and his friends were in their regular places for breakfast in the dining hall, beneath imposing portraits of noble Scottish philosophers and beautiful stained-glass windows, eating their fruit and granola, he invited the brunette to join him. Her name was Catherine, she told him, but everyone called her Kate.

When William began at the university, other students were notified in advance of his presence and warned that severe penalties would be imposed for any photographs, leaks to the media, or unwarranted intrusions. The college staff was fully on alert to deal with problems within the student body and, if necessary, to take steps to protect William, in order for him to study in peace. However, to everyone's surprise and relief, the Prince barely caused a ripple on the first day of classes. Students merely gave him a curious once-over before returning to their books. William's tutor, Professor Brendan Cassidy, told biographer Penny Junor, "I was so surprised. I was expecting some sort of buzz but there was nothing." In his seminars with Cassidy, where smaller groups of students met weekly with the tutor, William found himself the only male in a group of women and utterly tongue-tied. "His body language said it all," said Cassidy. "[Initially], he tried to wrap himself up, but within a couple of months, he was so much more relaxed."

During his first semester, William started dating Carley Massy-Birch, an English-language and creative-writing student. Carley was a true country girl whose warm and hospitable Devonshire family welcomed the shy Prince to their home for cozy family dinners. At college, the pair kept a low-key presence, keeping their relationship relaxed and easy. They hung out in local pubs, bars, cafés, and restaurants some of the time, or socialized with other students over a typical undergraduate dinner party of tuna bakes or spaghetti Bolognese.

"I'm a real country bumpkin," Carley told *Vanity Fair*. "I think that was why we had a connection. William was in the year below, and we just happened to meet through the general St. Andrews melee. It's such a small place that it was impossible not to bump into William, and after a while there was nothing weird about seeing him around. We got on well, but I think we would have got on well even if nothing had been going on romantically. It was very much a university thing, just a regular university romance."

The "regular university romance" hit the wall fairly soon, however. Carley was growing suspicious of William's true feelings about his summer romance with Arabella Musgrave, back in Gloucestershire. Despite the pair having broken things off before William went up to Scotland, a homesick Prince was keeping in regular contact with her and seeing her on trips home. It soon transpired that the life of studious stability and fulfillment he had envisaged in St Andrews wasn't working out. William was making friends in Scotland, and his tutors in his History of Art course recall a conscientious, if not dazzling, pupil. Yet, as the semester wore on, it became apparent to William that his heart was not in History of Art, and for all its charm and old-world appeal, St Andrews was a bit dull compared to the days of Club H or London's West End. Family issues were never far from his mind, or indeed the headlines. After all, this was the year in which sixteen-year-old Harry went, not for the last time, spectacularly off the rails and onto the front pages. William's brother was caught smoking weed and drinking underage at the Rattlesnake Bar in Gloucester, prompting a gleeful outburst of finger wagging from those models of temperance and sobriety, British tabloid journalists.

That Christmas, William told his father he didn't want to return to St Andrews for his second semester. He wasn't enjoying his courses, he missed home, and he didn't feel committed enough to warrant the massive upheaval his choice of university had caused numerous people, from his fellow students to the townspeople, college staff, and his own security operation. The college had even moved the configuration of the History of Art teaching buildings around, to accommodate William's security detail.

Charles was thoughtful. Many students experience uncertainty in their first year, and homesickness is also par for the course for the great majority, especially those who were used to livelier places than St Andrews. But given William's status and, yes, the huge amount of work that had gone into creating a safe space for him to work and live, Charles counseled caution. His own brother Edward had quit the Marine Commandos halfway through the induction year, much to the public's disappointment. Charles himself was no stranger to the trials and tribulations of adjusting to a new educational establishment, hundreds of miles from home. Despite availing himself of one of the finest collections of art in the country—that of his grandmother, where William had been immersing himself in the world of Old Masters and classical art—he hadn't clicked with the subject, and worse, he was terrified of public failure. He was preyed upon by the prospect of getting a reputation for weak work or an uninspired degree at the end of years of hassle and fuss for everyone.

But common sense (and a few motivating talks with his gruff but loving grandfather) prevailed in the end. "I don't think I was homesick, I was more daunted," William later said. "My father was very understanding about it and realized I had the same problem as he probably had. We chatted a lot, and in the end we both realized—I definitely realized—that I had to come back."

Charles told him that if he still felt the same way at the end of his second semester, they could talk again. In the meantime, William agreed to return to college and drop History of Art and major in Geography, a subject he felt a much deeper connection to. "It was really no different from what many first-year students go through," Prince Charles's former private secretary, Mark Bolland, recalled to

Vanity Fair. "We approached the whole thing as a wobble, which was entirely normal." But William's decision to return to St Andrews had also been motivated by another factor.

***

By now, Kate Middleton was a good friend. William and the girl from Marlborough School had grown close despite their mutual reserve, which concealed strikingly similar tastes and outlooks on life. Kate had also been on a Raleigh venture to Chile before college, of course, so she and William found much to talk about regarding their experiences there, as well as finding that they could make each other laugh and, increasingly, feel secure in each other's company. They both loved sports, and in his first term, William had enjoyed many tennis, swimming, and surfing sessions with Kate, followed up by drinks somewhere around town or in the university's grand common rooms. When William found himself unhappy and unsure of his future at school, the quiet Kate was a sympathetic and willing listener, letting him talk and not bullying or pushing him one way or another. William liked that. It reminded him of his mother's gentle demeanor and natural warmth.

Furthermore, while she was—and is—undoubtedly a beauty in the English rose mold, she wasn't at all glamorous or made up when she met William. Rather, William's attention was piqued by Kate's low-key, easygoing manner, her classic good looks, and natural personality. "They were instant companions," said a friend of Kate's, who lived at Sally's with her. "Kate is genuinely a very nice person. I actually felt bad for her having to deal with all of those other two-faced chicks. It's easy to see why a graceful person like Kate would charm Will."

Despite being something of a college heartthrob, Kate's friends and contemporaries from this time recall the future Princess as being a pretty normal girl, albeit one who was reputed to have had a picture of the Prince on the wall of her school dorm and would frequently talk about the chances of meeting him in a joking-not-joking kind of way.

"There wasn't just one, there was about twenty," smirked William years later when the pair was giving a television interview to mark their engagement.

"He wishes!" joked Kate. "No, I had the Levi's guy on my wall, not a picture of William, sorry!"

Returning to St Andrews, William made some changes. He planned to move out of his college accommodation in his second year, and in September 2002, he did—with a small group of trusted friends, including Kate.

He switched to a major in Geography, which immediately engaged him in a way his previous major hadn't managed to. The practical side of studying Geography—field studies, scientific analyses, and research—suited the Prince's personality and interests. He began to feel comfortable in his seminars, participating in lively discussions and overcoming his reticence in front of other students.

"He was a perfectly capable student," recalled his new tutor of Geography, John Walden. "The academic stuff was fine, he was no different from any other student in the cohort." He began to relax around his new classmates and made some more friends and started to let down his hair—now noticeably thinning. Meanwhile, as spring 2002 approached, his friendship with Kate, which had deepened during his minicrisis, grew steadily closer.

On March 27, 2002, William and his pal Fergus attended a fashion show in which Kate was to make an appearance as one of the catwalk models. The annual "Don't Walk" charity show at the college's student union was a fixture of the Scottish social calendar, with tickets going for two hundred pounds each. It was very much a last-minute decision to attend the event, which was how William liked to play things—avoiding any undue attention and fuss, slinking into the hall in his customary baseball cap and taking his place right by the catwalk.

When Kate emerged in the spotlight wearing a dress designed by fashion student Charlotte Todd, there was a collective intake of breath among the assembled crowd. Her lithe, toned body was barely covered by the skimpy outfit, which essentially consisted of black underwear and a see-through top. In a moment that has since passed into myth, William turned to Fergus and whispered, "Wow, Fergus, Kate's hot!"

"Kate was great on the catwalk," recalled one of the other models who appeared that night. "She and everyone, including William, knew it."

For William, it was the thunderbolt moment. After months of close friendship, in a flash, Kate's confident sexy strut down the catwalk lit a fire that confirmed what he had subconsciously felt from the start. For him, this was the girl who had it all: smart, funny, warm, serious, loving, kind, sympathetic, sporty, sociable, and very, very sexy.

That night, friends recall William being in something of a spin. At a party after the show, he gambled on making his move. In front of a roomful of people, William tried to kiss her, as they toasted her successful evening. Kate pulled away, slightly shocked at William's boldness. He well knew that she was dating another student at the time, Rupert Finch. According to one of their friends who witnessed the moment, Kate "played it very cool" because she didn't "want to give off the wrong impression or make it too easy for Will." Still, the friend told *Vanity Fair*, "It was clear to us that William was smitten with Kate. He actually told her she was a knockout that night, which caused her to blush. There was definitely chemistry between them."

It's uncertain when Kate finally allowed her Prince to sweep her off her feet for the first time, but this much is clear: by the time William returned to the university in September 2002, he had found a lovely old house to share with a small number of close friends at 13a Hope Street, in the center of town. One of their neighbors, Julian Knight, a fellow student, recalled the early days of the fledgling romance.

He said: "It became quite amusing because we were obviously in the circle of people who knew they were an item and we were just wondering when the press was going to catch on. I think it speaks volumes for the kind of protection he had, because there were a lot of people who knew they were together, but no one said anything.

"I think one of the main reasons why they were able to be together was because they were in the same hall of residence and then they lived together. Initially, they had time to get to know each other as friends. So, they were always spending time together, going down to Anstruther to go banana boating or playing golf or going for a walk. They were able to get to know each other as friends without anyone going, 'Ooh, what's going on there?'"

While some modifications had to be made to it, to ensure the royal security team was happy, the house gave William the privacy and comfort he'd been craving. By this time, his romance with Kate was well under way. Living under the same roof (although nominally in separate rooms) with discreet, trusted friends, the pair found a degree of privacy. Their intimacy deepened despite the prying eyes and telephoto lenses that lurked every day outside 13a Hope Street's bomb-proof front door.

Speaking some years later, the owner of the house, Charlotte Smith, said she had initially decided against renting to the Prince—she had instituted a "no-boys" policy after previous tenants caused property damage. When asked if William could move in, she initially said: "I still don't want to do it, thank you. I'd rather not do that . . . because I didn't know how he was going to behave off the leash, as it were. We arranged to meet Kate Middleton, Fergus, and Olivia before they moved in, but we thought we'd better not ask to see Prince William because we thought his credit rating must be quite good. But he was very friendly, very charming . . . a thoroughly nice man."

"He was just another very down-to-earth normal guy," echoes Julian Knight. "There were no real airs and graces if you like. It was just sort of, 'Alright mate, how are you doing?' and we had a relationship which was very matey [friendly] basically.'"

William embraced the relative normality of being an undergraduate. "I remember being in his room once and he [Prince William] had started to get into motorbikes, and he was looking at all these leathers," recalled Knight. "There were two on the screen and he was saying, 'I can't decide whether I want that one or I want that one.' I was like, 'Well, why don't you get them both?' and he looked at me and was like, 'No man, these are like £1,000 each.' At the time we were all on an allowance, but I think it genuinely seemed like he didn't have any more money than the rest of us. He wasn't flashy or didn't wear a big watch—he didn't rock up in amazing cars or motorbikes or anything like that. He'd buy the odd tray of drinks in the pub, or shots or whatever, but so would everyone."

With typical vagueness, William later reflected on the start of his real relationship with Kate, sharing the house at 13a Hope Street. "It just sort of blossomed from there, really. We just saw more of each other, hung out a bit more and did stuff."

The "stuff" often included trips to their favorite haunt, the Ma Belles wine bar at the town's Gold Hotel, where William and his friends would spend hours, enjoying drinks and laughs. Many years later, when William was giving a speech at a fundraiser for St Andrews, he jokingly warned "those of you who are parents of undergraduates right now, I give you one tip. Ask your son or daughter over the holidays if they know what Ma Bells is. If they answer yes, perhaps remove their wine glasses out of reach."

For a more romantic dinner à deux, William and Kate would go to the Oak Rooms, at the boutique hotel Ogstons on North Street, where staff remember him always making reservations under a cheeky alias and then arriving with the royal security team in tow. The Prince was said to favor the restaurant's chicken fajitas, said a source, adding that while the couple were often affectionate and "very smoochy," they did go Dutch when paying the check.

Other times, William would cook for Kate and his housemates, as she told the BBC's Mary Berry many years later. "In our university days, he used to cook all sorts of meals. I think that's when he was trying to impress me, Mary! Things like Bolognese sauce and things like that."

Compared to Harry's turbulent, high-octane love life at that point, William and Kate couldn't have been any calmer or more mundane. But like his younger brother, William had his demons, buried deep down inside. He had just learned not to show them in public. For her part, Kate, the product of an upwardly aspirational, fiercely tight family unit, was the stability, calm, and nurturing he needed—and she loved to provide. Their union was blossoming, but it wouldn't be an easy ride to the altar.

BETTER STAND BACK

In June 2003, William reached the grand old age of twenty-one. The British Poet Laureate Andrew Motion was commissioned to write a poem to celebrate the auspicious occasion:

> Better stand back
> Here's an age attack,
> But the second in line
> Is dealing with it fine.
> It's a threshold, a gateway,
> A landmark birthday;
> It's a turning of the page,
> A coming of age.
> It's a day to celebrate,
> A destiny, a fate;
> It's a taking to the wing,
> A future thing.
> Better stand back
> Here's an age attack,
> But the second in line
> Is dealing with it fine.
> It's a sign of what's to come,
> A start, and then some;
> It's a difference growing,
> A younger sort of knowing.
> It's a childhood gone,

A step towards the crown;
It's a trigger of change,
A stretching of the range.
Better stand back
Here's an age attack,
But the second in line
Is dealing with it fine.

William weathered the "age attack," with a specially commissioned photo shoot with Mario Testino, one of his late mother's favorite photographers. With typical William modesty, he claimed the choice was down to the fact that Testino was the only photographer who "could make a moose look good." Giving a press interview to mark the occasion, he played down recent reports indicating he had expressed misgivings about being King.

"Those stories about me not wanting to be King are all wrong. It's a very important role and it's one that I don't take lightly. It's all about helping people and dedication and loyalty, which I hope I have—I know I have.

"The monarchy is something that needs to be there—I just feel it's very, very important—it's a form of stability and I hope to be able to continue that."

In the months leading up to William's twenty-first, the Royals had been dealing with the particularly trying aftershocks of the dramatic trial of Paul Burrell. Diana's former butler had taken millions of pounds worth of items from Diana's residence following her death, claiming Diana had gifted them to him. There was also the small matter of a cassette tape, containing recordings of Diana that were said to be of a "sensitive" nature.

Due to a last-minute, rather bizarre intervention by the Queen, Burrell was freed, although his behavior during the trial seemed to reveal him as being something of a narcissistic drama queen, rather than the discreet and reliable "rock" he claimed Diana had called him. When the truth emerged at the trial that, far from relying on him, the Princess found his overweening attention somewhat creepy, he wrote a scurrilous tell-all book, much to the anger of the young Princes he claimed to be so fond of. Indeed, according to Prince Charles's biographer, Tom Bower, when raiding Burrell's house, police also found two thousand photographic negatives—including what he claims were images of "Charles in the bath with his children, and many others showing the young Princes naked."

While the Burrell affair rumbled on, Kate's quiet support by William's side helped as he grimaced through the agony of hearing his mother's name dragged through the courts, as the former butler detailed every intimate aspect of her life. Burrell's mealy-mouthed excuses that he was protecting Diana's legacy cut no ice with William and Harry, and the pair was in contact, united in fury that such a close member of the Royal staff should be so flagrantly betraying confidences and private conversations. When Burrell's book came out, the brothers took the rare step of issuing a public statement denouncing it and Burrell, accusing him of abusing his position "in such a cold and overt betrayal" and asking him to "bring these revelations to an end."

As genial as William might be in public, the world now knew that when it came to matters of privacy and trust, he was a tenacious opponent whose scorn could make or break a transgressor.

In their third year, William and Kate, plus Olivia and Fergus, moved into a house together. By now, their relationship was well known but the quartet was happy to continue living together, as they had formed a protective cocoon around the happy couple. The farmhouse, some distance out of St Andrews, provided ample privacy and beautiful countryside, ideal for the pair to enjoy long country walks and the soothing balms of nature. William was also enjoying his courses immensely even if there was the occasional unwelcome reminder of his "other" life. In June 2004, he was part of a field trip to Norway, to study the Jostedalen ice cap, in the west of the country. According to his tutors on the trip, the Prince was relaxed, happy, and thrilled to be in the anonymity of remote Norway, undisturbed and able to pursue his passion for the environment and geography.

The expedition went well at first. By day, William worked hard. At night, he regaled the company over dinner with funny and revealing anecdotes about life in the Royal Family. It all ended up with weary predictability, however, when on the third day, the team awoke to find much of the world's media camped outside along with them. Since the expedition's base was in the tiny remote village of Gjerde, it was a fair assumption a pack of journalists and photographers had assembled there all one morning for no other reason than to bay for quotes, interviews, photographs, and film of the young Prince. Though severely disgruntled, he immediately donned his baseball cap, shrugged, and acceded glumly to the shouted requests to pose and smile.

By now, the world had met Kate, albeit inadvertently. During Easter 2004, she had accompanied William on the traditional skiing break his father usually took, in Klosters, Austria. William often took friends along too, making for a large party. The Royals had long agreed to the usual form of posing for a photo call on the first day of their holidays in exchange for some peace and privacy. Once that was done, perhaps a little too trustingly, William took the opportunity to give his girlfriend a smooch on the lips. Too late, they realized that they had been caught in the act on camera. The pictures were a global sensation. The world wanted to know: who was the stunning brunette snogging the Prince?

THERE'S SOMETHING ABOUT KATE

Marlborough College is a coeducational independent boarding school for pupils aged thirteen to eighteen, set amid 286 acres of rolling countryside in Wiltshire, England. It was initially planned as a school for the sons of the clergymen who founded it in 1843, with 199 boys forming the first intake. But since then—following a rebellion by the pupils in the 1850s protesting the spartan conditions—the historical buildings have welcomed pupils from the upper echelons of British society, and around the world. Notable alumni include legendary nineteenth-century artist and designer William Morris, poets John Betjeman and Siegfried Sassoon, musicians Chris de Burgh and Nick Drake, and, of course, Royals, including Princess Eugenie of York and Princess Anne's former husband, Captain Mark Phillips.

The school tiptoed into the modern era by admitting women into the sixth form in 1968. When it was discovered that it did not collapse with the admittance of girls, nor did its inmates turn into a frenzy of carnal abandon, the college became fully coeducational in 1989, the first school of its caliber to do so. Today, Marlborough continues to flourish, with almost a thousand pupils enjoying a thoroughly up-to-date, well-rounded education that spans sports, scholarship, and extracurricular activity.

For a school that only turns out eighty female students a year, Marlborough has a considerable track record in producing notable female alumnae. In recent times, female Marlburians have numbered Kate Middleton; Samantha, wife of former Prime Minister David Cameron; Frances Osborne, wife of his Chancellor George; Sally Bercow, wife of the former Parliamentary Speaker John; and Diana Fox, wife of the Governor of the Bank of England, Mark Carney.

Members of the Royal Family view a fly-past and a Feu de Joie to mark the 100th anniversary of the Royal Air Force at Buckingham Palace, London, UK, on July 10, 2018. (James Whatling / MEGA TheMegaAgency.com)

The Duchess of Cambridge and the Duchess of Sussex watch the Women's Final at the Wimbledon Championships, London, UK, on July 14, 2018. (MEGA TheMegaAgency.com)

Members of the Royal Family attend Trooping the Colour at Buckingham Palace, London, UK, June 8, 2019. (James Whatling / MEGA TheMegaAgency.com)

The Cambridge and Sussex families watch as Prince William and Prince Harry take part in the King Power Royal Charity Polo Day for the Khun Vichai Srivaddhanaprabha Memorial Polo Trophy at Billingbear Polo Club, Binfield, Berkshire, UK on July 10, 2019. (James Whatling / MEGA TheMegaAgency.com)

Prince Harry, Duke of Sussex, and Meghan Markle, Duchess of Sussex, attend the European Premiere of *The Lion King* at the Odeon Leicester Square, London, UK, on July 14, 2019. (James Whatling / MEGA TheMegaAgency.com)

Prince Harry, Duke of Sussex, Meghan Markle, Duchess of Sussex, and their baby son Archie meet Archbishop Desmond Tutu at the Desmond on September 25, 2019 (James Whatling / MEGA TheMegaAgency.com)

The Duke and Duchess of Cambridge visit the Aga Khan Centre ahead of their Tour to Pakistan in King's Cross, London, UK, on October 2, 2019. (James Whatling / MEGA TheMegaAgency.com)

Prince Harry, Duke of Sussex, and Meghan Markle, Duchess of Sussex, visit Canada House to meet the High Commissioner and thank them for the hospitality and support they received during their stay in Canada, in London, UK, on January 7, 2020. (James Whatling / MEGA TheMegaAgency.com)

The Duke and Duchess of Cambridge visit City Hall in Bradford's Centenary Square, and meet the people of Bradford in Yorkshire, UK, on January 15, 2020. (James Whatling / MEGA TheMegaAgency.com)

The Duke and Duchess of Cambridge visit the Mumbles Pier and meet the public in Mumbles, Swansea Bay, Wales, UK, on February 4, 2020. (James Whatling / MEGA TheMegaAgency.com)

Prince Harry, Duke of Sussex, and Meghan Markle, Duchess of Sussex, attend the annual Endeavour Fund Awards at Mansion House, London, UK, on March 5, 2020. (James Whatling / MEGA TheMegaAgency.com)

Members of the Royal Family attend the annual Commonwealth Service, on Commonwealth Day, at Westminster Abbey, London, UK, on March 9, 2020. (James Whatling / MEGA TheMegaAgency.com)

Prince Harry and Meghan Markle are seen in Los Angeles wearing masks as they deliver meals to residents in need during the COVID-19 pandemic. The couple was pictured delivering packages after volunteering with the non-profit organization "Project Angel Food." The former Duke and Duchess of Sussex were seen linking arms and holding hands after dropping off deliveries to addresses in their new city. (P&P/Rachpoot/MEGA)

As for the shy, gawky girl who showed up with her parents to join the school in 1996, well, she would one day be married to the heir to the throne . . .

Kate had begun her secondary education at a small private school, Downe House, near her family home in Bucklebury. But she hadn't settled in, and Michael and Carole set their sights on posh Marlborough, a place where a girl could mingle with the aristocracy and make the crucial social connections that could only be properly forged in childhood.

As the family's party-supply business, Party Pieces, was flourishing, the eye-watering £29,000 annual fees could be managed. For ambitious Carole, the prospect of their daughter attending a school such as Marlborough was tantalizing. The historic establishment opened up a vista of social prospects for the Middletons.

Beginning a new school is nerve-racking enough for any child. But it's downright stomach-churning for a shy, quiet child showing up halfway through the first year into the intimidating environs of one of the country's most exclusive schools. For Kate—or Catherine, as she was more commonly known at that point—it was terrifying, said a source. Her nerves had been primed by her unhappy time at Downe House. When she arrived at Marlborough in the middle of the first year, crucial friendships had already been forged, alliances struck, and the unwritten social hierarchy found in any school had been established. On initial impressions, the other girls weren't particularly dazzled by the newbie.

The first friend Kate made, Jessica Hay, remembers the future Duchess as being rather "shy and gawky." Another girl, Gemma Williamson, recalls a quiet, homesick child who "looked thin and pale. She had very little confidence."

Meanwhile, Kate's house tutor at Marlborough, Joan Gall, was concerned for her new charge from day one. Kate was so stressed, she was suffering from eczema. "When she arrived she was very quiet," Ms. Gall remembers. "Coming into a big school like Marlborough was difficult, but she settled in quickly. It was like a big, happy family. We would do things like bake cakes and watch videos."

It didn't take long for Kate to get a handle on life at Marlborough. Her housemistress Mrs. Patching would later recall, "Catherine was able to settle in very easily. She got involved in school life and loved sport and music."

Kathryn Solari, who was in her Biology class, added, "Catherine was always really sweet and lovely. She treated everybody alike. She was a good girl and quite preppy—she always did the right thing—and she was very sporty. I wouldn't say she was the brightest button, but she was very hard-working."

Another friend from her year recalled a girl who was "ordinary, hard-working, athletic, and easygoing. Media depictions swing between a snooty Sloane and a dastardly commoner. Both are wrong."

Kate soon showed off her sporting prowess, becoming joint captain of the tennis team with her friend Alice St John Webster, as well as excelling in swimming, high jump, netball, and hockey. She was a giggler, fun-loving, and mischievous, but never a serious rule breaker. "Even when we all passed our exams and were partying, I never saw her drunk," recalled another fellow student. "Kate only had a few glugs of vodka."

Having achieved a solid set of eleven passes at her GCSEs in 1998, Catherine enjoyed a well-earned family break in the Caribbean that summer. And it was now, with her exams over, that she turned her attention to a personal makeover. Guided by her mother's unerring eye and sense of style, Kate put together an entire new look, eye-catching and dramatic, yet tasteful.

When she returned to school that autumn, fellow pupils, who had never considered Kate to be one of the school's glamourpusses, were stunned. Gone was the mousy, pony-tailed, knock-kneed geek. Now, Middleton swept back into her dorm rooms an elegant and charismatic young woman.

"It happened quite suddenly," remembered her friend Gemma Williamson. "Catherine came back from the long summer break an absolute beauty. She never wore particularly fashionable or revealing clothes, but she had an innate sense of style."

A teacher at the school remembers how Catherine had quietly managed to upstage her boisterous and cheeky younger sister, Pippa, who joined Marlborough in 1997: "Pippa was a boyish girl; however, Kate had lost her props and looked dazzling. She was wearing makeup and looked astounding."

This characteristic sense of panache and decorum was to become a Kate characteristic. Friends and staff noted that Kate had a strong moral compass instilled by her hardworking and socially ambitious parents, and now, this maturity stood her in good stead throughout her teens. As she moved up the school, friends recall how she was careful around the typical teenage high jinks that would go on, such as sneaking out of school at night for trysts with boys or illicit dorm parties with smuggled wines, spirits, and cigarettes. She would always be part of the gang, often obligingly keeping an ear out for a passing teacher. But she would generally avoid drinking, smoking, or getting up to any sort of forbidden peccadilloes.

She did, however, have a childish love of pranking, which saw her go through an uncharacteristic phase of mooning surprised male students from her dorm windows, a habit that inspired the affectionate nickname Middlebum. Clambering up to the dormitory windows, to the amazement and disbelief of her chums, Kate would drop her pants and treat passers-by to the sight of her bum, wiggling comically in the window. Kate would scream with laughter as cheers from the appreciative crowds outside egged her on. "She kind of got addicted to it," Jessica Hay recalled. Over the course of one year, Hay estimated Kate flashed her rear in the window for anyone to see no fewer than ninety times.

As the once-nervous young girl moved up through the school, she was becoming a confident, outgoing, and charismatic young lady. This was in keeping with the school's well-founded reputation for turning out graceful, resourceful, and accomplished young women who go on to great things. According to another alumna, Kate Reardon, former editor of British society magazine *Tatler*, Marlborough played a huge role in nurturing Kate's inner core of steel and outer mantle of calm.

"A good education gives you confidence to stick up your hand for anything—whether it is the job you want, or the bloke," she says. "And the more you stick up your hand, the better your chances are that you will get what you want. Also, a good school teaches you resilience—that ability to bounce back."

This last quality would certainly hold Kate in good stead in the years to come.

Another Old Malburian, Sasha Howard, recalled how the school taught her positivity: "We were taught to be proactive, to push ourselves, get things done, and be happy, too. I can talk to anyone of any age or gender with total confidence."

While many of her peers enjoyed hectic love lives with their male counterparts at posh schools around the country, building the connections that would sustain the next generations of the aristocracy, Kate kept herself more or less out of the dating frenzy. "She was very good-looking and a lot of the boys liked her," recalled Jessica Hay. "But it used to just go over her head. She wasn't really interested, she had very high morals."

When it came to the all-crucial matter of gentlemen friends, Kate kept a discreet profile, for the most part. Despite not wishing to be seen to be an easy catch, she had no lack of admirers, following her 1998 makeover, but still managed to avoid any public affairs or romances. "I got the distinct impression that Catherine wanted to save herself for someone special," said her friend Gemma.

There were rumors of affairs with handsome male Marlburians Charlie von Mol, Willem Marx, and Oliver Bowen—all sporty, popular chaps, much lusted after by the school's female contingent. However, there was one young man for whom Kate's crush was well known. Over late-night microwaved Marmite sandwiches with friends Jessica and Gemma, Kate would semicomically rhapsodize over Prince William. "We would sit around talking about all the boys we fancied," said Jessica. "Catherine would say, 'Oh I don't really like any of them, they're all a bit of rough.' Then she would joke, 'There's no one quite like William, I bet he's really kind, you can tell just by looking at him.'"

Kate ended her time at Marlborough a polished and popular graduate. Her younger sister, Pippa, had also proved a resounding success at the school, following in her sister's footsteps but from the outset exuding a glamorous confidence and pizzazz that came to be synonymous with the Middleton family. The arrival of the youngest Middleton, James, established a minidynasty at the school that was not always entirely viewed with uncritical adoration. One mother of a girl in Kate's house told *Tatler* magazine: "There was always something slightly galling about having your child at school with the Middletons. It made other families feel rather hopeless."

Having achieved high marks, with "A" grades in Mathematics and Art and a "B" in English, the time had come for Kate to decide on her university options. Initially, Kate considered Edinburgh University. But for reasons that are still being debated, she changed her mind at the last minute. The decision would change her life, that of her family and friends, and ultimately the course of British monarchy history. Instead of rushing off to Edinburgh as planned, Kate decided on taking a gap year out, before starting at St Andrews University, on the north coast of Scotland. This ensured that when she returned to the United Kingdom and began her degree course, she would be at the same university, on the same course, and at the same time as one William Arthur Philip Louis Windsor—better known to the world as His Royal Highness, Prince William.

WAITY KATIE

The royal romance continued apace after the world saw William kissing Kate at the Swiss resort of Klosters. The gentleman's agreement brokered between Clarence House, the official London residence of the Prince of Wales, and the British newspapers had been transgressed, however, and Charles and William were furious. However, the damage had been done. The press had a field day, unearthing details about Kate bit by bit, pressuring fellow students for juicy tidbits about the pair. Some students even reported being bribed with having their student loans paid off, in return for exclusive stories.

William and Kate now took their mutual passion for privacy to the next level. They rarely appeared in public together, and when they did so, they resolutely refused to so much as hold hands, let alone kiss or cuddle. Both of them knew this relationship needed air to breathe and grow, rather than be crushed at first bloom by the oppressive, relentless media spotlight. To that end, the pair retreated to the Royals' rural idyll, Balgove House, on Strathtyrum, a sprawling private estate a quarter of a mile outside the town center, owned by Henry Cheape, a distant cousin of the Prince's. While William's protection officers were nearby in various small houses, the pair was pretty much left to their own devices unless they specially invited friends over—Pippa and James Middleton were frequent guests as were close friends from college.

Unlike William's mother, Diana, Kate was eased gently into the hidebound world of the Royals. While Kate quickly had to adapt to being in the spotlight, after the headlines around the world following the press scoop at Klosters, she already enjoyed visiting Royal homes at Highgrove, Balmoral, and Sandringham, where she would often join in with shooting weekends, during the season. The Queen had also allowed William to use a Balmoral cottage, Tam-na-Ghar, during term time as a private retreat. There, Kate was becoming an increasingly familiar sight as she and William wandered the moors or took romantic walks along the river Dee. Most evenings, the pair would stay home, cooking a meal and cozying up in front of a roaring fire.

The circumstances were near-perfect. But barely a few months since the kiss at Klosters, cracks were beginning to appear in the couple's relationship. Perhaps they had spent too much time together alone, perhaps they needed to both go through a period apart before proceeding further or simply—they each needed some time alone to process what was clearly a major and significant step for them both.

The pressure on the couple, both barely out of their teens, was immense. Since the world had gotten to know about the relationship, Kate and the Middleton family had come under the expected scrutiny in no time at all. Even at Buckingham Palace, some of the snootier of the Palace staff looked down on Kate's self-made family and mocked their new money, their ambitious social climbing, and their relentless pursuit of status. Carole Middleton's past came in for ribbing too, with some staff at the Palace making barbed comments about "setting cabin doors to manual" and "trolley dollies" when her name came up. If Kate was serious about William, this could turn the family upside down. Was she committed enough— and was he?

Ricocheting like a sparkling firework through both Princes' teens and twenties was the boisterous and impish figure of Guy Pelly. Ever since their schooldays, where Pelly and William were classmates, he had been a source of mischief and fun, from buying porn for William at school, to encouraging and ably abetting wild drinking sprees. He was always up for a party and a prank. Now, as the 2004 summer holidays loomed, William announced to Kate that he and Guy would be taking a boys-only sailing holiday, with a few other friends and an all-girls sailing crew. Kate pursed her lips and accepted her boyfriend's wish, wisely realizing that whatever William had to get out of his system, he might as well go off and get it out. Still, Kate felt a chilly displeasure toward Guy, according to a source. At the very least, she felt, he was a bad influence on the Prince.

Compounding Kate's unhappiness, the sailing trip in Greece was to be preceded by a solo holiday in Nashville. William and some pals had accepted an invitation to visit the 360-acre family ranch of a friend studying at Edinburgh, the twenty-two-year-old heiress Anna Sloan. It was his chance to have fun in the sun with the rangy American, on whom, it is fair to say, he had a massive crush.

Friends have since claimed he was "head over heels" for Anna and was "desperate to woo her" on his Tennessee holiday, but Sloan turned him down. According to royal biographer Katie Nicholl in her book *William and Harry*, it was partially due to Prince William's friendship with Sloan that Kate and William's relationship hit the skids around this time, even though nothing—so William claimed—happened between the pair.

"Kate was beginning to question William's commitment to their relationship, and she also had her own creeping doubts about their future after St Andrews," wrote Nicholl. "A number of things had caused her to question William's commitment, although she had not raised them with him yet."

Kate's suspicions that William was feeling frisky deepened when another girl popped up on the scene that summer. A member of the aristocracy with a sparkling personality, stunning looks, and part of one of Britain's richest families, Isabella Anstruther-Gough-Calthorpe was a shoo-in for the young Prince's wandering attention. Sadly for William, she too felt that the life of a royal lover was not for her and she gently let him down, too.

While William was busy attempting to seduce girls in the United States and the United Kingdom, Kate joined housemate Fergus Boyd for a family holiday at the Boyds' house in the French region of the Dordogne with some college friends. Kate had not confided in her pals about the extent of her and William's troubles, until one night, after a few glasses of wine, she most uncharacteristically poured her heart out to the gang. "She got quite drunk on white wine and really let her guard down," said one of those present. "She was debating whether or not she should text or call him. She said how sad she was and how much she was missing William—but she never mentioned it after that."

That November, William and Kate reunited at college, but there was still a distance between them, even as they continued to share their house. The tensions that had surfaced that summer were still in the air, and the couple was struggling to decide how they should move forward, especially after they graduated the following summer. William didn't help matters much by talking about how much he'd like to fly to Kenya to meet up with his old buddy Jecca Craig, which must have made Kate's eyes roll yet again in frustration at her dithering boyfriend. At this stage, William seemed to simply not know what he wanted. It was here that Kate's mother Carole stepped in with some sage advice, a family insider recalled, urging her daughter to give William a bit more space and allow him to come to terms with his feelings.

It worked. By Christmas 2004, William and Kate were officially back together, after some tough talking from a defiant Kate, said the source. William would stop making hopeful booty calls to the likes of Isabella and show that he was serious about Kate. Now, it was time for them both to knuckle down and prepare for their finals, in summer 2005.

To cement their reunion, William and Kate flew to Verbier, Switzerland, for a brief holiday with friends in January 2005. She and William enjoyed skiing and socializing with their pals. The abundance of kissing and canoodling between the two confirmed beyond doubt that things were definitely back on track.

In March 2005, there was more skiing when Charles invited Kate to Klosters again. This time it was for a holiday that served as a prewedding break for the happy Prince of Wales, who on April 9 would finally marry the love of his life, Camilla Parker Bowles. Everyone around Charles, not least his sons, were delighted for the old man, who was clearly thrilled to be making an honest woman of the person who had been such a major part of his life for decades. There had been some talk of the holiday being a lad's only affair, but given their recent reconciliation and the prospect of looming finals, Charles knew it would make William happy to have Kate along.

The trip was a success. Kate and Charles bonded easily and warmly, and Kate's natural sportiness and game attitude ensured that she fit into the group from the outset. Charles found himself liking her more and more. Clearly, had William been looking for paternal approval for his girlfriend, he would have been pleased with his dad's enthusiastic reaction. Kate and William had learned the lesson of the previous year and made a point of avoiding PDA where possible, and instead adeptly fended off stories about their recent time apart with smooth rebuttal. In fact, the only downer of the whole trip was when Charles, irritated at the obligatory press call, was overheard making exceedingly uncomplimentary remarks about the BBC's royal correspondent, Nicholas Witchell, which were spread widely and caused more than a few red faces among the royal party.

William invited Kate along to the party, but she kept a respectful distance from the intimate family ceremony, by mutual consent. William was thrilled with his new stepmother, with whom he had built a warm relationship over the years, unimaginable at one time when their mother portrayed her as a homewrecking witch. While the family celebrated the formal addition of the newly ennobled Duchess of Cornwall, Kate was preparing for the imminent finals, which she and William were due to take in May that year. The four years of study, which had been a constant throughout their budding romance, their flourishing love, the arguments and splits, the happy evenings alone together, the uncertainty and anguish—all came to a head that month. Just before the exams started, they attended the annual May Ball, as tradition dictated. Kate, full of nerves, drank so much that Fergus Boyd had to step in and hoist her aloft and take her home, early in the evening, said one onlooker.

After a nail-biting few days, by May 25, the final exams were done, and William and Kate each breathed a huge sigh of relief. But like final-year students everywhere, they were also apprehensive about what the outside world had in store for them once they had graduated. Of course, in their case, the eyes of the world would be following their every move. For two control freaks, things had to be perfect. No pressure there, then.

On June 23, 2005, "William Wales" and Catherine Middleton graduated from St Andrews University, each gaining a 2:1 degree in Geography and History of Art, respectively. At the graduation ceremony, the Queen, Prince Philip, and Prince Charles and his new wife Camilla all turned up to watch William receive his degree. In the custom of the university, he and Kate received a tap on the head with a piece of cloth believed to have come from the breeches once worn by renowned Calvinist, reformer, and founder of the Presbyterian Church, John Knox. After they both had accepted their degrees and posed for photographs, University Vice Chancellor Brian Lang addressed the fresh graduates, ahead of their heading out into the world.

"You will have made lifelong friends and I say this every year to all new graduates: You may have met your husband or wife. We rely on you to go forth and multiply," he said.

That day, a photograph, which has since been seen by millions worldwide, was snapped. It shows the couple, radiating happiness and joy, in the euphoric moments following their graduation ceremony. William, his hair thankfully still present and abundant, grins openly, while Kate nestles into her boyfriend, a broad smile radiating simultaneous relief and happiness, neither betraying any sign of anxiety about the turbulent years that lay ahead.

LEARNING TO FLY

Following graduation, twenty-two-year-old William undertook his first solo royal tour to New Zealand, where crowds turned out to see the handsome young graduate Prince, as he joined the country's then-Prime Minister Helen Clark in commemorating the sixtieth anniversary of the end of World War II. He was accompanied by his old friend, Thomas van Straubenzee, and his private secretary, Jamie Lowther-Pinkerton. Amid the formal events marking the solemn occasion, William found time to hang out with his beloved British Lions rugby team and explore some of the beautiful countryside of the nation he had last visited twenty-two years before, as a baby with his parents on his first-ever overseas jaunt.

When William's trip was done, he flew to Mount Kenya, where he had arranged to meet Kate. Kate had been looking forward to seeing William away from St Andrews, from the London nightclub scene, and from the United Kingdom's increasingly inquisitive press. In the shadow of Mount Kenya, at the exclusive Ngwesi ecolodge in the Mukogodo Hills, the couple reunited under a gibbous moon and reaffirmed their love for each other.

William was staying a month in Kenya, with friends, at Lewa Downs, the Craigs' nature reserve where he had paid previous visits since his gap year. Any lingering reservations Kate had had about William's relations with Jecca were put firmly to rest when the couple hung out with Jecca and her boyfriend, Hugh, during the month William worked on the ranch and reservation, putting his newly acquired geographical knowledge to good use. At the end of the stay, he spent two thousand pounds on hiring the lodge for a big group of friends for an exuberant blowout.

The party flew back to the United Kingdom weary but glowing with the aftermath of a brilliantly stimulating month in the wilds of Africa. The couple's paths were set to diverge. William, now an adult Royal with a schedule to match, had a packed diary of engagements and obligations. Kate had—well, not much, really. Her position was difficult. She had to find a job that would challenge and stimulate her but also be flexible enough to allow her to continue her relationship with William. Following in her parents' footsteps, she attempted to start up an online children's clothing line, which soon failed. However, her immediate problem was, inevitably, the media.

Kate was being virtually stalked around the clock by paparazzi, whether it was hanging out at Boujis nightclub with William, Harry, and the gang or shopping casually at Topshop, Peter Jones, or Miss Sixty. Shopping trips to the local Waitrose supermarket or department store with Carole became frenzied games of cat and mouse, as the pair dodged long-range lenses and persistent pressmen. Occupying the gray area between being a formal royal consort and a member of the public, Kate found the Palace offered protection only when she was physically with William. The rest of the time, she was left to fend for herself.

Matters came to a head on her twenty-fifth birthday, when her house was swamped with a media circus. Lawyers were instructed, and the press warned, to back off. But as shrewd as ever, Kate didn't create enemies of the media. She knew that there was a very good possibility she would need to keep them on her side for many years to come.

In a rare exchange of events, Prince William had to follow in his younger brother's footsteps when he applied for Sandhurst, since Harry was already there. Undertaking the RCB entrance process at the Westbury barracks in Wiltshire, William passed with distinction, ensuring his path to a career in the military was assured. Kate was at his side when he received his results and celebrated with him at the Purple nightclub in Chelsea. They let their hair down and caroused until the early hours.

William was easing his way into the role of a senior Royal, but he was also planning ahead. His life was to be one of duty and service. Like every male member of the family, a stint in the military awaited. But mindful of his position as a future King, he wanted to develop as much as possible. To that end, ahead of his term at Sandhurst, William embarked on a sort of postcollege gap year, in which he undertook three stretches of work experience.

First up was a spell at the stately Chatsworth House, where he spent a fortnight shadowing various staff and learning how the 35,000-square-acre ranch estate worked, from the inside out. He then spent a week at HSBC in the city of London as an intern, studying the machinations of the financial services at the heart of the UK economy. Finally, and most aligned to his immediate future, was a two-week attachment to the RAF's rescue team in North Wales. William came in for some criticism when it was revealed that he had flown from Anglesey to RAF Lyneham in Wiltshire in a Hawk jet so that he could collect a pair of boots.

William needed to break in the boots, it was explained, ahead of his arrival at Sandhurst, scheduled for January 8, 2006, the day before Kate's twenty-fourth birthday.

Like Harry two years previously, the Prince arrived at Sandhurst with his father to be deposited with his iron, ironing board, and shoe-shine kit (and his presumably now-comfortable boots).

"I can assure you," boomed the commandant of Sandhurst, Major General Andrew Ritchie, "He will be treated the same as ever other cadet. Everyone is judged on merit, there are no exceptions made."

William's experience at Sandhurst largely followed the same lines as Harry's. He would be up every morning at 5 a.m., brush his teeth (leaving toothbrush and toothpaste at right angles), and make his bed with military precision. His room and floor had to be spotlessly clean. He would arrange his clothes in the wardrobe by color, leaving a space of exactly four fingers between each hanger. His shoes were given a new coat of polish and the soles scrubbed with a toothbrush. It would now be 6 a.m., and Cadet Officer Wales would be obliged to stand at attention outside his bedroom door, to sing the national anthem and await inspection.

His day would be taken up with military, strategic, and fitness training, including handling weapons such as the SA80 5.56mm rifle, light mortars, and hand pistols. In deference to the augmented protocols the royal cadet necessitated, extra precautions were put in place, such as fake training schedules to throw the media off the scent, while the real programs were printed out and circulated to a limited few.

Nevertheless, the prospect of seeing the future King going through his paces during training was irresistible to the press, and so, as with Harry, there were several attempts by photographers to break into the grounds, using near-military levels of cunning and perseverance themselves.

After a grueling five-week immersion period, William had a weekend off. He celebrated in style with Harry—"passed out" from the Academy, ranking him above William for once—by staying out late partying at a London nightclub. The following night, William and Kate enjoyed a huge night out at Boujis with friends, managing to run up a bar tab in excess of two thousand pounds. Undaunted, the couple flew out for a week's luxury holiday in Mustique, following in the notoriously decadent footsteps of his late aunt Princess Margaret, whose villa had hosted some wild scenes in the 1970s.

William returned to Sandhurst and Kate continued with her life, going to fashion events, swanky parties, balls, receptions, and, in September, another week abroad with her boyfriend, aboard a yacht sailing around the Balearics.

The lather of excitement over Kate in the press had settled to a steadily bubbling froth of speculation on when the by-now inevitable proposal would take place. The couple was being snapped together at every possible opportunity, whether at the races, on holiday, or emerging rosy-cheeked from Boujis in the early hours. But given William's perceived slowness in proposing, the unfortunate sobriquet "Waity Katie"—which Kate loathed—became a running joke in the papers.

By autumn 2006, Kate had found a job as an accessories buyer at Jigsaw, the high-street chain, run by a friend of hers, Bella Robinson. The role was flexible and challenging, ensuring Kate could juggle her increasingly public profile by William's side with a meaningful and creative career.

That December, William was watched by a beaming Kate and their proud families as he passed out from Sandhurst. The festive season saw William and Kate spend Christmas day with their respective families, before William was due to join up with Kate in Scotland with the Middletons, for the traditional Scottish Hogmanay celebrations. For whatever reason, he didn't make it.

Life for William was now all about his military career. Like Harry, he was relishing the relative freedom he paradoxically found in the most controlled environment he had yet been in, and with alacrity, he embraced his new life as a second lieutenant in the Blues and Royals, a regiment of the Household Cavalry.

William considered a number of regiments before applying to join the Household Cavalry. He based his decision on the variety of roles that the regiment undertakes, from reconnaissance support to airborne forces, right through to ceremonial duties. The Prince was also attracted by the regiment's outstanding record in recent decades, most notably during the Falklands Conflict, the 1991 Gulf War, Bosnia and Kosovo, in Iraq and in Northern Ireland.

The Prince spent the first year or so continuing his training to become a fully qualified armored reconnaissance troop leader and experiencing life as a young officer at regimental duty.

He also spent much of his downtime helping maintain the regiment's reputation as a hard-partying, boisterous bunch. Known appropriately as the "Booze 'n' Royals," the soldiers enjoyed themselves to the fullest, on weekends, letting off steam after a week's tough training.

***

There is a wonderfully concise and accurate means of discerning the key differences between William and Harry: their military training. For Harry, the military was intended to be a lifelong career that could fulfill his childhood ambitions of being a soldier as well as providing him with a strict routine and structure to his life, and above all, the blissful anonymity in its ranks that he craved and within which he thrived. Harry confessed in 2017 he had been so disillusioned with being part of the Royal Family that at some point he simply wanted out. The army, he revealed, was "the best escape" he had ever had until he had to abandon his military career, finding himself at a crossroads between royal duties and the military life.

For William, however, his years in the army served as little "more than window dressing," according to royal biographer Duncan Larcombe. In his biography of Harry, Larcombe asserted accurately that William's military career was never really going to be more than part of his long-term strategy, preparing for his reign as King. William told the biographer, in 2005, that it was important for him to "understand the military and to be able to look soldiers in the eye with at least a tiny bit of knowledge of what they have gone through."

To this end, when William graduated from Sandhurst, he decided to spend the immediate future gaining experience across the military. He knew that his destiny decreed that he would one day be the commander in chief.

This is why, at the start of January 2008, William, or rather, Flying Officer William Wales, began a four-month spell with the Royal Air Force at RAF Cranwell. During an intensive sixteen weeks, he spent time across the entire RAF network, learning to fly light aircraft, and then, following his spell at Cranwell, flying helicopters at RAF Shawcross. He was regarded as a steady and reliable pilot, not given to flashy air acrobatics. William gravitated toward search and rescue operations, initially observing and then participating in rescues at sea.

He also fulfilled a personal ambition and made it to the front line in Afghanistan—if only for thirty hours. Flying as part of a crew to Kandahar, to return with the body of a young paratrooper killed in action, William took the controls of the massive Globemaster plane for part of the flight and spent a few hours on the ground at the Afghan airbase, meeting troops. When he landed back in the United Kingdom, he sought a private audience with the soldier's parents, to express his condolences.

While stationed at Odiham, he managed to hit the headlines when he flew a Chinook helicopter to the Isle of Wight, for cousin Peter Phillip's stag party—picking up Harry on the way, in London. At a cost of over eighty thousand pounds to the taxpayer (the cost of flying a Chinook for about an hour), William beat the traffic and arrived at the weekend in style. The newspapers tutted their collective heads, as it seemed William was using expensive RAF vehicles as a personal taxi service.

As it turned out, William had actually been offered a lift by the pilots of the Chinook, who had flown up to Odiham and were returning to Cranwell, so there had been no breaking of rules, just bending them in the case of picking up of Harry en route as well as not properly informing his supervisors about the exact nature of the flight.

But the story broke around the same time as another apparently flagrant flouting of the rules, when William landed a Chinook in a field by Kate's house. It was seen as showing off. But William hadn't descended from the helicopter to sweep up an adoring Kate in his arms—he had just taken off again. He was simply doing what every flying student did and practicing his takeoffs and landings using familiar landmarks, such as properties belonging to friends and family. Admittedly, not every student had a girlfriend with a country manor conveniently outfitted with an adjacent field.

That April, William also decided to buzz over Highgrove, to surprise his dad, a 106-mile round trip to Gloucestershire and back. A few days after that, he undertook more low-level flying training by swooping over his grandmother's Sandringham estate in Norfolk. (She wasn't home at the time.) More controversially, he appeared to be trolling entirely when he traveled 260 miles to Northumberland, from where another pilot took the chopper back to base while the Prince popped up to Scotland to attend a friend's wedding with Kate. A slightly sheepish Ministry of Defense told the press it was a "legitimate training sortie" although there were plenty of rumors that behind the scenes, top brass had hit the ceiling when news of William's little jaunts had become public. There were further grumblings in the media about the time and money spent on William's training, given that his position made it highly unlikely he would ever be seeing active service.

Once he had his wings, William followed in his father, grandfather, great-grandfather, and great-great-grandfather's footsteps and joined the Royal Navy, to undergo their training program. This was a young man who really intended to scrutinize the inner workings of the British military with unprecedented commitment. He completed a grueling four-week induction, which included wargaming on a nuclear sub, and then was sent to the West Indies, where he joined the crew of the frigate HMS *Iron Duke*. There, William roughed it with the rest of the crew, sleeping in cramped cabins with other recruits, participating in all manner of sea exercises, including swooping on a boat loaded with narcotics heading for Europe, and gaming a disaster scenario on the island of Montserrat. He also was consistently punished for running late for his PT classes, meaning he had to invariably do extra push-ups in front of everyone else.

The final stage of William's military training came when, after two years of fairly entry-level stuff, he took full advantage of his position to intern at the Ministry of Defense, under the direction of the secretary of state. He attended high-powered meetings among Chiefs of Defense staff and witnessed the nuts and bolts of the running of the military. Now, after years of hands-on learning and experiencing, William was uniquely qualified to empathize with the needs and challenges facing Britain's twenty-first-century military, from the lowliest Army recruit to the commander and Field and Air marshals at the very top.

In January 2009, William returned to his beloved helicopters and began training in earnest as a Sea King pilot with the RAF's Search and Rescue team. Once he passed his initial tests in helicopter rescue, he moved to Anglesey in North Wales, where he joined the Search and Rescue Training Unit at RAF Valley. Based in Wales, the country of his surname, he settled into a spartan military issue cottage, which was to be his base for the next few years. Assigned to C Flight, 22 Squadron, he started out undertaking copilot duties.

On October 2, 2010, William's months and months of training all came to a head when he undertook his first rescue mission as the copilot of an RAF Sea King. Following an emergency call from the Liverpool Coastguard, William and three crew members flew from their base at RAF Valley to an offshore gas rig where a worker had suffered a suspected heart attack and needed to be airlifted to a hospital. The man's reaction to knowing his mercy flight was being piloted by the future King might have had an adverse effect on his cardiac health, so that little fact wasn't relayed to him at the time. William performed splendidly and went on to participate in further rescue missions, including one in November 2011, when he rescued two sailors who were on board a cargo ship that was sinking in the Irish Sea.

Between February and March 2012, the Prince was seconded to 1564 Flight to Argentina, much to the annoyance of the Argentinian government, who clearly remembered the 1982 Falklands War, even if the Royals didn't. In any event, it turned out that rather than promote British sovereignty over the once-disputed islands, he just occasionally rescued Argentinian fishermen stranded at sea. But his steady and calm presence at the helicopter controls, his knack for teamwork and easygoing manner, and his diligence in adhering to exacting military standards ensured his popularity and success. All of this led to his promotion to becoming captain, or pilot in command, of a Sea King helicopter, in June 2012.

"The training has been challenging, but I have enjoyed it immensely," he told the press when he qualified to fly rescue missions in the Sea King. "I absolutely love flying, so it will be an honor to serve operationally with the Search and

Rescue Force." With typical clipped military briefness, Officer Commanding 22 Squadron, Wing Commander Mark Dunlop, barked, "Flt Lt Wales demonstrated the required standards needed for the award of Operation Captaincy."

Barely two months later, William captained his Sea King for a dramatic rescue of two teenage girls who had been swept out to sea while bodyboarding off the Anglesey coast. The RAF announced that the rescue was one of its "fastest and shortest" operations, with the helicopter taking only a remarkable thirty-eight seconds to arrive. William would continue to excel in his career as a search and rescue pilot, until September 2013.

THE SPLIT AND THE REUNION

Initially, William did his best to be a conscientious boyfriend to Kate, who was working most weeks at Jigsaw, while he was stationed near the South Coast. He would drive the 130 miles up to the capital on weekends and squire his girlfriend to the usual parade of clubs, parties, and events, much to the continued delight of the media, whose frantic panting at the couple's every move was increasingly irritating them both.

Also becoming a source of irritation to Kate was William's slowly waning lack of passion and energy for the relationship, according to one snitch. She was dealing with a horrendous amount of intrusion and stalking from the media on a daily basis, despite legal warnings—and receiving barely any help from the royal media machine. Her family was also being subjected to intense scrutiny, all thanks to her choice of partner. Meanwhile, William was gallivanting around seemingly unconcerned about Kate's problems and taking her, in her eyes, for granted. The festering tension was exacerbated by the distance between them and William's reluctance to make a commitment.

Matters came to a head during March 2007, thanks to William's boorish antics at Elements nightclub in Bournemouth. Two girls with whom the future King was drunkenly flirting sold their stories to *The Sun* tabloid.

"Word went around that William was in [the club]," eighteen-year-old Ana Ferreira told the paper. "There were a lot of girls hanging around him and he was posing for pictures. He had me on one arm and my friend Cecilia on the other. I was a little bit drunk, but I felt something brush my breast. I thought it couldn't be the future king, but now when I see the pictures, it's no wonder he's got a smile on his face."

Worse was to follow. Another young woman, nineteen-year-old Lisa Agar, told *The Sun*'s rival tabloid, *The Mirror*, that William, after numerous shots of sambuca, had tugged at her arm onto a podium to dance with him.

"He was being very flirty," she said. "I was quite taken aback, but just went for it. He was laughing his head off and waving his hands in the air." Agar and some other friends were persuaded to join the Prince and his chums back at their barracks for a drunk afterparty, but, according to Agar, she left after only twenty minutes. "Strangely, I felt a bit sorry for William and I thought that maybe he was cheering himself up."

Unsurprisingly, Kate, beset upon from all sides, was said to be furious.

The royal brothers were certainly letting off a bit of steam at this point. Harry was also enjoying life to the fullest at this time, falling in and out of his usual haunts around London's Mayfair district, popped to the eyeballs with his favorite Crack Baby cocktails—a blend of vodka, passion fruit puree, syrup, Chambord, and champagne. Allegedly, he even headbutted a paparazzo outside Boujis nightclub at 3 a.m. Needless to say, the tabloid cycle of persecution and condemnation of the brothers' behavior reached fever pitch.

That Easter, Kate and William's relationship reached its lowest point. William turned down an invitation to stay with the Middletons over the holiday, and instead, the pair met up for a serious talk. Kate, badgered by her mother, wanted a firm commitment from her partner, said the family insider. He wasn't prepared to be pressured. The following week, their relationship ended with an afternoon phone call from William while Kate was at work at Jigsaw. Kate fled the office that afternoon and stayed away all week, going back to her parents' house in Berkshire. That Friday, April 13, 2007, William formally notified his grandmother, the Queen, that he and Kate had split up.

***

Many have speculated on why the couple split in 2007. Some blame Carole Middleton's apparent interference in the relationship, urging a commitment from William. Others, such as royal biographer Christopher Anderson, laid the blame more in the direction of the Royals themselves and, specifically, Camilla. Speaking to the *Daily Beast* some years later, he explained his theory: "Camilla is a bit of a snob. She never really felt that Kate Middleton as an individual and the Middleton family as a whole were going to be worthy of entering into the Royal Family. I was told at the time of the breakup, and later on as well, that Camilla basically whispered in Charles's ear that it was really time to make—to force—William to make a decision one way or the other. She was the instigator of this."

Whoever was behind the split, at face value, it was clearly a stalemate between the two youngsters that was the primary cause. It's still unclear whether William was indeed disinclined to commit and Kate, frustrated, simply had had enough, or whether their respective families had weighed in and urged a resolution. What is evident is that Kate and William knew that a commitment meant a wedding and the unique role of King and Queen. Having seen the chaos and heartbreak a hasty decision to wed had caused his parents, the Prince was clearly in no way going to repeat that mistake.

In the first decade of the twentieth century and ten years after the paparazzi had hounded William's mother to her death, it was completely unrealistic to expect Kate—who had been continually harangued by the press—to fall in line and meekly behave with subservience and obedience to the Royal Family and the country while William's girlfriend. William's larking around while off duty from military training was oafish, but Kate knew she had to be sure what she was taking on.

A "close friend" of the couple told *The Sun* soon after the split, "As far as Kate is concerned, William simply hasn't been paying her enough attention. Kate feels hugely frustrated that their relationship just seems to be going backwards at a rate of knots."

William hadn't had much in the way of significant relationships before Kate, unlike Harry, who had had at least two serious long-term girlfriends before he met Meghan. But while William and Kate were apart, he in Dorset and she in London, William wanted to break loose and act like a frat boy in heat, noted one aide. Kate retreated to her parents' house, sought refuge with family and friends, and then behaved in a most un-Kate manner. She got out her sauciest pairs of heels and her most glamorous outfits and strutted her funky stuff around town.

"Actually, it [the breakup] made me a stronger person," Kate admitted some years later. "I really valued that time for me, although I didn't think it at the time!"

The separation proved something else to William, aside from his unexpected jealousy at seeing Kate having fun. He realized what a rock she had been to him, over the seven years they had known each other. From being there for him when he was agonizing over whether to stay at St Andrews, to patiently accepting the hounding from the press. From coping with the fact he would one day be King, to putting up with being forever a consort. Kate's discretion, immaculate comportment, and polite, equable temperament had won her many supporters within the Firm. Never once had Kate confided in anyone outside her family about her relationship, far less even consider selling her story. This sensible and grounded girl was clearly a potential huge asset for the Royals, as they faced the closing decades of the Queen's reign.

Kate wasn't such a soft touch that William could expect her to come running at his merest whim. No, this Prince would have to work to get his lady back. To fill in the time and take her mind off things, Kate signed up for a charity challenge with an all-female dragon boat racing crew called the Sisterhood, who billed themselves as "an elite group of female athletes, talented in many ways, toned to perfection with killer looks, on a mission to keep boldly going where no girl has gone before." The twenty-one girls taking part in the venture were aiming to row across the English Channel to raise money for children's hospices. The team trained on the River Thames from 6:30 each morning. Fellow rower Emma Sayle told the *Daily Mail* about their teammate: "I think the training became her therapy. Kate had always put William first and she said this was a chance to do something for herself. It wasn't a case of oh, she's Kate Middleton so she makes the team. She had to prove herself." Emma Sayle, incidentally, was the founder of Killing Kittens, a sex party in London, and a director of operations at the Fever swinger parties. Kate's horizons were certainly broadening beyond pizza and DVD nights in with William.

If that didn't make William quake in his immaculate Army boots, then the news that Pippa had just finished university and moved into Kate's Chelsea flat would have made him spill his bedtime cocoa in horror. Kate's party-loving, gregarious younger sister would be leading Kate into all sorts of diversions and activities that certainly wouldn't involve sitting around at home in PJs, misery-eating ice cream, and watching *Bridget Jones's Diary*. No, together, the pair was tanned, toned, and up for trouble. William was shaken to see tabloid pictures of his once-demure ex-girlfriend's bronzed limbs and sexily tousled brunette hair, emerging from—and later sliding into—taxis outside London's most exclusive hot spots and nightclubs.

William had rather expected Kate to pine for him, waiting patiently for him to call. Kate was made of sterner stuff, though. If William thought he was the only one who would be out having fun in clubs, he had another thing coming. Seeing Kate in the papers, looking like she was having a wild old time, flirting with handsome men, and dancing the night away, William was said to be piqued. This wasn't what was meant to happen.

William realized he had to move fast and man up. Kate had gone to Ibiza for some sun and fun with her brother, James, and friends. They stayed at the villa of Kate's uncle Gary, where Gary's wife noticed that Kate spent a lot of time on the phone, reassuring a frantic William that no, she wasn't dancing on podiums all night at legendary nightclub Pacha's infamous foam parties. William was fast coming to terms that in breaking up with Kate, he had lost a very special woman. Now, there was no doubt she was the one. Even when dumped, she had firmly refused to talk to anyone outside her family about William—yet another profound example of just how well suited the calm and dignified Kate was to the notoriously private Royals.

Pals said he felt the bust-up was "a terrible mistake." "She's not about to wait much longer—and he knows it," a friend confided.

Over the summer of 2007, Kate had enhanced her reputation to the extent that with or without William at her side, she had become a hot catch on the society A-list. Feted for her discreet sense of style and panache, liked by everyone for her down-to-earth natural charm and giggly humor. She was at countless posh garden parties, making the scene at lavish dinners and receptions and frequently making the society gossip columns as she navigated her way through the upper echelons of London society.

Kate knew that if they were to reconcile, this would have to be a journey that led down the aisle. And then, she had to be sure that she could handle everything that lay beyond that aisle, as did William.

He and Kate met and began discussing their future. They realized what they had was special and, crucially, a strong enough foundation to build a successful partnership.

"She told William she wanted a commitment," a royal source said at the time. "Either he agrees to wed by next summer or she's leaving him to get on with her life."

At a fancy-dress party on June 9, with William done up in hot pants, vest, and a policeman's helmet, and Kate going as a "naughty nurse," the pair was seen back together again for the first time since April.

"We were both very young," William later said of the split, to ITN. "It was very much trying to find our own way and we were growing up."

One month later, Princes William and Harry walked onto the stage at Wembley Stadium in front of 63,000 people, where they were hosting a concert to celebrate what would have been their mother's forty-sixth birthday and marking a decade since her death. In the royal box, Harry was accompanied by his partner, Chelsy Davy, and William sat next to his best friend, Thomas van Straubenzee. But Kate was present, discreetly sitting a few rows behind William, accompanied by her brother, James, and clearly happy to be there.

After a spectacular concert, featuring a host of celebrities, musicians, and statesmen, there was an extravagant party at a London nightclub, where tropical fish swam beneath a Perspex dance floor, oysters and raspberry vodka jelly shots were downed, and dancers in cages leapt and boogied. Harry was with Chelsy, while Kate and William dominated the dance floor, before sneaking off into a corner to sip cocktails, canoodle, snuggle, and snog the night away.

A few weeks later, they were together again. At Camilla's sixtieth birthday party at Highgrove, a black-tie event for which Kate was smuggled in to avoid the paparazzi, she shimmered in a cream-colored dress and smiled patiently and even put up with William asking the orchestra to play "It Had To Be You" and goofily mouthing the words to her, in front of everyone.

That September, they flew to the Seychelles in the Indian Ocean. Finally, they had time alone, to gaze into the beautiful sunsets and dream of their future together. They stayed at the Desroches Island Resort, checking in under the names "Martin and Rosemary Middleton," where they spent their days kayaking and snorkeling in the shallow coral reef. At night, over candlelight, they discussed their relationship and made a deal with each other.

As William and Kate returned from the reconciliatory break in Desroches, the tenth anniversary of Diana's death came around. Tactfully, Kate left William space in which to mark the difficult period. Some months later, the paparazzi got their shot when the couple partied all night long at Boujis nightclub, tumbling happily out of the doors at a spectacularly early hour and zooming off into the hazy dawn. The message to William's family, friends, and the wider world was clear: the couple was back and, by all appearances, even tighter than ever.

The following April, Kate was firmly back in the Firm when she was photographed at William's graduation from Royal Air Force College Cranwell. Accompanying William's aunt, Lady Sarah McCorquodale, she watched William graduate in a ceremony presided over by none other than his father. Flying Officer William Wales was presented with his wings and then attended a drinks reception with his dad and stepmother—with Kate very present at his side.

In May, Kate made another huge leap further along her path toward the royals inner sanctum, when she represented William at the wedding of his cousin Peter Phillips (for whose bachelor party William had cheekily appropriated that lift in the Chinook helicopter). William was off in Kenya at the wedding of his old friend Batian Craig, brother of Jecca. Kate, meanwhile, joined fellow royal girlfriend Chelsy Davy at St George's Chapel in Windsor, in the presence of the Queen, to celebrate the Phillips's marriage (which ended in divorce in 2020).

At the wedding, Kate's relaxed demeanor as she chatted and laughed with Chelsy and joined her and Harry on the dance floor added fuel to the fire. Rumors and speculation about Royal nuptials continued to accumulate. The press, who had come to cover the wedding, couldn't believe their luck at scoring a double scoop. Here was Harry presenting his girlfriend to the Queen for the first time. Nerve-rackingly, Kate was making her debut solo appearance at a royal function without William at her side.

"[William] sent out a message," wrote the *Daily Mail*'s Richard Kay, quoted in *Vanity Fair*. "[He's saying,] 'I'm not there, but this girl is very important in my life. She's representing me. Read what you like into that.' And, so, one tends to read into that, well, the girl is almost in the homestretch to be his wife."

The event was also notable for being the high point of Kate and Chelsy's rather muted relationship. According to royal biographer Katie Nicholl, prior to the Phillips wedding the pair had never quite clicked.

"[Kate]'s friendship with Chelsy was lukewarm," wrote Nicholls. "They were completely different characters and the bubbly Zimbabwean got along better with Pippa. Kate had made an effort to befriend Chelsy, inviting her clothes shopping, but Chelsy had turned the offer down, leading to a coolness between them."

The wedding heralded yet another first—this one, a less happy one, for certain guests. It emerged that the wedding couple had sold the picture rights to the wedding for £500,000 to *Hello!* magazine. This was the first time in history a Royal had sold the media rights to such an occasion, and the Queen was not pleased at all—especially when it transpired that Peter Phillips had discussed the proposal with his mother, Princess Anne, but had not gained his granny's all-important approval. Informal shots of the Royals letting their hair down at the party and reception made their way into the magazine's copious coverage of the event, including shots of the monarch herself. When she learned of this, ice formed on the upper slopes of Queen Elizabeth II. Such tawdry monetization of her family's name and unashamed hunger for publicity and self-promotion went against everything she stood for. The Queen let it go for now, making her displeasure known, and assured that henceforth surely none of her grandchildren would exploit their position and heritage in such a similarly tacky manner.

In June 2008, William had joined the Navy for training. Aware of his renewed commitment to Kate, he now dutifully made the two-hundred-mile trip to see her at every chance, making up for his previous, neglectful ways.

That same month, the Queen bestowed the most distinguished honor it was within her gift to give—she appointed the twenty-six-year-old Prince William as Royal Knight of the Garter. At the formal investiture ceremony, disaster struck when Harry and Kate, in front of all the senior Royals, were hit with an attack of the giggles. "Oh my God!" squeaked Kate, as William sailed regally by, trying to muster up as much dignity as was possible while crowned with a gigantic bunch of ostrich feathers and wearing a velvet cape over his shoulders. Harry, his face as red as his hair, snorted and coughed, trying to contain his laughter. It was Kate's first formal royal event in front of all the family—and she had collapsed into laughter.

As Kate's slow but steady progress into the heart of the Royal Family continued, it was now a given that a wedding of their own wasn't far off. Yet the couple continued to move slowly, adjusting their lives step by cautious step. There could've been no greater contrast to the courtship of William's parents.

WILL AND KATE GET HITCHED

On Friday, April 29, 2011 at 11 a.m., HRH Prince William of Wales and Miss Catherine Middleton were married in Westminster Abbey, central London, just a shade under a decade since they had first bumped into each other one September morning back at St Andrews in 2001.

The wedding had come at a time when the Royal Family was feeling optimistic and upbeat about the future. With William's nuptials, the second in line to the throne had found his future Queen. The following year, the current Queen would celebrate her Diamond Jubilee, having survived sixty years in the hot seat. For her, it was an especially heartwarming moment, after the disaster of her eldest son's marriage, to see her quietly determined grandson finally make an honest woman of the lady who would clearly be such an asset in taking the Royal Family into a new era.

To the country at large, there were strange parallels with that day almost exactly thirty years before, when William's father had married Diana, in the same place, with pretty much the same level of media hysteria. Back in 1981, the emphasis was on the impossibly romantic fairy tale that had seemingly brought the handsome Prince and his blushing bride so swiftly to the altar and the inevitable long life they would enjoy together, ending up as King and Queen. At the time of William and Kate's wedding, Britain was once again in the grip of an economic recession, the government was wildly unpopular, poverty and crime were on the rise, and in general, there seemed little to celebrate.

But a royal wedding can always unite Britain, even a miserable, broke, penny-pinching, austerity-ridden Britain. And so, on that bright spring morning, everyone came together to celebrate, from flag-waving grannies to cynical young Republicans.

This being Britain, the celebrations had actually begun well in advance, causing not a few sleepless nights for certain people. "They were singing and cheering [outside] all night long, so the excitement of that, the nervousness of me and with everyone singing—I only actually slept for about half an hour," William recalled, of the night before the big day.

The lack of sleep didn't help with his nerves. After arriving at the Abbey, William had a moment's blind panic, and Harry had to settle his older brother down. "Before Kate arrived, William went to compose himself with Harry in a room just off Poet's Corner [an area in Westminster Abbey]," wedding guest and former royal editor Duncan Larcombe told *Elle* magazine. "We were sat near there, so they both walked straight past us and William looked absolutely terrified. They came out afterwards and gave a deep breath."

Meanwhile, Kate had had her fair share of prewedding jitters, too. Everyone was on tenterhooks to know about her wedding dress, which was to be a surprise on the day. But months before the wedding, the details were somehow leaked to the public. According to biographer Katie Nicholl, Kate freaked when the press revealed Alexander McQueen designer Sarah Burton was making her wedding dress. Burton had previously designed a stunning red dress worn by Michelle Obama, but Kate's interest was actually piqued by an off-the-shoulder wedding dress for Sara Buys, a fashion journalist, who married Tom Parker Bowles, son of Camilla, Duchess of Cornwall, in 2005.

"Behind the scenes, I think that caused tears at the Palace because Kate had done everything she could to keep the wedding dress a secret," said Nicholl. "Subsequently, a fashion source said that the dress will be a combination of Middleton's own design ideas, and Burton's deep knowledge and understanding of high fashion."

The final result was simply breathtaking. Sarah Burton had used traditional Carrickmacross stitching—a form of lace like a decorated net—to make the dress, a technique that dates back to the 1800s, to represent something "old." There was exquisite, hand-cut Chantilly lace on the sleeves, lace appliqué on the bodice, and individual lace roses, thistles, daffodils, and shamrocks hand-stitched on to the silk tulle. The skirt itself was crafted with white satin pleats reminiscent of an opening flower. The dress was rounded off with a silk tulle underskirt and 2.7m train, while Kate's veil, created at the Royal School of Needlework, featured hand-embroidered flowers. The whole thing was fastened on the back of her dress with fifty-eight buttons of gazar and organza, in rouleau loops. Those who had waited weeks to see the outfit were dazzled. It was definitely in the McQueen mold, but with a rare elegance and quirkiness, perfect for Kate's personality.

From dawn, news networks had been broadcasting hours and hours of helicopter camera shots of an unmoving Buckingham Palace, or the exterior of the Goring Hotel, where the Middleton entourage was staying. Innocent tourists stepped nervously past the massed banks of cameras and lights already set up around Westminster Abbey. Other less fortunate reporters had been dispatched to Kate's home village of Bucklebury to "capture the mood" of the village. That mood brightened considerably when the pubs opened especially early, to allow ruddy-faced locals a chance to sink a few breakfast liveners. John Haley, the landlord at Kate's local boozing spot, the Bucklebury's Old Boot Inn, even had an invite to the wedding. "I've got the morning suit, top hat," he boasted to the roving reporters. "It's fabulous."

Back in London, there were the obligatory crowds that traditionally turn out for royal events to line the Mall, the vast historic boulevard leading up to the gates of Buckingham Palace. As is usual on such days, they camped out with sleeping bags and flasks of tea and that slightly hysterical bonhomie that the British manage to muster during such times of self-imposed hardship. Many had arrived days in advance, to secure a position as close as possible to a police security barrier.

Reporting for Oprah, former royal bridesmaid India Hicks, who had been on the legendary Palace balcony for the wedding of Charles and Diana, observed how the day had echoes of the past, while being completely different.

"When Princess Diana got married, she was only nineteen years old," said India. "But at twenty-nine, Kate is the oldest royal bride in history, and probably better prepared to take on the role of princess than her late mother-in-law was. If there's anything that can be drawn from the terrible, terrible past history that we've seen, it is that William is protecting and preparing Kate. However, the tiny, little glimpse that I've had into that world shows that nothing, but nothing, can prepare you for it. Nothing can prepare Kate for what she has to face. The press is relentless . . . "

Despite the global frenzy around the wedding, William had been emphatic in interviews with his advisors that the wedding was to be as personal and intimate as could be hoped for. "What we want," he reiterated. "is a personal day that is going to be special to us. But we want it to be a day which will be as enjoyable as possible to as many people as possible."

It's clear that the self-effacing, low-key couple would have been happy with a quick registry office wedding and a pie and pint for lunch. But they knew that in their case, a low-key, ordinary wedding was as likely as Prince Philip limboing down the aisle.

The first sight the world had of Kate that morning came when she emerged from the Goring and traveled by vintage Rolls Royce with her father, down the Mall to Parliament Square and the Abbey. She emerged to raucous cheers, looking composed yet with vivid emotion animating her features. As every head in the Abbey craned to catch a glimpse of Kate, Michael serenely escorted her up an aisle lined with eight twenty-foot-high trees—six English Field Maples and two Hornbeams—while Kate's neat but opulent bouquet consisted of myrtle, lily-of-the-valley, sweet William, ivy, and hyacinth.

"The whole of Westminster Abbey fell completely silent when Kate made her entrance," recalled Duncan Larcombe, in *Elle* magazine. "There were over 1,000 people sat there in absolute silence and all we could hear was the echoes of the crowds outside. In terms of the build-up for the bride's arrival, they probably don't come much bigger than that."

As Kate walked down the aisle, the DJ dropped "I Was Glad" by Sir Charles Hubert Hastings Parry. "Here she is now," observed Harry correctly, as the pair gained the nave of the Abbey, with William's best man, Harry, standing at the front. Cameras deciphered William quietly reassuring his wife-to-be with a whispered, "You look beautiful, babe." To her father, he gave the ghost of a wink and said, "So, just a quiet family wedding, then . . . " before the horns blared out the triumphant clarion call, signaling the start of the proceedings.

The Archbishop of Canterbury performed the actual wedding ceremony, uttering the vows everyone was agog to hear. The couple had decided on traditional vows, but Kate did not promise to "obey" her new husband. Instead, the couple vowed to "love, comfort, honor, and keep" each other. After, William tried to slip the ring onto Kate's finger but couldn't get it to fit. For several eternal, ago-nizing seconds, millions around the world watched, open-mouthed, in anticipa-tion. The ring was fashioned from the same block of Welsh gold that had spawned rings for the Queen, Charles and Diana, and Princess Anne. Sweating, William managed to finally shove it onto Kate's finger, announcing as he did so, "With this ring, I thee wed, with my body I thee honor, and all my worldly goods with thee I share, in the name of the Father, the Son and the Holy Ghost. Amen."

"Kate had asked Wartski, who made the ring, to make it a size smaller so it didn't slip off," Kate Nicholl explained in the *Daily Mail*. "She had her engage-ment ring resized because she'd lost weight and didn't want the same problem with her wedding ring slipping off."

Following the signing and some brilliant brass numbers by the Fanfare Team from the Central Band of the Royal Air Force, the Bishop of London stepped up to address the 1,900 guests and newly married couple with a rousing yet comfort-ingly Godly speech. "In a sense every wedding is a royal wedding with the bride and the groom as king and queen of creation," he said, "making a new life together so that life can flow through them into the future."

After the ceremony the Duke and Duchess of Cambridge left the Abbey in true Cinderella fashion, in the same carriage that had transported the groom's parents after their 1981 wedding, a 1902 State Landau originally made for the coronation of Edward VII. They were driven off to the sounds of "Crown Imperial" by William Walton, "Toccata from Symphonie V," and "Pomp and Circumstance March No. 5" by Elgar. Later on, the wedding bouquet was discreetly placed on the tomb of the Unknown Soldier at the Abbey.

As they traveled the short distance, they were cheered lustily along the streets by the thronging crowds. There was a slight hiccup along the way when a horse tripped on the parade route to Buckingham Palace, throwing its rider to the ground. He valiantly attempted to rein in the horse and pull it off to the side, but instead it bolted and ran down Whitehall until it was stopped by guards before anyone was hurt.

That afternoon, a beaming Queen hosted a reception for the couple and their guests at Buckingham Palace, attended by all the Royals and a select gathering of VIP guests. The mood was light-hearted yet formal, with the customary family photographs and the traditional balcony appearance and RAF fly-past by William's brother officers. The crowds, numbering some 500,000 stretching back down the Mall, were treated to the sight of not one but two royal kisses, to full-throated roars and applause. Memories flitted between the Royals, memories of a similar summer's day in 1981, and the couple who had kissed that July day on the balcony. One could feel the painful, aching emptiness in the hearts of William and Harry over the absence of the one person they would most love to have been there.

Then it was time for the wedding cake, almost as big a part of the day as the dress. And big it was. Made by Fiona Cairns, it was a multitiered traditional fruit-cake decorated with cream and white icing in the Joseph Lambeth technique. The cake was decorated with the couple's new cipher, and each tier had a different floral theme. The English rose, Scottish thistle, Welsh daffodil, and Irish shamrock were all featured, as were Sweet William, lilies of the valley, and acorns (that grow into mighty oaks, William's idea, apparently). Speaking to the BBC, baker Cairns said, "It's a traditional cake but also quite delicate and modern. All the tiers will have a different theme."

Following their first reception, stuffed with cake, blessings, champagne, and love, the newlywed Duke and Duchess rode off into the spring sunset in an Aston Martin decorated with ribbons, bows, balloons, and a license plate printed JUST WED. Finally, Kate and William were man and wife.

The newlyweds spent their wedding night at Buckingham Palace, in the opulent Belgian suite. They had thrown the party of all parties that night, once the older members of the family had toddled off to bed. The Queen had wisely (and kindly) told William that the Palace was at his disposal for revels that night and to have fun. The couple's friends then, done up in their party finery, arrived in the early evening for a lavish gala dinner, prepared by top chef Anton Mosimann and featuring the compere without compare, the master of ceremonies himself, Prince Harry. Harry delivered a masterful evening's entertainment, ribbing his brother about everything from their childhood fights to William's balding head, his long road to marriage and his general unworthiness of an angel like Kate. The angel's father also gave a humorous speech in which he recalled, with wry chuckles, that time the groom had landed his helicopter in his back garden, blowing the tops off his prize azaleas.

The carousing carried on into the early hours, with much singing, dancing, drinking, and feasting, before the DJ brought matters to a close at 3a.m., with the Beatles' "She Loves You." The pair then climbed into a chic little Fiat, to be driven around the side of the Palace and off to their honeymoon suite, while guests filtered away into the early morning.

It had been an exceptional day. "It was simply magical," one guest was heard to say, a bit tipsily. "The best party ever imaginable." The hardcore knew that rather than risk being seen carousing in the usual royal haunts in Mayfair, the after-party was taking place back at the Goring hotel. There, Harry hosted a number of close pals who toasted the happy couple's health, in absentia, until past 5 a.m.

The next day, when much of Britain finally awoke, blearily put the kettle on, and took an aspirin for the hangover, speculation was buzzing about the destination for the royal honeymoon. The Bahamas? Botswana? Kenya? Outer Mongolia? In reality, the helicopter's secret destination was rather more prosaic: William and Kate's cottage, in RAF Valley in Anglesey, Wales.

The couple returned from London to workaday life on the military base, where Kate was now an RAF wife, away from the spotlight. She would join the wives' club at RAF Valley and enjoy coffee mornings and social events while their husbands were away, on active duty or training.

The actual honeymoon itself, which was paid for by William and Kate, finally took place some weeks later, on an island in the Seychelles archipelago. The North island was remote, hidden, and allowed the pair to enjoy some of their favorite activities, including scuba diving, swimming, windsurfing, and kayaking. The couple enjoyed ten days of blissful privacy in paradise.

THE DIAMOND JUBILEE

Kate's first official engagement as the Duchess of Cambridge was in Canada—a country that would later assume significance for William's brother. When they arrived on June 30 in Ottawa, the reception for the young Royals brought back more memories of the hysteria that had greeted William's parents in the early days of their marriage. Diana's presence could not have been greater in the air, on that first visit, as the trip coincided with what would have been her fiftieth birthday.

The nine-day trip to Canada covered Alberta, the Northwest Territories, Prince Edwards Island, Quebec, and the capital, Ottawa, where a ceremony at Rideau Hall saw the new Duke and Duchess plant a tree next to the one planted by Prince Charles and Princess Diana in 1983.

The couple helped out with Canada Day celebrations, dressed in cowboy duds for a rodeo in Calgary, escaped on a romantic canoe ride to Eagle Island in the Northwest Territories, and undertook countless walkabouts, meet and greets, tours, photo ops, and more. It was a baptism by fire for Kate, but to everyone's delight, she handled the grueling schedule like an old pro. Kate had selected a wardrobe that carefully curated a dynamic cross section of Canadian fashion designers, blending in some of the country's most exciting talent with her own signature, low-key style.

Throughout the whirlwind trip, Kate and William's body language sparkled with love and joy in each other's company. Traveling across the country, they met literally hundreds and thousands of people: victims of natural disasters in a remote town in Alberta, politely ignored anti-Monarchist protestors in Quebec, and members of the Canadian air rescue services, who delighted William by teaching him some nifty new tricks with his old favorite, the Sea King rescue helicopter.

Leaving Canada, Kate must have breathed a sigh of relief. She had leaped, with characteristic accuracy and precision, over the first major hurdle of her married life.

Following Canada came a lightning trip to Los Angeles, where the couple's media firepower was harnessed by charities for fundraising opportunities. In two days, wealthy Angelenos paid up to sixty thousand dollars each to have the chance to hang out with Kate or play polo alongside William, thereby raising colossal sums of money for charities affiliated to the Prince's causes.

Life had settled into a comfortable pattern for the Duke and Duchess of Cambridge by the time 2012 rolled around. William continued his day job, as part of the RAF search and rescue, while Kate got accustomed to her new life, doing the shopping, cooking the supper, and watching a DVD snuggled up with "Big Willie" when he returned, exhausted from another backbreaking rescue shift. In between these moments, the royal diary would call, necessitating a superhero style makeover and reemergence as Britain's de facto First Couple. Their first Christmas as a married couple had seen Kate join her husband for a traditional family celebration, and in the New Year, she was out and about with William, at the usual round of receptions, parties, cinema premieres, and the countless less-glamorous events, the visits to provincial old peoples' homes, hospital visits, schools, and countless more.

The Cambridges enjoyed a vacation with the Middleton family in Mustique in early February. Upon their return, William was headed to the Falklands with his Search and Rescue crew for six weeks. Meanwhile, Kate was seen at the launching of a new Lucian Freud exhibition in London, which marked her first solo engagement as a Royal.

Kate's confidence and easy rapport with crowds meant she was a natural when it came to be going about the usual round of engagements. A few months later, Kate joined the Queen and Prince Philip for a visit to Leicester, as part of their 2012 UK Diamond Jubilee tour. Kate admitted she missed her husband "desperately" but was being "very well looked after." The contrast with Diana brought sighs of relief within and outside the Palace. Those with long or guilty memories recalled the bulimic Diana in the immediate aftermath of her wedding, haunting the corridors of Buckingham Palace, drifting unhappily around her suite of rooms, while Charles went out night after night alone, making small talk with courtiers and Palace staff, to while away the time. They looked at Kate, happy, confident, and clearly enjoying herself with and without William at her side and knew that the marriage was off to a fine start.

That summer, the Queen's Diamond Jubilee consumed the country—the parts of it that revered the Royals, at least. Commemorating Her Majesty's sixty years on the throne, it revived the national sense of celebration that Kate and William's wedding the year before had begun. Jubilee parties were held around the country, while in London, the Thames Pageant saw over one thousand boats gather on the River Thames from all around the world. The flotilla measured seven miles from end to end and was the largest fleet of ships assembled on the Thames in over 350 years. Leading the way was the boat containing the monarch and her immediate family circle, which now included Kate. As the Queen basked politely in the after-glow of fireworks, surveying the hordes of crowds cheering her, and noting at her side her purposeful grandson and his steady regal wife, she must have felt well pleased with the state of the family.

Barely had the celebrations for the Jubilee died down than London was at the epicenter of global attention yet again as host of the Olympic Games. In a James Bond spoof, the Queen apparently leaped out of a helicopter alongside actor Daniel Craig in a sketch that summoned up the mood of fun and excitement that the Games brought to Britain. At the heart of it all were William and Harry, the official ambassadors for Team GB. This was one appointment for which the sports-loving brothers were united in their enthusiasm, eagerly agreeing to attend over thirty Olympic events. Pictures show a beaming Harry alongside William and Kate, cheering British athletes on from the stands, yelling and shouting their encouragement and generally having a wild old time. Pundits noted how at ease Harry and his new sister-in-law were, a tight trio of grins, laughter, and charm.

During the games, Harry repeatedly paid tribute to the athletes, singling out the female beach volleyball players with special interest. Meanwhile, in interviews during the games with the BBC's Sue Barker, William revealed worrying about being caught on the "Kiss Cam" with Kate and also revealed his wife is a "sight to behold with a hockey stick."

For royal watchers, the highlight of the Games came when Team GB's sprint team won gold in cycling in record time. In the ecstatic applause, William and

Kate embraced each other in full view of the world. The spontaneous moment of pure elation summed up the optimism and youthful energy now at the center of the Royal Family. With Britain's spirits buoyed by the future King and his new wife's all-devoted love for each other, the hugely successful Diamond Jubilee, and now the Olympics, the outlook for the future was optimistic. Things could only get better—couldn't they?

ANOTHER PAIR OF HEIRS

The world saw more of the Royals than ever before in 2012. Not only did they see the "Queen" billowing down from a helicopter, but for good measure, Harry's genitals and Kate's breasts were exposed, too. Even Prince Philip got in on the act. While sporting a kilt during the Highland Games, he accidentally managed to flash his own one-eyed Loch Ness Monster to cameras. The "wardrobe malfunction" answered the question of whether ninety-one-year-old Royals go commando under their kilts.

Harry was snapped naked as he cavorted in Las Vegas, playing some sort of nude billiards with a gaggle of girls. Kate's topless sunbathing, meanwhile, was immortalized when an enterprising photographer with a very long lens infiltrated the couple's private holiday at a hunting lodge deep in the French countryside.

St James's Palace growled a response of rage over the "grotesque and totally unjustifiable" violation of Harry's privacy, calling the incident "reminiscent of the worst excesses of the press and paparazzi during the life of Diana, Princess of Wales." In a show of patriotic pride, and to spare both Harry and Kate's blushes, the British media refused to buy and print pictures of either of them. Such restraint was a rare moment of unity in the notoriously febrile UK media and an indication of the fondness with which they—then—held the brothers.

St James's Palace went on to issue legal proceedings against *Closer*, the French magazine that had printed the photographs, for breach of privacy; its editor stood by the decision to publish, saying, "These are pictures that are full of joy. The pictures are not degrading." In May 2017, the magazine lost the case and was forced to pay $119,000 in damages, with the magazine's editor and owner each having to come up with an additional $53,000.

For the most part, Kate and William's home life progressed peacefully in the year after their wedding. Based in Anglesey, where William was flying his RAF Search and Rescue missions as a copilot in the Falkland Islands, the couple generally kept a low profile outside of royal engagements.

As one historian had famously put it, the first "duty and ambition" of someone in the Duchess's position was to produce an heir. December brought the news everyone had been waiting for. Shortly before her twelfth week, when an announcement usually would have been made, Kate's morning sickness reached worrying levels, and the decision was made to go public. The news was received with elation. Harry, on tour in Afghanistan, was notified by email, while the courtiers at St James's Palace high-fived and issued a statement of congratulations from the Queen, Philip, Charles, and fam.

The pregnancy was especially important, because the Queen had tweaked the laws of primogeniture. Now, regardless of the tot's gender, it would be third in line to the throne.

On July 22, 2013, a hot, muggy summer's day in London, George Alexander Louis—Prince George of Cambridge—was born. The world celebrated the arrival of the future King with gun salutes in Bermuda, the United Kingdom, New Zealand, and Canada, church bells pealing in celebration across Britain. Kate had suffered in her first pregnancy, and her extreme morning sickness elicited sympathy and admiration for her stoic continuation of her Royal duties until the last possible moment.

After a day of global rejoicing and congratulations, Kate was on the steps of the Lindo Wing at Paddington's St Mary's Hospital, clutching the eight-pound, six-ounce tot for his first photo call, in front of a phalanx of global media, as was traditional for new royal births. Looking thrilled, Kate was immaculate. Her hair was blow-dried and styled, and she wore a polka-dot dress by British designer Jenny Packham. Above the yells of photographers, the flashing of cameras, and distant cheers of crowds who had been keeping vigil outside the hospital, Kate grinned widely and was overheard saying she "couldn't be happier. It's a moment that any parent having just given birth will know what this feeling feels like."

William radiated pride for his son and wife and was eager to begin cracking dad jokes straightaway. "He's got a good pair of lungs on him, that's for sure," he bantered. "He's a big boy but he has got her looks, thankfully." The couple, mindful of newspaper deadlines, bypassed tradition to announce the birth initially by Twitter, much to the gratitude of newsrooms around the nation, who had been on standby for over a week now. But William also placated traditionalists by ensuring the news was also delivered in the old-fashioned manner of a placard, set on an easel by the gates of Buckingham Palace.

The Queen was the first visitor to meet her new great grandchild and someday successor, the following morning, back home at Kensington Palace. Harry gave an interview later on, saying it was "fantastic to have an addition to the family," even though he had been knocked down the line of succession. "I only hope my brother knows how expensive my babysitting charges are," he deadpanned.

In August that year, the Cambridges released a series of amateur snaps, taken by Kate's dad, of the proud new parents, George, and dog Lupo enjoying the summer sunshine. The sharing of the relaxed, informal shots sent a clear message: George was the first close heir to the throne of the modern digital era, but his childhood was going to be loving, secure, and as normal as possible, something Diana always prioritized with her own boys.

As William's commission with the RAF drew to a close at the end of August, so did the best part of a decade spent in service across nearly every part of the military. It was time for him to assume his full-time royal duties. That September, he and Kate moved back to London, to apartment 1A at Kensington Palace. They settled into the comfortable, calm rhythm of royal life, with Kate engaging with a variety of causes and charities.

The couple's first full year of marriage concluded with a heartbreaking moment when, on December 5, they attended the red-carpet premiere of *Mandela: Long Walk To Freedom*, the long-awaited biopic of Nelson Mandela. During the gala screening in central London, the royal couple was seated next to the film's star, Idris Elba. As the film screened, he noticed Kate suddenly seemed distracted and upset.

"The Duchess, Kate, sort of turned to me and looked at me as she had her phone," he recalled in an interview. "I wondered what was wrong with her because she looked quite emotional. And my girlfriend looked at me and handed me the phone and I looked down and there it was, Mandela had passed. I looked back at Prince William and Kate and they were just in tears with me."

Exiting the cinema to gathered masses of reporters, William looked shocked by the news that Mandela had died in Johannesburg, bizarrely during the London premiere of the film of his life.

"I just wanted to say it's incredibly sad and tragic news," he addressed the media. "We were just reminded what an extraordinary and inspiring man Nelson Mandela was. My thoughts and prayers are with him and his family. It's very sad."

The sad news aside, the couple and George rounded off the year with a traditional Christmas at Granny's, in Sandringham. It had been a magnificent year, full of accomplishment and achievement, the new Royal slipping easily into her role as wife, Duchess, Queen consort-in-waiting, and charity campaigner. The British press, soothed by her pragmatic approach to their role in her life, yet suitably impressed by the no-nonsense way she had faced down the French editors who had printed the topless pictures, was united in approval.

Barely a year after George's arrival, Kate was pregnant again. In September 2014, it was announced that George would soon be joined by another wee Cambridge. And so it was, on May 2, 2015, Charlotte Elizabeth Diana was introduced to the world with the traditional photo call outside the Lindo wing, barely ten hours after she was born. "It's very special having a new little girl . . . I feel very, very lucky that George has got a little sister," Kate said in an interview.

Later, in 2020, Kate admitted that these photo calls outside the Lindo wing were nerve-racking, implicitly sympathizing with her sister-in-law's much-criticized reticence following baby Archie's birth.

"Yeah, slightly terrifying, slightly terrifying, I'm not going to lie," she told the Happy Mum, Happy Baby podcast. But pointedly, in contrast to Meghan, Kate was careful to acknowledge the expectations of the public when it came to royal babies: "Everyone had been so supportive and both William and I were really conscious that this was something that everyone was excited about and, you know, we're hugely grateful for the support that the public had shown us, and actually for us to be able to share that joy and appreciation with the public, I felt was really important."

THE PRINCE'S PARTNERS IN CRIME

Harry's years at Eton were packed with incident and action. Unlike his comparatively stable brother, Harry was cheerfully unacademic, but they shared a love of sport and enthusiastically participated in the school's Combined Cadet Force. But while William had learned to be dignified and dutiful during his time at Eton, Harry found himself increasingly in the news, crashing in and out of parties, pubs, nightclubs, and trouble. The recently bereaved adolescent entered Eton in September 1998, barely a year after his mother's death and still traumatized. Throw in his increasing royal profile, and Harry would find himself caught between the staid tradition of his family and the hedonistic lifestyle of a boisterous young Etonian.

By the time Harry settled into the school, he'd bonded with a tight circle of privileged friends. In addition to his and William's long-trusted circle from home, the "Glosse Posse," the Princes had kept close to a number of youngsters who had journeyed with them from primary school to secondary school. By the time Harry was in his midteens, the Glosse Posse were notorious around the pubs and clubs of rural Gloucester with the teenage Prince often seen staggering around with a beer bottle in one hand, cigarette in the other. Trouble brewed in 2001 when British tabloid newspapers exposed after-hours sessions at the gang's favorite bar, the Rattlesnake, where Harry partied with girls, booze, and dope. Further details revealed that Harry and William had even created their own private nightclub in the basement of Highgrove, dubbed "Club H," where all manner of frolic and fun apparently took place on a regular basis during the Princes' school holidays. To the media, and the wider country, which generally tended to regard the Royals with a very British mixture of affection, respect, and contempt, Harry was clearly a troubled youth, running wild.

But back at school, chastened by the media coverage and away from the distractions of life at Highgrove, Harry soon got back on track. The young Prince discovered that he thrived on structure, routine, discipline, and activity, whereas when left to his own devices, he floundered. His friends from school supported him, understanding the impossibility of Harry and William's life. Adolescence is hard enough, going away to an elite boarding school even harder. Having your family's intimate secrets splashed all over the world's media as you try to navigate both is unbearable. The necessity of security at the school and communications with the Clarence House's Press Secretary Colleen Harris to contain the perpetual media intrusion, with door-stepping journalists attempting to bribe fellow pupils and friends into divulging juicy tidbits, stalking the boys and their friends with zoom lenses in the bushes or covert surveillance in search of a headline—one could see why the Princes kept a tight lock on their faithful core of friends.

There were two in particular—Tom "Skippy" Inskip and the boisterous Guy Pelly—who were Harry's perennial partners in crime, when it came to partying, boozing, and bad behavior. Other members of the inner sanctum were Thomas and Henry van Straubenzee, sons of Diana's close friends and old accomplices of William and Harry, respectively. The pair had holidayed with the van Straubenzees on idyllic, boisterous vacations in the Cornish town of Rock, where lengthy evenings touring the local bars were balanced with days surfing and chilling with other kids from wealthy backgrounds.

It was eighteen-year-old Henry van Straubenzee who unexpectedly shook Harry's world to its core toward the end of his time at Eton. In December 2002, Henry and a friend were at a party to celebrate the end of the school year at Ludgrove Prep, where he had been teaching to fill in time, before heading to university and then military training at Sandhurst. A bright, spirited scamp of a boy, Henry was drunk when he and an equally intoxicated friend volunteered to drive to a nearby pal's house to fetch a CD player. The short journey ended in tragedy when, after skidding off the dark road, Henry was killed outright, his friend at the wheel severely injured. That year had also seen the death of Harry's great-aunt Margaret and great-grandmother, the Queen Mother. Now he was ending 2002 in shock and grief at the death of one of his closest friends. The emotional toll of that year hit sensitive Harry in the gut. Between the press scandals about his alleged drug taking and heavy drinking, the deaths of family members and now his clos-est friend, and the pressures of entering adulthood with all the expectations his position required of him, the Prince was shaken, fragile, and in need of some time to reflect on the turbulence of the past few years.

In 2003, Harry left Eton with two A-levels, in Art (B) and Geography (D). Making the best of the situation, Prince Charles issued a statement claiming he was proud of his son's academic achievements, but it was clear to everyone that the Prince was never going to linger in academia, once he had the choice. In the tradition of royal men, he eagerly signed up to join Sandhurst Military Academy.

Ever since childhood, Harry had been obsessed with the military. He had watched the film *Zulu* so many times that his father took him to Africa for the first time in November 1997, in the immediate aftermath of Diana's death, to visit Botswana and South Africa and see the infamous site of Rorke's Drift, immortal-ized in the classic war film. Now, as he graduated from Eton with a stellar career in the school's military wing, the Combined Cadet Force his greatest success of the past five years, he knew there was only one future for him. First, though, there was the little matter of a round-the-world gap year adventure. The boy who left London in September 2003 would never return. He came back the next year a Prince, a man, a troubled soul, a conflicted individual, but a youngster who had discovered the world, met countless people from all manner of backgrounds—and had met his first, great love.

OUT BACK OF THE PUBLIC EYE

There are few tougher, or emptier, environments than the Australian outback at the height of summer. Tooloombilla was smack-dab in the heart of nowhere, and between September and November 2003, the Tooloombilla Station cattle ranch was home to the third in line to the throne.

The forty-thousand-acre property, owned by friends of Diana, Annie, and Noel Hill, gladly welcomed Harry to experience life as a "jackaroo," an Australian cowboy. Being so far from home, there were some concerns at Clarence House about how the eighteen-year-old Prince would cope with conditions on the ranch. The intense heat, the grueling routine, working from 6 a.m. to 6 p.m., herding cattle, mending fences, and generally getting stuck in—would Harry be able to handle it?

Predictably, the biggest challenge Harry faced in his early weeks at the ranch turned out to be none of the above. For locals, many of whom had voted for retaining the monarchy in the Australian referendum in 1999, news of Harry's presence raised barely a sunburned brow. But, despite a formidable security operation (costing the Australian taxpayer £240,000), the British media were soon gathered at the gates of Tooloombilla Station, clamoring for a glimpse of the Prince on horseback. Already nursing a deep loathing for the press following his mother's death, Harry was torn between fury, frustration, and resignation at the chaos, threatening to leave unless the media did. Rather than herding bulls between the parched gum trees on wide dusty paddocks, the Prince found himself stuck sitting indoors, watching videos.

"I've got a young man in there in pieces," said Mark Dyer, the senior aide who arranged Harry's visit. "He can't do his job as a jackaroo, he can't go out, he can't even muster cattle in the yards near the road without having his photo taken."

Back in London, Prince Charles's press secretary and long-term confidante of William and Harry's, Colleen Harris, warned that Harry might walk unless the papers retreated. She explained, "He's gone to the outback to acquire new trades and have new experiences, but if he's hindered by the media and it's disruptive to his work on the farm, then we will have to look at the options."

Fortunately for all concerned, the issue was resolved by a compromise, allowing the press a couple of photo opportunities with the Prince, in return for leaving him alone for the rest of his stay. Once this small hiccup had been resolved, Prince Harry was free to enjoy his first solo trip abroad. He attended rodeos, herded cattle on his favorite horse, Guardsman, and took regular trips across the country to follow the English rugby team. Earning one hundred dollars a week and roughing it with fellow jackaroos and jillaroos was heaven for Harry, despite the scorching heat wave that gripped the region that summer, with temperatures soaring past a hundred degrees.

DIRTY HARRY

The Prince had first traveled to Africa in September 1997, with Charles and his nanny, Tiggy. There, in the immediate bleak aftermath of Diana's death, the young Prince found something new and immediately fascinating—a continent alive with people, stories, cultures, and experiences unlike anything he had previously encountered. The Royals have long cherished their connection to the African continent, and Harry is no exception. To this day, he is regularly seen in countries across the continent, and speaking up on social, environmental, and ecological issues pertinent to the region. In 2019, he told Reuters how the continent had soothed, inspired, and fascinated him over the years since Diana's death.

"I have often talked about Africa as my second home, and I've often been asked why I love it so much. Ever since I came to this continent as a young boy, trying to cope with something I can never possibly describe, Africa has held me in an embrace that I will never forget, and I feel incredibly fortunate for that," he said.

"I always feel that wherever I am on this continent, that the community around me provides a life that is enriching and is rooted in the simplest things—connection, connections with others and the natural environment."

In February 2004, Harry, a friend named George Hill, and his father's communications secretary, Patrick Harverson, touched down in Lesotho, a tiny nation kingdom enclosed by South Africa that had been a British protectorate state from 1869 to 1966. The mountainous kingdom is one of the highest in the world, home to an astonishing array of rare flora and fauna. It also has the world's second-highest rate of HIV; poor medical facilities, infrastructure, and sanitation; appalling levels of infant mortality; grim statistics on child abuse and gender inequality; rampant unemployment corruption; and food shortages. In short, the country was a shocking landscape of suffering, hardship, and misery. It was a world away from Club H.

Harry's visit began with trips to some of the country's numerous orphanages, home to thousands of children, many of whom had HIV. He played with them in a manner that reminded onlookers of his mother—that same easy approachability and sense of fun that immediately charmed and disarmed strangers. He mucked in with manual labor too, helping out with renovations and building work as well as kicking footballs around with the youngsters and befriending them. The country's Prince Seeiso became a close friend, showing his British counterparts around the country and making no secret of the numerous challenges and obstacles Lesotho faced in defeating its many issues.

Speaking to CBS a few years later, Seeiso reflected on the extraordinary impact Harry made on his country. He said, "You go to any part of Lesotho where Harry has been and you get a truthful, honest, and a straight answer. Do you love Harry? We love him, he's just one of us. Everywhere he goes, I think he bonds a lot faster with the children. Harry is one big child basically. He wasn't afraid to pick up a child who is HIV positive. He wasn't afraid to step into and talk to a disabled person who, who is mentally or physically disabled."

While playing with children in the orphanages over his two-month stay, Harry took the time to learn about their life stories, often in tragic detail. The sensitive young man often found himself in tears when he heard why this or that boy or girl had found themselves there. Some had been abandoned by their parents, others orphaned at an early age. Some had been sexually abused. (One superstitious belief had it that HIV could be cured by intercourse with an extremely young child.) Harry spoke to them all, often gaining the children's trust with his gentle manner and genuine concern. He became fascinated by the country's history and frustrated at the lack of resources and facilities available. By the time he left Lesotho, at the end of April 2004, he had gained invaluable insights and experiences that would profoundly shape the way he was to lead his life. He also began toying with an idea that would ultimately bring hope and relief to thousands of children in Lesotho and neighboring states in the years to come. But Harry's life-changing trip to Africa had one more major surprise to come.

Arriving with Paddy Harverson and George Hill in Cape Town, South Africa, that April, Harry had a wicked glint in his eye, a glint that would have been very familiar to the regulars at the Rattlesnake Bar or Club H. He wasted no time in looking up a girl he'd met in London the previous year, Zimbabwe-born Chelsy Davy, a gorgeous blonde who had been a pupil at the ultraexclusive Cheltenham Ladies College before attending the equally posh Stowe school where she had met the Prince through mutual friends. By the end of school, she missed Africa so much she returned to the continent, to the University of Cape Town, to study Politics, Philosophy, and Economics. When Harry arrived there on his gap year, he tracked her down. Thus began the longest relationship of his life to date.

The instantaneous attraction was apparent to them both—Harry was smitten by Chelsy's blonde allure, her athletic physique, and her raucous, sharp wit, as well as her toughness and love of the wide-open plains of her childhood. Her father, Charles Davy, was a millionaire safari operator, and the family lived on 1,300 square miles of African savannah teeming with wildlife such as giraffes, lions, and snakes. "At my preschool there were monkeys everywhere," she recalled, "stealing your crayons."

Harry hadn't met many girls who made him laugh, were unimpressed by his status—the Royal thing was a bore for her—oozed raw sex appeal, and could kill a snake with their bare hands, so when he met up with Chelsy in Cape Town, he didn't hold back. Her beachfront apartment in Camps Bay became a home to him, as the pair tore around the city in her Mercedes coupe and hung out with Chelsy's friends and family. It was only a couple of hundred miles from Lesotho, but in Cape Town, Harry found another side of Africa that was equally appealing and exciting and in Chelsy, the perfect girl to discover it with. By the time he finally bade Africa farewell and headed back to the United Kingdom, Harry had made two new important discoveries. They would both go on to profoundly reshape his life.

Harry flew back to the United Kingdom that spring, drunk on love. Friends recalled him gabbling excitedly about the willowy blonde who'd captured his heart and were amused and touched to see how deeply Harry had fallen for her. Chelsy was equally smitten with her Prince. The pair had enjoyed a wild, whirlwind romance, and in most cases, Harry and Chelsy would have left matters at Cape Town Airport. But for the two of them, this was something big.

That autumn, Harry turned twenty. By now, the Prince was a familiar face at London's more ritzy nightclubs such as Pangaea, Mamilanji, Mahiki, and Boujis (home to Harry's favorite "Crack Baby" cocktails), often snapped in the early hours, emerging red-faced, disheveled, and bleary.

In the early 2000s, London was awash with cash and jet-set Eurotrash, behaving badly and drawing a motley assortment of young British aristocrats in their wake. "It was the height of that period of people spending a lot of money and of there being a big influx of Russians and Italians into the London social scene," explained nightclub promoter Roger Michael, a familiar figure on the London circuit at the time. The young Princes held court for an endless stream of mainly Russian girls, intent on making some sweet royal memories of their own.

"William and Harry would have tables reserved at the back of the club next to the VIP area, and at one time they even had their own barman called Gordon," biographer Katie Nicholl said. "They were always relaxed at Boujis, they knew the owner Jake Parkinson-Smith, but they still had to abide by the rules. Like everyone else, they had to take their baseball caps off, which made them instantly recognizable. Women would always be approaching them and asking them to dance. There were always a gaggle of stunning, long-limbed beauties on prince watch."

The tabloid fascination with "bad boy" Harry, whose partying antics were now far exceeding those of his elder brother, started sounding faint alarms among staff and officials at Clarence House. In October, there was an unseemly altercation with a press photographer outside the Pangaea nightclub. A drunk Harry lunged at the particularly persistent photographer, giving him a cut lip. The press reacted with horrified delight.

Had Harry been dispatched to the strict environs of Sandhurst Military Academy to begin his Army career, as planned in autumn 2004, there would have been little to worry about. But disaster had struck after Harry passed the rigorous entry procedures, the Royal Commissions Board, with flying colors. While coaching a group of kids during a game of rugby, Harry sustained a serious knee injury. His start at Sandringham was delayed until spring 2005.

Nevertheless, much to the relief of the Royal Family and much to the regret of London's paparazzi, Harry flew off that November to Argentina, where he participated in a six-week stint at a polo ranch in Buenos Aires, enjoying the demanding routines and the plentiful riding. That Christmas he jetted off to Bazaruto, in Mozambique, to visit Chelsy, who was holidaying with her family on the picturesque island. The pair enjoyed a passionate reunion amid the idyllic setting, and the young Prince returned to the United Kingdom for a Royal Christmas, apparently refreshed and relaxed and looking forward to making 2005 a year of achievement in his personal, public, and romantic life.

Early in January 2005, William and Harry were invited to a birthday party for a close friend, Harry Meade, who, like much of their close gang, had something of a penchant for fancy dress and themed parties. Meade chose the rather questionable "Natives and Colonials" as a theme, perhaps not the most sensitive topic for a bunch of posh, privileged British kids. Among the lion suits, cowboys, safari suits, Indians, and Royals (the irrepressible friend of the brothers, Guy Pelly, came as the Queen), one certain guest took it all a bit too far and wore a Nazi swastika armband while lurching around with a cigarette and a beaker of strong drink constantly in hand. When the inevitable pictures made their way to the front pages, all hell broke loose.

The timing could not have been worse. Harry was still in the headlines, following his recent punch-up with a photographer outside Mahiki. Added to that, a major ceremony to mark the sixtieth anniversary of the liberation of Auschwitz was imminent. Aghast at the reaction, Harry's office issued a heartfelt apology that went some way to quelling public outrage, but the damage had been done. The world saw a drunken, louche young man, soaked in booze and ignorance, parading around a party in a swastika armband. The fact that no one had been on hand to advise the headstrong young Royal on his decision to wear the outfit did not go unnoticed. Neither did the fact that Harry was barely challenged for his choice of outfit by his peers at the party.

Senior figures in the establishment rushed to play the affair down. Rabbi Dr. Jonathan Romain, of the Reform Synagogues of Great Britain, said to the BBC: "The fact that the palace has issued an apology indicates that this was a mistake by the prince. But having been given, the apology should now be accepted."

But the Queen's former assistant press secretary, Dickie Arbiter, weighed in with an admonition: "This young man has got to come up front and be seen in person making an apology." The former Armed Forces minister, left-winger Doug Henderson MP, said the picture showed the prince was "not suitable" for Sandhurst. "If it was anyone else, the application wouldn't be considered. It should be withdrawn immediately," he thundered. Fortunately for Harry, and mindful perhaps of the profound ramifications of such a decision, a spokesman for the Sandhurst Military Academy explained that the school was minded to let this one go.

"He is most emphatically not a liability," read a statement. "We take the same attitude to the prince as any other cadet. I am quite sure there are plenty of cadets who display a lack of judgment, but we never hear of them because they do not end up in [tabloid newspaper] *The Sun*."

Harry spent the next few weeks penitently mucking out stables and undertaking backbreaking chores at his furious father's farm in Highgrove. It seemed that for now, the chastened Royal had learned his lesson.

On May 8, 2005, Prince Harry arrived at the Royal Military College at Sandhurst, accompanied by his proud father, a newly-acquired kit bag, and that mandatory item for each new recruit—an ironing board. Harry was excited, apprehensive, and determined. He'd just scraped into the prestigious academy with his less-than-impressive grades and results from his entry exams. He knew he was lucky to have made it in, his acceptance being the culmination of his lifelong obsession with the military. Most of all, Harry was said to be craving anonymity and uniformity. His wildness at school and carousing around the bars of London's West End and Gloucestershire had led to the media taking a ghoulish delight in watching him wobble erratically through his teens, barely containing the festering anger at the world, following his mother's death.

But now, away from home and Eton, and thanks to the delicate negotiations by Buckingham Palace's press team with national media, Harry was set to enjoy a period of growth and development.

Each of the 270 newbies was allocated miniregiments in which they would undergo the grueling forty-four-week induction course. Officer Cadet Wales was placed in the Alamein Squadron, with twenty-nine other recruits. He had to adjust fast, as there was little time for niceties. From being waited on hand and foot as a senior Royal, or as a privileged Eton schoolboy, Harry was now expected to look after himself and his quarters, keeping them spick and span as well as being inspection-ready at 5:30 a.m. each morning.

His bed made with precise hospital corners, his small room spotless, his trousers ironed with razor-sharp creases, and his boots polished to a gleam, Harry would nervously await the eagle eyes of an irate sergeant major who would bawl him out should there be so much as a smudge on his shoes, a carelessly-tucked bed sheet, or an impudent molecule of dust floating around the floor.

But Harry was delighted. This was exactly what he had craved—being one of the boys, one of the crowd, mucking in with everyone else and no special treatment or singling out. The staff at the academy knew they would treat Cadet Officer Wales as they would any other wet-behind-the-ears rookie and instructed his peers to do the same. By and large they did—there is a story about one unfortunate lad who decided to have a bit of fun teasing the Prince and ended up being briskly booted in the nuts by him.

Likewise, the training took no shortcuts or special privileges for Harry. Despite having to have his personal protection officers within sight at all times while out on exercises, Harry underwent the same tough routines and tasks that everyone did. His NCO would gleefully hurl abuse and lively reprimands to the Prince at every opportunity, which Harry came to value and respect. The course was so demanding and degrading that on average, despite the coveted places at the academy, 15 percent of new recruits would drop out in the first two weeks.

The training was the making of Harry. For the first time, he was being shouted at, pushed around, forced to be on his toes at all times, worked from dawn to dusk, and treated exactly like everyone else. He found what had been lacking in his life so far—stability, discipline, self-reliance, and comradeship, according to a friend. Until now, William had been the only other person who truly understood what Harry might be feeling at any one time. Now he had a whole platoon of fellow recruits, all going through the same ordeal and drawing strength and motivation from one another.

"My father's always trying to remind me about who I am and stuff like that," he said some years later. "But it's very easy to forget about who I am when I am in the army. Everyone's wearing the same uniform and doing the same kind of thing. I get on well with the lads and I enjoy my job. It really is as simple as that."

The following year, to mark his twenty-first birthday, Harry gave an interview in which he recalled those early weeks of his training, shocked and jolting through each grueling day: "You're marched around in a green overall, half like a gardener, half like an inmate. I do enjoy running down a ditch full of mud, firing bullets. It's the way I am, I love it."

Harry spoke in glowing terms of his comrades in his platoon, and it became obvious to everyone in his family that, to their great relief, after an uninspiring academic career so far, he was finally finding his niche.

However, trouble was never far away. It emerged some years later that, despite the binding of the Official Secrets Act upon all Academy staff, a pharmacist called Tracy Bell, who worked at the school's healthcare facility while Harry, and later William, were attending, sold five articles about the royal Princes between October 2005 and July 2006. Furthermore, in a High Court trial years later, it emerged that the notorious phone-hacking scandal involving the British tabloid *The News of the World* had extended to members of the Royal Family. It explained why another minor scandal reached the front pages, when Harry bent some rules and reached out to his private secretary, former soldier Jamie Lowther-Pinkerton, for information about the 1980 Iranian hostage siege in London, when he was under pressure to write an essay on the event. No one could understand at the time how the story reached the press, as only Lowther-Pinkerton and Harry had known of the request.

Likewise, it baffled everyone when photographers and journalists would suddenly pop up when Harry was out in the countryside on training exercises.

While Harry was charging through swamps firing machine guns, back in South Africa, his girlfriend Chelsy was finding out what it was like to be romantically linked to one of the most eligible young bachelors in the world. Speaking in 2015, Chelsy recalled the "terrifying" experience of being relentlessly tailed by the paparazzi, having her car tracked and the world's media lying in wait for her wherever she went: "I found it very difficult when it was bad. I couldn't cope. I was young, I was trying to be a normal kid and it was horrible."

For a relatively carefree teenager, this was a rude awakening to something of what Harry went through day to day. She remembered how Harry had been reluctant to go public with their romance at the start, and how she didn't understand. Now she did.

In his twenty-first birthday interview, Harry expressed his anger and frustration with the press's intrusion into his private life, saying of Chelsy: "That does irritate me, I see how upset she gets . . . that is my private life."

The relationship was a struggle on many levels—the six thousand miles between them, the diverging paths in life, Harry committed to all-encompassing military training, and Chelsy to studying law. Harry would pine for Chelsy when he was alone. She was sensible and level-headed and would support him without being remotely bothered by his position and status. Chelsy loved Harry, despite the trappings of his family, although her concern for him was frequently perceived as neediness. In the phone-hacking trial in 2015, it was revealed that Chelsy called and texted Harry, during his training, sometimes up to sixty times a day. As Harry was forbidden to use his phone during the days (along with laptops, televisions, and any other gadgetry), he couldn't respond to her. (For his part, the same trial revealed that around 2006, Harry would often call Chelsy up late at night when he was drunk and bellow endearments at her.)

When the ten-month training course ended in April 2006, Harry and his new friends celebrated in style, with a raucous night out that ended up in a tacky strip club, Spearmint Rhino, in Slough, a dull town on the outskirts of London and the last place one would have expected to bump into a senior member of the Royal Family at 3 a.m. The inevitable media scandal blew over quickly when one of the dancers present that night sold her story but admitted Harry had politely, if woozily, turned down the offer of intimate entertainment.

Chelsy, though irritated with Harry's boorish behavior, was smart enough to realize he was just letting off steam with his mates after a challenging year. Once the hangover had dissipated, Harry "passed out" again. This time it wasn't due to booze; it was at the annual graduation parade at Sandhurst, in front of a beaming Queen, Princes Charles and Philip, and his brother William, now himself a new recruit beginning life at the Academy.

PART FOUR

A STAR IS BORN

Whatever it was, they married and had me.

—Meghan Markle

Barely a year after marrying in a Hindu ceremony at the Self Realization Fellowship Temple, off Sunset Boulevard, Los Angeles, in 1979, Doria Ragland and Thomas Markle announced they were expecting a child. Their union hadn't been easy, in a state where barely fifty years ago, mixed marriages were still regarded as unconstitutional. While the laws had changed, society was still catching up, and by the end of the 1970s, Thomas and Doria still attracted plenty of attention, suspicion, and casual racism.

Doria's deep spirituality informed the couple's choice of wedding venue. As a follower of the Hindu yoga guru Yogananda, Doria joined the likes of Steve Jobs, Mariel Hemingway, George Harrison, and Linda Evans in following the great man's scriptures. She wanted to get married to Thomas in a place where color and background were irrelevant. "I like to think he was drawn to her sweet eyes and her Afro, plus their shared love of antiques," Meghan wrote on her blog some years ago. "Whatever it was, they married and had me."

A year after the wedding, Doria was pregnant. Thomas was delighted. His two grown-up kids, Thomas Jr. and Yvonne, fought like cats and dogs, and neither showed much interest in anything other than themselves. Partly, this was down to their turbulent childhood since Thomas and their mother split. Partly, it was down to the environment in which they were living. Teens in LA weren't especially woke at that time, and what with Thomas Jr.'s reported fondness for weed and indolence and Yvonne's bizarre flirtation with Satanism and the goth lifestyle, it was no surprise that Thomas found so much comfort and strength in the diminutive, yet solid presence of Doria Ragland.

The pregnancy was hard. Los Angeles in the summertime is a swampy hot mess, and for Doria, the daytime temperatures in the mideighties were painful and difficult to bear. But it was all worth it when, at 4:46 a.m. on the morning of August 4, 1981, Doria delivered a baby girl. They called her Rachel Meghan. She was quickly nicknamed "Flower" by the family.

"He was just so, so happy," recalled Meghan's stepbrother, Thomas Jr. "He spent every single minute he could with her. My dad was more in love with her than anyone else in the world and she became his whole life. He was just blown away by Meghan."

Yvonne, meanwhile, aged seventeen and more interested in her gang of friends and social life than her father's new baby, clearly resented the newcomer. Thomas's regular absences during her traumatic childhood were no doubt fresh in her mind.

As Thomas delighted in the first years of his youngest daughter's life, his professional profile grew significantly. The long hours and hard work were paying off, as Tom won an Emmy for his work on *General Hospital* after two nominations. This meant he was now spending almost ninety hours a week at work, something his young wife was understandably less than ecstatic about, especially now that she had a baby to look after.

The neighborhood, meanwhile, was still predominantly white. Out and about with baby Meghan, alone as usual while Thomas was at work, Doria soon tired of passers-by stopping to admire the young baby and assuming Doria was hired help—Meghan's nanny.

As had been the case in his first marriage, Thomas's long hours and devotion to his job at the expense of family life began eroding the secure domestic unit the couple had created. Despite his love of his daughter and his joy in watching her thrive, Thomas just couldn't find a way to make it work with Doria. Arguments between the couple began to dominate their marriage, much to the weariness of Thomas's two elder children, who had been here before. By the time Meghan was two years old, the couple had separated, divorcing five years later.

Thomas seemed heartbroken by the split, even though Doria cited his long absences from home as being its primary cause. He claimed Doria hadn't given the marriage enough time to work. Whatever it was, the couple was now living separately, Meghan with her mother during the weekdays and with her father on weekends. The latter often provided the young girl with the chance to hang out on sets of popular TV shows, doing her homework and reading or playing around with other members of the cast and crew.

Some years later, Meghan reflected, with amusement, on how her worlds would collide in those years. "Every day after school for ten years, I was on the set of *Married . . . with Children*, which is a really funny and perverse place for a little girl in a Catholic school uniform to grow up," she said. Nevertheless, her after-school afternoons on set with her father gave Meghan an invaluable insight into the machinations of the process. She absorbed the world of studios, actors, crew, and technicians and the extraordinary levels of patience, skill, and talent required by all. The lessons would stand her in good stead in her own television career.

As Meghan grew older, she and her mother's bond deepened, the pair coming to rely on each other for emotional and spiritual support during the hard years following the breakdown of the marriage. Doria had moved to Los Feliz, just south of Hollywood, where she was training to be a social worker. Later, she would return to her first love, yoga, and run classes around the neighborhood.

"My mom has always been a free spirit," recalled Meghan. "She's got dread-locks and a nose ring. She just ran the Los Angeles Marathon. We can just have so much fun together, and yet, I'll still find so much solace in her support. That duality coexists the same way it would in a best friend."

Thanks to Thomas's then-healthy income, young Meghan attended crèche (daycare), and later classes, nearby at the exclusive Little Red School House. There, she excelled in sports and drama, appearing at the age of five onstage to sing "The Wheels On The Bus" and school productions of *Bye Bye Birdie* and *West Side Story*. She took a lead role in *How the Grinch Stole Christmas,* too (the chorus line of which also featured an unassuming blonde kid named Scarlett Johansson).

Living in a modest home with Doria but attending a posh girls school instilled a strong appreciation of the broad spectrum of privilege, wealth, and snobbery that was part of Hollywood society. Unlike many of her peers, Meghan went out of her way to befriend fellow students who were struggling with bullies or racial discrimination. At school, in the company of children from a wide range of ethnic and economic backgrounds, Meghan's awareness about her ethnicity began to materialize into a major issue for her for years to come. According to a fellow pupil's anecdote, some of Meghan's snootier classmates asked if she would join their new "White Girls Only" club. Young Meghan's reaction was stinging.

It wasn't just fellow pupils who found themselves in Meghan's firing line. After watching commercials in a social studies class, Meghan was appalled by a spot for a dishwashing liquid that ended with the tagline "Women of America are fighting greasy pots and pans." A letter-writing campaign followed, in which the ten-year-old expressed her anger not only toward Procter & Gamble, the corporation behind the ad, but also to First Lady Hillary Clinton, Nickelodeon newsreader Linda Ellerbee, and feminist lawyer Gloria Allred. While Procter & Gamble never formally acknowledged Meghan's letter, the wording on the offending commercial was swiftly amended to "People all over America."

Meghan's successful activism led her to join the National Organization for Women, the equal-rights group founded in 1966. Speaking many years later, she looked back on this time with pride. "It was at that moment I realized the magnitude of my actions. At the age of eleven, I had created my small level of impact by standing up for equality."

By the time Meghan had reached her early teens, she had traveled with Doria to some of the most poverty-stricken parts of the world, including slums in Mexico and Jamaica, where she had been dismayed to encounter children literally scrabbling for food in the dirt. The experience left a deep impression on the thirteen-year-old, and when she returned home to Los Angeles, she went to see if she could volunteer at the Hippie Kitchen, a nondenominational charity running soup kitchens in the city's dire Skid Row district. "It was rough and raw," she remembered. She stayed away for the time being, intimidated by the drug-crazed homeless people who would line up for bread and beans and feeling a little out of her depth.

By now, Meghan had an after-school job at a frozen yogurt shop, the rather wonderfully named Humphrey Yogart. She also, by now, was attending a secondary school, Immaculate Heart, and had moved to live with her father, whose home was nearer to the school. Thomas's fortunes had dipped, and it was only a lucky $750,000 win in the California lottery in 1990 that allowed him to send Meghan to the highly ranked all-girls school. (As of 2019, the school costs $16,850 annually to attend.) Even though his daughter was unaware of his win—as was Doria, from whom Thomas Sr. especially wanted to conceal it, lest it affect their divorce settlement—she repaid his investment abundantly.

Immaculate Heart in Los Feliz is a girls' school steeped in religious and philosophical teaching. According to its motto, its aim is for students "to become women of great heart and right conscience through leadership, service, and a lifelong commitment to Christian values."

At Immaculate Heart, Meghan built on her successful academic record and extracurricular activities in music, sports, drama, and activism, as well as becoming something of a leader among the girls. "Meghan was the kind of student who, even though she had a circle of friends, she was friendly and welcomed everyone," remembers teacher Christine Knudsen, who taught a senior elective Markle took on spirituality and literature. Immaculate Heart was a place where independence, toughness, and spirit were encouraged, not smothered.

Former student Kate Sullivan, interviewed by Charles A. Coulombe in the *Catholic Herald*, remembered the school's feisty spirit: "As I recall, the line between political assembly and liturgy was fairly thin in my early days at Immaculate Heart—and that felt perfectly natural. It was no big deal to receive Communion from the nuns, or to hear a sermon delivered by a woman, or to sing 'We Are a Gentle Angry People.'"

"[Meghan] had a lot of depth, probably because of her own experiences and hard knocks growing up," Knudsen added. "She'd take conversations to a deeper level."

Another Immaculate Heart teacher, Maria Pollia, also recalls Meghan with admiration and fondness.

"Meghan was always happy, raising her hand to ask questions and engaged in class discussions," said Pollia. "She was also a very unusually compassionate person and developed that compassion quite early in her life."

It was Pollia who inspired Meghan to return to Skid Row and the Hippie Kitchen, where she herself was a volunteer. Meghan explained how, three years prior, she had tried a day's volunteering at the Kitchen but had been nervous. Now, as Pollia sought to instruct her charges in the ways of Catholicism and the necessity of helping others over one's own fears, Meghan asked her for advice.

"Meghan approached me after class and said, 'You know, when I was about thirteen, I volunteered at a kitchen on Skid Row and I was really scared. But I really, really, really want to go back. How did you do it?'"

Interviewed for the book *The Game Changers: Success Secrets from Inspirational Women Changing the Game and Influencing the World*, Meghan remembered how Pollia inspired her to volunteer again.

"I remember [Maria Pollia] told me that life is about putting others' needs above your own fears," she said. "Yes, make sure you are safe and never, ever put yourself in a compromising situation, but once that is checked off the list, I think it's really important for us to remember that someone needs us."

"She created relationships with the people who were at the Kitchen because she would come back," Pollia recalled. "Not once, but throughout her entire junior and senior year at Immaculate Heart."

"Meghan was really charismatic and was a very hard worker and very focused and you could tell she was going to do something special with her life," another of Meghan's fellow pupils recalled. "She was bubbly, optimistic, and positive. She was also very focused and had her eye on the prize—she knew where she wanted to go to college and she knew she wanted to do drama."

It's hardly surprising that such an accomplished, popular, and outgoing girl as Meghan was inundated with requests for dates and romantic trysts during her time at Immaculate Heart. Despite the school's innocent name, there was no lack of activity buzzing between the school's students and those neighboring boys' establishments such as Loyola High School and St. Francis.

Meghan dated her first serious boyfriend, Luis Segura, for almost two years between 1997 and 1999, becoming close to the Segura family. She was remembered as "sweet and fun" by Luis. In April of 1999, she began seeing Giancarlo Boccato, her date for the Immaculate Heart Junior Senior Prom in April that year. However, despite the buzz among the guys that Meghan encountered wherever she went, from stage to soup kitchen, school to sorority club, she kept her rep for composure and flourishing sense of style. Interestingly, in these ways, she echoed that of another student, some four thousand miles away in the United Kingdom, one Catherine Middleton.

MEGHAN: STEPPIN' OUT

Meghan's love of theater and drama got serious at Immaculate Heart. At this time, her acting ambitions were confined mainly to practicing award speeches in front of her bedroom mirror, using a hairbrush for a microphone, according to those who knew her at that stage of her life. At Immaculate Heart, she embraced the drama department, becoming president of the Genesian Society, a group of students who followed drama festivals and stage plays. Meghan had found the perfect environment to turn her dreams of acting into reality and even roped her father into bring his lighting skills to school productions. It gave Thomas a chance to appreciate his daughter's innate drama talents. He would often throw in the odd bit of advice learned from his own theater and television work, instructing her how to stand, move onstage, and project.

"She had the talent and focus to back it up," said a fellow member of the Genesian Society. "You could tell she knew the work it would take and she was willing to put in the work."

The school's proximity to Hollywood meant that Immaculate Heart had no problem getting well-known acting coaches to visit the premises. One such luminary was Gigi Perreau, whose films in the 1940s and 1950s had made her one of the best-known child acting stars of all time. Perreau recalled Meghan as one of the most responsive and dedicated students she had taught. Speaking to Meghan's biographer Andrew Morton, she remembered a "skinny kid who developed and blossomed into a beautiful and confident young woman.

"She was spot-on, learned her lines when she had to, very dedicated, very focused. She was a wonderful student, a lovely girl. I knew she would be something special."

Meghan's acting roles grew in range during her time at Immaculate Heart. From appearances in productions of *Annie*, she went on to tackle meatier roles in *Stage Door, Steppin' Out,* and *Back Country Crimes.* However it was outside Immaculate Heart where Meghan took on the most challenging acting roles she had yet encountered. In January 1999, she blazed through auditions to secure the role of Jocasta, the lead in the Greek tragedy *Oedipus Rex* at the nearby boys' school, St. Francis High School. "She had charisma," recalled the school's drama director, Manny Eulalia. "Meghan was a standout. A lot of pupils went to the show just to see [her], she certainly had a fan club."

If Meghan had impressed the boys of St Francis with her performance in *Oedipus Rex*, it was her next role, at the neighboring Loyola High School's production of the 1955 comedy musical *Damn Yankees* that made her a local sensation. Taking the star role as slinky seductress Lola Banana, she wowed audiences in a sequined leotard, performing a risqué song and dance routine. Audiences were stunned with Meghan's mastery and control. Maria Pollia was present backstage that evening, in raptures. "That night, a star was born."

In June 1999, Immaculate Heart held its annual graduation ceremony at the Hollywood Bowl. That year, among the soon-to-be alumnae of the school, one individual made a characteristic splash, gathering up the biggest cache of end-of-year prizes and awards reflecting her proficiencies from theater to sports to charity work. Who else could it have possibly been?

At eighteen, Meghan Markle's future was sunny. She had left Immaculate Heart one of its most celebrated, popular, and accomplished students, having overcome her earlier shyness, insecurity, and uncertainty over who she really was. The trauma of her parents' separate lives had healed for the most part (yet her relationships with her parents and siblings could still hit rocky patches). She had become a regular at the Hippie Kitchen, a friendly face serving beans and salad to the inhabitants of Skid Row, never making a big deal of it and taking the time to get to know the men and women who lived in the most appalling poverty and hardship. Her acting career had taken off and was building up momentum. Meghan was discovering she had a natural flair and presence onstage and, crucially, the ability to project and perform. She and Doria were solid, a little partnership that balanced and grounded them both as it had done over the vicissitudes of the past eighteen years. Now, as she gained acceptance into Northwestern, she planned to study English, perhaps pursue a career in law, politics, or civil service. Everyone agreed, Meghan was one to watch. She felt positive and energized about her future. It was almost time to go to college—but first, there was a gap year to enjoy.

INTELLIGENT HOT MESSES

"Meg always wanted to be famous. She just loved to be the center of attention."

Meghan and Ninaki Priddy had been best friends since the age of two. The pair had met at Little Red School House and bonded immediately. At the age of eleven, they both moved to Immaculate Heart, where their friendship deepened as the pair navigated adolescence and the trials and tribulations of everyday teen life. They both came from divorced households and supported each other emotionally. The pair remained close after leaving school, and during Meghan's gap year, they flew to Europe with Ninaki's family, touring France and the United Kindom, where, one day, the pair were snapped laughing and posing outside the gates of Buckingham Palace, just two ordinary American tourists, among the crowds, on a sunny day in London.

"It was always Niki and Meg. We were so close-knit, we came as a two," said Ninaki. "We were both honorary daughters in each other's homes. We were like family. The idea of having a family was something Meg very much wanted, particularly because she was from a family that felt very disjointed. I think when you're an only child in that situation your friends do become your family."

Despite their sisterly relationship that had endured since babyhood, the time was fast approaching when the pair knew their paths were to diverge, with Ninaki heading to Paris to study at the Sorbonne. For Meghan, after lots of speculation from her teachers and friends, it was eastward to Chicago and the elite Northwestern University, where she would study English.

Northwestern comprises a dozen colleges and schools across three campuses—a 240-acre campus in Evanston, a twenty-five-acre campus in Chicago, and the newest campus, in Doha, Qatar. A renowned center of research and learning, it had been established in 1853, with a 379-acre tract of land on the shore of Lake

Michigan, twelve miles north of Chicago. After completing its first building in 1855, Northwestern began classes that fall with two faculty members and ten students.

Meghan's early days at the university were a challenge. She'd mentioned to friends and teachers at Immaculate Heart in her final year that her goal was to use Northwestern as her springboard toward a bona fide acting career.

The gregarious, open, ambitious young woman found herself out of the comfortable surroundings of Los Feliz and into a vast new world, where she was a fish out of water. Back in Los Angeles, Meghan was the teacher's pet, theater star, and boy magnet. Here in Chicago, Meghan was one of a handful of nonwhite students. Her dorm was in the Mid Quads, where, as she recalled in an article she wrote for *Elle* in 2015, one student introduced herself to Meghan by sneering at her divorced parents, implying this was a result of Thomas and Doria's mixed marriage. "To this day, I still don't fully understand what she meant by that," wrote Meghan. "But I understood the implication. And I drew back—I was scared to open this Pandora's box of discrimination, so I sat stifled, swallowing my voice."

"In my memories of Meghan at Northwestern, she was very clear about the need to think about the experiences of people who are not only biracial but of people of color," one of her former teachers, Drama Professor Harvey Young, told *Elle*. "She was mindful of the need for gender equality and the importance of championing for women's rights."

The specter of racism was never far away. During one trip home from Northwestern, Meghan and Doria encountered a traumatic experience, coming home from a concert. Writing in *Elle* in 2015, Meghan recalled the event:

> I was home in LA on a college break when my mom was called the N-word. We were leaving a concert and she wasn't pulling out of a parking space quickly enough for another driver. My skin rushed with heat as I looked to my mom. Her eyes welling with hateful tears, I could only breathe out a whisper of words, so hushed they were barely audible: "It's OK, Mommy." I was trying to temper the rage-filled air permeating our small silver Volvo. Los Angeles had been plagued with

the racially charged Rodney King and Reginald Denny cases just years
before, when riots had flooded our streets, filling the sky with ash that
flaked down like apocalyptic snow; I shared my mom's heartache, but
I wanted us to be safe. We drove home in deafening silence, her chocolate knuckles pale from gripping the wheel so tightly.

Meghan continued, "I took an African-American studies class at Northwestern
where we explored colorism. It was the first time I could put a name to feeling too
light in the black community, too mixed in the white community. For castings, I
was labeled 'ethnically ambiguous.' Was I Latina? Sephardic? 'Exotic Caucasian'?"

She rushed the coveted Kappa Kappa Gamma sorority, which was founded in
1870 and was the home to some of the school's most influential young women. A
fellow KKG, Melania Hidalgo, remembered Meghan fitting in perfectly. She said
that the girls identified as "intelligent hot messes, all very driven, ambitious, and
passionate."

Meghan soon found her feet and began participating fully in university life,
not only following her English program, but a number of minors and ancillary
classes that catered to her broad scope of interests. Front and center was the ongoing investigation into her identity and heritage. She also found time to continue
her charity work. In March 2000, she undertook the grueling dance challenge,
boogying for thirty hours straight in the annual Dance Marathon at the Norris
University Center. (She reflected later that the typical weight gain experienced by
first years—the "freshman fifteen," occasioned by plenty of drinking, trips to the
campus Burger King, and late nights—didn't spare her, despite such exertions.)

"Meghan was the recruitment chair of the sorority during her time here,"
Hidalgo said. "She was in charge of bringing in the new girls. You have to be a
very friendly and outgoing person for that role. I lived in the house for a year and
it's a very fun experience, you end up becoming friends with people you never
thought you'd mix with."

The sorority was a hard-partying, hard-working crew, with a reputation for
living it up. "Meghan had a fake ID during her time at the university and told us
about it when she visited the campus," said a student who met Meghan on a return
visit to the campus in 2014. "She said she used it to drink at the Keg, which was a

popular student bar for years, and she also got a job at a club in the city. You can get two fake IDs for about $100 in Chicago—it's a little bit sketchy though and not everyone has one."

Meghan's charity work continued while at the university. She volunteered for numerous initiatives, such as the Glass Slipper Project, a nonprofit organization that collects donated dresses for teens who are unable to buy their own prom attire.

The university, which counted the likes of David Schwimmer, Warren Beatty, Stephen Colbert, Julia Louis-Dreyfus, and Zach Braff as alumni, clearly held a huge appeal for the budding actress, who would refer to herself as both Meghan (her original middle name) and Rachel (her Christian name) when attending auditions on and off campus, or casting calls for television commercials. On campus, she explored the history of black theater, as her interest in both black history and drama escalated. Professor Young, who taught Meghan in a seminar on contemporary black theater, recalled her as one of his most engaged pupils. "She was one of those people that I would highlight for students," Young remembered. "I would say, 'This is a possibility. This is a path you can pursue if you work hard.'"

Meghan was so committed to theater that during her second year, she pivoted away from studying English. "I knew I wanted to do acting, but I hated the idea of being this cliché—a girl from LA who decides to be an actress," Meghan told *Marie Claire* in 2013. "I wanted more than that, and I had always loved politics, so I ended up changing my major completely, and double-majoring in theater and international relations."

After that change, Meghan began spending more and more time rehearsing and practicing stagecraft at the school's Virginia Wadsworth Wirtz Center for the Performing Arts, making full use of the faculty Theatre and Interpretation Center.

She also developed some close friendships, which would endure way past graduation. One of her closest friends from the early days at Northwestern was a flamboyant African-American, Larnelle Quentin Foster, who was soon confiding in and being emotionally supported by Meghan. Once Meghan made the switch to theater studies, she and Larnelle would visit plays and performances. They also made weekend trips to Larnelle's family home, where Larnelle's mother fell in love with Meghan immediately, begging her son to couple up with her. Larnelle was in fact gay and closeted to his family for fear of upsetting his mother, so Meghan was an extra welcome distraction.

Genevieve Hillis, another member of the Kappa Kappa Gamma sorority, has remained a tight buddy to the Duchess, to the present day, notably coorganizing Meghan's lavish baby shower in New York in 2018 with Serena Williams. During a literature class in her first year, Meghan met Lindsay Roth, a New Yorker whose raucous sense of humor, warmth, and energy matched Meghan's own, ensuring the pair were to become solid friends. Recalling Meghan to *People* in 2017, Roth said she was "still the same girl I met years ago, with the same values and priorities. She's selfless, and that's just a part of who she is and who she was raised to be."

In a birthday Instagram post to Meghan the year before, Lindsay had paid tribute to her friend as "the most kind, generous, wickedly smart and gorgeous (inside and out) maid of honor a girl could have."

Meghan's love life also blossomed at Northwestern. Throughout her time at school, she enjoyed a number of discreet romances, such as her freshman year affair with hunky basketball player Steve Lepore, who was a campus hottie extraordinaire. Unfortunately, Steve had to transfer to North Carolina on a sports scholarship, leaving Meghan momentarily distraught, but she was too busy with university life to get too down.

As Meghan stretched her wings at Northwestern, she embraced the wide range of studies available to her, from classes in ethnic diversification and politics, to a course in industrial engineering. But theater remained her priority. In her final year, she managed to secure an appearance on *General Hospital*, thanks to Thomas's intervention. The role was brief—but Meghan had finally made it onto the small screen.

SOUTHERN SOJOURN, HUSTLE TO HOLLYWOOD

Despite her hectic academic and extracurricular schedule, Meghan's final year at Northwestern saw her seeking to broaden her horizons. Balancing her theater work, Meghan's joint major in International Relations led her to seek work experience in the US State Department, as she pondered a possible career in politics or diplomatic service. Like many of her classmates, she scoped around for a suitable berth and luckily—through the Markle family's connections—found one.

Just as her father had discreetly pulled a string here and there to secure Meghan's television debut on *General Hospital*, so did his brother Mick, who was rumored in the family to be a CIA spy—although his official role was that of a governmental communications systems specialist.

When his niece sweetly asked if he could help find her an internship, he obligingly arranged for Meghan to take a six-week role as a junior press assistant in the US Embassy in Buenos Aires.

Meghan's adventure in South America was memorable. Joining the team at the embassy, she quickly adapted to the strange, limited existence of US embassy staff in the dangerous city. At the time, the terror risk was reasonably severe, meaning Meghan's movements had to be monitored. And, according to Meghan's biographer, Andrew Morton, talking to London's *Daily Star* newspaper, the threat almost turned seriously nasty on one occasion:

"One of the scariest things for her was when she was traveling with a convoy in Buenos Aires. She was with the American convoy that was attacked by demonstrators. She wasn't hurt but they whacked placards on the vehicles. It was the scariest moment of her life. It really was a horrendous experience for her, it really scared her to death."

But for the most part, Meghan's time in Buenos Aires consisted of fairly routine office work, filing, copying, answering phones, and helping out wherever she could. Her cheery, positive approach and dedication impressed itself upon her colleagues, who were so enamored of their intern, they pressed her to take the Foreign Service Officer Test, a rigorous three-hour examination, a daunting hurdle for any prospective candidate for the Diplomatic Corps, that tested a vast spectrum of knowledge. Most uncharacteristically, Meghan failed the test. Still, she had completed six weeks with the embassy and survived the hardships and challenges the role had brought with it. Rumors also had drifted back to the States that Meghan and one of the embassy's guards, a burly US Marine, had gotten pretty friendly during her time there. Nevertheless, while confident now that a career in frontline diplomacy might not be her calling, she was happy to focus on theater and drama as she returned to Northwestern, for the final time, to graduate.

***

Meghan graduated from Northwestern in 2003. After she blazed through school and college, it would have been understandable if Meghan had felt somewhat let down about spending the days chasing up auditions and screen tests back in Los Angeles, in a tattered old SUV. Most of her auditions for roles in advertisements, television, and movies went nowhere. But knowing the acting world was a tough nut to crack, Meghan made sure to stay upbeat, keeping up with friends from college and home, exercising, hanging out with Doria, and having fun.

It was around this time that her bosom college buddy Lindsay Roth, now a casting agent, got Meghan a few lines in an Ashton Kutcher comedy, *A Lot Like Love*, where she talked the director into expanding her total on-screen dialogue from a "Hi" to five whole lines. Further blink-and-you'll-miss-it appearances followed, in TV shows *Century City*, *Cuts*, *CSI*, *Without A Trace*, and *Castle*.

To generate some income and keep afloat while she trudged from one television audition to the other, Meghan resourcefully reactivated her calligraphy skills that would later become on show in the infamous letter to her father, offering friends and acquaintances handcrafted wedding invitations. Among her satisfied customers were Robin Thicke and Paula Patton, whose 2005 wedding invites were Markle originals. "I just thought Meghan did a beautiful job," Patton recounted. "It really is a lost art, and it was so nice to create something without a device that doesn't use a battery or need to be plugged in."

Such was the demand for Meghan's skills that for around a year between 2004 and 2005, she also taught a class in calligraphy, gift-wrapping, and bookbinding at the Paper Source store in Beverly Hills. "It was her part-time job as she was going through auditions," said Paper Source CEO Winnie Park. "She talked about being a big fan of custom stationery and thinks it's the best gift to give a friend. She hosted a group of customers and instructed them during a two-hour class on how to do calligraphy." Writing a few years later on her blog *The Tig*, Meghan reflected on her enduring love of the written word and how this passion had come to mean so much to her: "I think handwritten notes are a lost art form. When I booked my first [TV] pilot, my dad wrote me a letter that I still have. The idea of someone taking the time to put pen to paper is really special."

Meghan has since acknowledged that while during this time she projected optimism and ebullience, in private, she had her doubts. Was this the life she'd dreamed of? Hustling from audition to audition, barely bagging roles of more than a few words, and writing fancy wedding invitations for other people? As the 2000s wore on and Meghan headed into her midtwenties, it seemed at times as if she'd made a huge mistake. But as usual, the Markle determination powered through moments of self-doubt and worry. Things might be tough for this budding actress, but as Winston Churchill once famously said, "If you're going through hell—keep going!"

ONE-WOMAN PITY PARTY

Tall, loud, brash, and confident, Trevor Engelson was the kind of guy friends describe as the "life and soul" of a party. Big, handsome, and charismatic, he had a larger-than-life personality and zest for life that drove a fierce ambition to make it big in the movies. He was the archetypal frat dude, typically found surrounded by a gaggle of friends, in a bar or a club, in the middle of things.

It was at a bar in West Hollywood, where Meghan was hanging out one night in 2004, that she first heard Trevor's strident New York vowels booming out across the room. Unexpectedly, the pair collided and began chatting. A flirtation somehow sparked into life. Soon after that, neat, precise Meghan was dating the loud, louche New Yorker. They would be together for the next seven years.

Trevor, from Great Neck, New York, had studied journalism at the University of Southern California, before starting out in Hollywood as a production assistant. Spunky and ambitious, he moved into talent management and founded a production company, Underground, in 2001.

His ultimate goal was movie production, an ambition he was to achieve with varying degrees of success during and after his time with Meghan. Initially, though, his irrepressible energy and go-get-'em spirit was like a shot in the arm for Meghan.

Her friends were initially baffled by the romance. Sure, Trevor was a graduate of the Annenberg School of Cinematic Arts at the University of Southern California. Yes, he came from a wealthy Jewish family. Being tall, blond, tanned, and handsome, he was undoubtedly a catch. But whereas Meghan was cerebral, intelligent, well-read, and thoughtful, Trevor was a spur-of-the-moment kind of guy, a fast-moving figure who embraced fun, spontaneity, and impulse. Above all, he was a born hustler, focused on his dream to make it as a Hollywood producer.

It was that iron-clad will and determination that drew Meghan toward him. She admired his get-up-and-go, his indefatigable zest for success, and the lengths he would go to to ensure he came out on top. He had, she surmised, the balls to make it big, and she wanted some of that.

However, when Meghan and Trevor began dating in 2005, both their careers were still very much in first gear. A year later, Meghan hadn't managed to get much further than the odd walk-on cameo here and there, on daytime TV shows and low-budget TV movies. She fervently hoped her hotshot new boyfriend would help change all that. Meanwhile, Trevor's big, breakthrough project, a humorous action caper feature called *Zoom*, had not only flopped, it had crashed monumentally. Its lead, Tim Allen, was nominated for a Razzie award, for Worst Actor. For a hungry film producer, this was not the best start to a career.

Meanwhile, Meghan was waiting tables in a Beverly Hills restaurant to make ends meet. But the pair knew Hollywood well enough to know that perseverance and luck were the keys to success. Meghan was also aware that her mixed heritage was equally capable of being a negative, as well as a plus point. "I wasn't black enough for the black roles and I wasn't white enough for the white ones," she wrote in *Elle*, in 2015. Again, she began wondering what sort of future she had in show business and how she would find success. However, she was at least happy in love, with her partner, whom she lovingly referred to as "Trevity-Trev-Trev."

By now, Meghan and Trevor were living together. "She was definitely a curator of a beautiful life," recounted Ninaki Priddy. "She liked to throw dinner parties with beautiful menus that complemented flavor profiles with amazing wines."

Priddy, who still enjoyed a sister-like closeness to Meghan, remembers the fairy-tale romance between Meghan and Trevor. "She loved him. He was very doting. They were a great support system for each other through difficult times, like the death of her grandma, her father's mother, Grandma Markle. Meghan was really close to her."

Suddenly, a lucky break came her way. Meghan Markle—the prize-winning pride of Immaculate Heart, the double-major in Theatre and International Relations, who had built up an impressive resume of charity works and interned with the Civil Service, who had wowed audiences with her dynamic stage presence, and who had worked around the clock to advance her career—was invited to become a high-heeled, miniskirted, smiling assistant on the popular TV show *Deal or No Deal*. It was, tragically, the best thing she'd been offered to date.

Over 2006 and 2007, in thirty-four episodes, Meghan appeared on the popular show as a briefcase model. She beamed beside one of twenty-six numbered brief-cases onstage, as a contestant tried to choose a winning one or chickened out and accepted a low cash prize.

But for the briefcase girls, the rewards were fairly decent and consistent. Meghan would have made eight hundred dollars per episode, and when the show was in full production swing, she could clear over twenty thousand dollars a week. She earned every cent of her paycheck, though—for all the glamour and excitement of the show, Meghan was standing in high heels for hours in a freezing TV studio, going through endless takes and keeping a professional smile plas-tered to her face. The girls were decked out in skimpy, revealing clothes, without any lines to speak of. The ardent feminist in Meghan was appalled and humili-ated. But it was a reasonably well-paying gig and afforded her chunks of down-time during which she could travel with her jet-setting partner.

Plus, there were other compensations. Being in the public eye on a popular show on a weekly basis was doing Meghan's profile no harm. Unlike most of the girls on the show, Meghan kept a low profile offscreen, avoiding the C-list Hollywood party scene that many of her fellow briefcase girls were involved in. The women attracted their share of attention, with the likes of Donald Trump visiting the set a few times to leer at Meghan and her friends. One fellow briefcase girl, Tameka Jacobs, told Andrew Morton: "He was a creep, supercreepy. But some girls were attracted to his money and power, so took his number."

During this time, Meghan scored a small role on *CSI: NY* but little else of note. It rankled her, said one friend, that while she was scuffling for any role she could get, Trevor was producing another comedy movie, this time starring Robin Williams and Mandy Moore. Despite this, he had nothing for his future wife. Meghan's innate sense of dignity and propriety prevented it from becoming a major deal, but at the same time . . . the man she had hoped for so much from was delivering so little.

As 2006 shaded into 2007, some glimmers of hope began emerging. Meghan met an agent, Donna Rosenstein, who was influential at ABC. She got Meghan an audition for a planned crime thriller, *The Apostles*. The character was Kelly Calhoun, a former hooker who'd married a born-again Christian policeman, played by Keith Robinson, living a superficially respectable life in Southern California. Speaking some years later, Robinson remembered his erstwhile screen wife with affection. "Sometimes you don't jive with every actor or actress you work with, but with her, it was very seamless," he told a BBC radio interviewer. "She was very into it, very giving. It wasn't a hard sell for me at all. We had some pretty intense scenes. I think we did a pretty good job. She was very laid-back."

It was a meaty role, with potential for Meghan to explore her full range. She shot a pilot, felt positive, prayed for good news, and then—Fox studios declined the pilot episode in June 2007. Despite having told herself to stay cautious, Meghan was devastated. So close . . . yet so far. *Again.* As her husband's career began to flourish—he was now coproducing a Bradley Cooper/Sandra Bullock vehicle, *All About Steve*—it looked as if Meghan's would never get going at all.

Although *The Apostles* hadn't been picked up by the network, Meghan's ease on set and natural screen presence didn't go unnoticed. She soon got a part in another pilot, this time a mafia comedy for ABC, *Good Behavior*. Unfortunately, this too met the same fate as *The Apostles*.

Trevor's career was bouncing from strength to strength. While Meghan continued picking up small television roles and the occasional bit part in a movie, he was being tipped by the *Hollywood Reporter* magazine as one of the faces to watch in 2009. The accolade finally spurred Trevor into throwing a few small roles to his girlfriend, in middling movies like *Remember Me* and *The Candidate*. But Meghan failed to cut through, languishing deep in the closing credits.

Around this time, Meghan began writing an anonymous blog, Working Actress, which was a litany of self-pity and maudlin reflections from an actress who was clearly not making her mark. Only outed as the author some years later, it was a sobering look into a world of days spent miserably huddling beneath the duvet, beaten down, confused, and downcast by the endless stream of rejection: "I've spent many days curled up in bed with a loaf of bread and some wine. A one-woman pity party. It's awful and ridiculous."

"THIS IS THE ONE"

I had no idea that this late August morning of 2011 would change my life. Suits *stole my heart. It's the Goldilocks of my acting career—where finally I was just right.*

—Meghan Markle

In 2010, Meghan's agent, Nick Collins, sent her the script for a new drama that he felt had some potential. Meghan was mildly excited, but cautious, after her recent slew of disappointments. The show was to be called *A Legal Mind*. Meghan was asked to audition for the part of a kick-ass paralegal in a high-pressured corporate law firm, who was also the love interest for the main character, Mike Ross, played by Patrick J. Adams. Aaron Korsh, the showrunner, wanted the character of Rachel Zane to be a tough cookie, in a hypertestosterone world of corporate law, a sassy woman who could deal with the guys in her office yet still manage to evoke a blend of inner vulnerability and grit.

One hot August morning, Meghan turned up for her audition. She was dressed in a casual, everyday outfit. When she arrived, she quickly determined that her getup wasn't quite right. Panic. Dashing out of the studio offices, she rushed into the nearest store she could see—a branch of H&M—and grabbed a simple, black $35 dress. Running back to the offices, she managed to get changed and audition.

It was a disaster, she wailed on her phone on the way home. She'd screwed up. She hadn't nailed it at all. Her agent soothed her, as he had soothed countless other clients on their way home from auditions, convinced they'd messed up. He ignored Meghan's pleas to call the producers and arrange a fresh audition. He'd heard that a lot, too. Nothing could be done now, he counseled, just try and forget it and look forward to the next audition. There'd be more—eventually.

But Meghan knew in her heart that her days of auditioning for roles she wanted were starting to run out. She didn't know how much longer her nervous system could cope with the constant emotional grind of preparing, showing up, undergoing all manner of indignities and requests, before the inevitable rejection arrived in her inbox. Or, in many ways worse, getting a role—only for the entire production to be canceled after a harrowing shoot for the pilot.

But unbeknownst to Meghan, Jeff Wachtel, the president of USA Network, and Aaron Korsh were in fact blown away. Meghan's presence and chemistry with her costar Patrick J. Adams had crackled on tape. She brought that essential cocktail of qualities to the character that exceeded anything anyone else had managed to impart. Her striking appearance, her innate professionalism, her blend of charisma, steel, and grace all coalesced into Rachel Zane. They had found their perfect actress. Talking to writer Sam Kashner years later about the audition, Aaron Korsh recalled: "We all looked at each other like, 'Wow, this is the one.' I think it's because Meghan has the ability to be smart and sharp, but without losing her sweetness."

On August 24, it was announced that Meghan had the role and the pilot would begin shooting in New York that autumn. She was elated but thoughtful. This had happened many times before. Would the show make it past the all-important pilot?

In the meantime, there was more excitement in Meghan's life. Immediately after Meghan had wrapped the ninety-minute pilot in Manhattan, Trevor whisked his girlfriend off on holiday, to Belize. There, a diamond solitaire ring and a typically Trevity-Trev-Trev proposal—half-chaotic, half-laughing, but loving and sincere—charmed Meghan utterly. She squealed a delighted yes.

The couple's joy was complete when, the following January, it was confirmed that the USA Network would commission the show, now named *Suits*, and shooting would begin that April in Toronto.

THE RING RETURNED TO SENDER

In 2011, two life-changing events took place in Meghan's life. First, *Suits* debuted on June 23, to widespread critical acclaim. Meghan was singled out for praise for her portrayal of Rachel Zane—a sparkling presence, fizzing with energy and sexual tension with her costar. She was now what she had always dreamed of being—a bona fide star in her own right, after years of minor roles, failed pilots, dashed hopes, and broken dreams.

The show soon gathered a dedicated following that tuned in week after week to keep up with the high-powered legal drama and, of course, the twists and turns of Rachel Zane's on-off romance with her unpredictable colleague, Patrick Ross. The steamy scenes between them inevitably led to speculation around the actors' real-life relationship. (Despite their sizzling on-screen chemistry, it was resolutely platonic.)

The wedding of Meghan Markle and Trevor Engelson, at the Jamaican port of Ocho Rios, took place on September 10, 2011, a day of friends, family, sunshine, drinks, laughter, and much love. Busy shooting *Suits*, Meghan had turned over most of the organization to a professional wedding planner, who was given a generous budget for a four-day party at the town's Jamaica Inn. It certainly would not have been cheap—the Jamaican Inn's custom marriage packages start at $1,500, and then there was the Herculean task of arranging family and friends' flights and accommodation.

Meghan's wedding dress was a long, white, strapless floor-length gown with a short V-plunge, accessorized with an encrusted silver belt. (Coincidentally, the same year, Kate Middleton wore a similar design for her wedding to Prince William.)

Meghan kept things simple, with some dark eyeliner and natural lipstick, and wore a gold bangle that, in due course, was joined by her wedding ring. Trevor, meanwhile, was cool and breezy, in a white shirt with matching trousers.

The couple was married in a rapid ceremony on the beach, the bride's hair still wet from the swimming pool. They'd written their own vows. Once the short ceremony was over, everyone set about getting pleasantly oiled on copious quantities of wine and spirits. There were "human wheelbarrow" races across the sand and later that night, a jolly dance with the couple held aloft on chairs, in honor of Trevor's Jewish heritage. Three more days and nights of partying followed, with guests including Meghan's immediate family, close friends, and some of the cast and crew from *Suits*. After the celebrations were finally done, Trevor and Meghan flew home to Los Angeles for some quality time together. This was all the more important, as *Suits* had been confirmed for a second season, and Meghan would soon be jetting back off to Toronto, where filming took place. The happy couple faced a future in which they would be living and working in different cities. After seven years together, the pair had committed to each other for life, at a time when their personal fortunes were twisting and turning with increasing velocity.

Ninaki Priddy's ringside seat to Trevor and Meghan's marriage afforded her a unique perspective on the pair's internal dynamics. "After the wedding, it was like a light switched off. There's Meghan Before Fame and Meghan After Fame."

Meghan started to fully embrace her notoriety as the filming of the second season of *Suits* got underway. The crackling sexual tension between Rachel Zane and Mike Ross had fans hooked, alongside the brilliantly crafted story lines and gripping plots. Furthermore, as the show's writers evolved Rachel's backstory and introduced her biracial heritage into the mix, she became something of a poster girl, when leading characters of color were still a rare sight on mainstream television dramas. Meghan was encouraged by the studio to develop her own brand, such as launching her Instagram account, which reflected not only her hectic filming schedule, but a carefully curated selection of images that showed off her esoteric reading lists, her globetrotting life, food, fashion, and everything else that went into creating Brand Meghan. She soon attracted a huge following, with judicious use of hashtags, links, and likes. Soon, Meghan had an enviable online presence. Marketers and big brands began to sit up and take notice.

Like many people who have struggled and slogged to achieve success, its arrival turned Meghan's head. As her fame grew, old friends such as Ninaki Priddy noticed how the actress's behavior was getting markedly more selfish.

"The tone of her voice, her mannerisms, the way she laughed—didn't seem real to me anymore," she recognized. "By season two of *Suits*, she was turning down lunch with us because she said she'd be recognized. I felt if I questioned her behavior, I'd be left on the outside."

Ninaki noticed also that Meghan expected friends to change their own plans to fit in with hers, or to drop prearranged appointments or engagements to accommodate Meghan's. It raised eyebrows with her old gang, and there was a feeling that Meghan's success was going to her head in no small way. But also, as with any old friends, there was a tolerance and loving acceptance. Privately they thought she was being difficult. She'd struggled for years, so she would return to normality. It would be OK, eventually. "Wouldn't it?" questioned one pal.

To Trevor, it was becoming increasingly obvious that his own schedule would also have to bend to his wife's a little more than he had anticipated. As Meghan's filming got underway, he found himself having to travel to Toronto each week-end, to spend time with her. "It's not up to me to speak for Trevor, but I know he was traveling to Toronto every few weeks," recalled Ninaki. "[He] would have walked the earth to make their marriage work."

Still, the couple managed to spend some quality time together engaged in their favorite pastime of traveling. In late 2011, they rented a campervan and took off around New Zealand on a low-key adventure, which provided plenty of cozy romantic moments.

Then there was the dog. In 2013, Meghan engaged her friends and *Suits* colleagues to petition a local dog rescue center to allow her to take an abandoned pup. Ninaki was one of the people cc'ed on Meghan's begging emails to the adoption center.

"She'd fallen in love with [the dog], but found someone else wanted the dog, too," Priddy recalled. "So she emailed the pet adoption people and explained how she could provide a great life for it. She spoke of what a great time the dog would have in the *Suits* family. I felt that she was playing the *Suits* card to try to get what she wanted."

Whatever swayed the center's decision, Meghan successfully adopted the

Labrador pup, whom she named Bogart and who would become a regular star of Meghan's Instagram stories. Two years later, in 2015, Bogart would be joined by another pooch, a rescue beagle mix whom she named Guy.

While Meghan continued to thrive and flourish in Toronto, Trevor was continuing to expand his own operations, opening up a New York office so he could reach Toronto quicker. But his easygoing personality, which had always been at odds with Meghan's controlled perfection, was beginning to severely impact Meghan.

In his biography of Markle, *Meghan: A Hollywood Princess*, author Andrew Morton wrote that Markle effectively froze husband Trevor out of her life while her star was rising in Toronto. Quoting a friend of the pair's, he reported: "[Engelson] went from cherishing Meghan to feeling like he was a piece of something stuck to the bottom of her shoe."

Morton also wrote that, as Markle gained professional success, she left the home she and Engleson shared, taking a blender with her, to move to Toronto to film *Suits*, because of his "scattered approach to life."

Meghan's friend, actress Abby Wathen, concurred, concluding the *Suits* star simply felt the relationship wasn't right for her anymore.

"She always knew she would be successful, she just knew it," she said. "She knows what she wants and she gets it. We both went through divorce, so we bonded on that too. I was destroyed, but she was empowered. She took her power back. She moved on."

Remarkably, Meghan signaled the end of the marriage by sending her wedding ring back to Trevor—by mail. The couple filed for divorce in 2013, citing irreconcilable differences. Many of Meghan's friends were disappointed in her, seeing her high-handed behavior and lack of input into the marriage as key factors in the unexpected split.

Trevor was devastated, confirmed a source: "She suddenly had no more time for him. Meghan broke Trevor's heart, pure and simple. Meghan's desire to be a big actress seemed to be the end of them. The more successful she got, the more they drifted apart."

Trevor continued to pursue his production and screenwriting career, but with notably less success than he previously enjoyed in the late 2000s. The last major headlines he generated were back in 2017, when Fox commissioned a pilot of a show in which a Hollywood couple divorce, with the wife remarrying a British prince and the subsequent trials and tribulations of coparenting their children. The premise was enough to raise many eyebrows around Hollywood—Trevor's utter heartbreak at being dumped was well known—but as of the time of publication of this book, no further updates are available.

***

By now, with *Suits* a television smash hit, Meghan was undoubtedly a star. Rachel Zane was considered cool, sexy, and sassy—and was one of the series's major assets. Meghan was seen making the scene, high-stepping around town and working the star circuit—including the obligatory glam shoots for *Men's Health* magazine that most young female film and television stars still have to endure, in order to soothe any male viewers threatened by a strong female lead character.

She then flew to London in November 2013, where she was interviewed by the *Daily Mail*'s Katie Hind, to whom she claimed the notorious "love-rat," footballer Ashley Cole, was chasing her for a possible date. Katie filled Meghan in on Cole's hectic love life, making Meghan decide against accepting Cole's desperate attempts to spend some quality romantic time with the star. Speaking to Andrew Morton later, Hinds admitted she sensed that Meghan was now very much open to auditioning gentlemen for the vacancy in her private life. Before she found her next love, though, the unexpected success of a little idea she came up with to fill in time between shoots and boost her profile took her completely by surprise.

The Tig, launched in 2013, was a powerhouse of a blog. The "little engine that could," in the characteristically self-deprecating words of its creator and chief editor, *The Tig* set out to be a "hub for the discerning palate—[aimed at] those with a hunger for food, travel, fashion & beauty." This loosely translated as a fairly relaxed, (i.e., fiercely curated) insight into Meghan's life, with her friends, music, pets, travel, and thoughts on various topics making up the blog's daily updates.

Suits was now cruising along at high altitude, and despite Meghan's acclaim, fame, and frequently professed love of theater and acting, she was getting a little bored. She was starting to feel slightly limited by her television filming schedules, the endless press junkets and interviews about Rachel Zane, the inanities and indignities of being a mainstream star, and the endless grind of having to look good and keep quiet. Meghan had never claimed to be anything other than an opinion-ated kind of gal, and now with a potentially colossal global platform, she knew she had to find a way to get her thoughts, ideas, and reactions across to the wider world.

Initially, Meghan flourished on Instagram, posting pictures of lovely suppers, cool travels, beaming pals, and her dogs being adorably dumb. Around the time *Suits* reached its second season, she began to look around for other ways to grow her online branding and decided to build a website, cashing in on her celebrity status. But Meghan being Meghan, after some thought she knew she could kick it up a level and do something a bit better than a run-of-the-mill celeb site.

That feeling became an exciting possibility when she met and befriended the tennis ace Serena Williams, one of the most accomplished athletes in the world. Serena's massive online operation encompassed pretty much every platform, in a bid to bring her millions of fans together and reach out to them in such a way that each reader felt like part of Serena's inner clique. It was an extraordinary talent Williams had, of spreading her values, ideas, and causes, like her friend Oprah Winfrey could also do, with conviction and intimacy, all the while touching the hearts of literally millions of people worldwide.

Meghan wanted a piece of the action. She saw how creating a close connection with her audiences—a one-on-one relationship that saw her sharing her life with her subscribers—could really make them feel they were hanging out with Meg every day. A few ideas were kicked around before Meghan came up with what effectively became *The Tig*. Quick and easy, short and juicy chunks of content on a daily basis, anything from a girl's weekend party to working through her family heritage, travel, and shopping to debating the Middle Eastern peace process—whatever the topic, Meghan's trademark thoughtfulness and desire to debate rose to the occasion every time.

A recurring part of Meghan's daily grind were the chic, exclusive eateries to be found around the Toronto hipster circuit. One such joint, the Harbord Room, was a favorite hangout. Its boss, the charismatic chef Cory Vitiello, then thirty-five, was soon to be a favorite of Meghan's in another sense.

Vitiello was young, successful, and handsome. The Harbord Room was a roar-ing hit, as was his chain of quirky chicken shops, Flock. He also had a string of high-profile (in Canada, at least) celebrity romances to his credit. Now, as Meghan popped in more often, ostensibly to chat him up for *The Tig*, she found herself becoming more and more drawn to the sexy hash slinger and his unbelievable way with a burger. Cory was a child prodigy cook whose mixed Italian and Scandinavian heritage created a truly hard-working and inspiring character. "And maybe that's part of it," gushed Meghan on *The Tig*'s effusive review of the Harbord Room: "[Cory's] small-town charm and moral compass of someone who doesn't come from the big city but dreams big thoughts and makes them happen—that makes his food so approachable yet inspired."

In late July 2014, the pair embarked on a sizzling romance, shortly after Meghan had published her glowing tribute to Cory's restaurant. Friends of Meghan's saw their pal once again go head-over-heels for a tall, good-looking alpha male, with frat-boy overtones. It had been a year since she and Trevor had divorced, and Meghan was feeling perky and up for some fun.

Cory was something of a cult celebrity in Canada, his low-key cool credibility easily eclipsing Meghan's fame. It couldn't have escaped her notice that he moved in the sort of circles she herself aspired to occupy. Once they began seeing each other, she gained entrée into the most elite echelons of Toronto society, with connections that stretched across the world's movers and shakers.

Toronto socialite Shinan Govani got to know Meghan well, having hosted the pair at a dinner party in the early days of their relationship. "She was just a cable actress to me and didn't mean much," he told David Jones, an investigative journalist. "Cory is pretty much liked by everyone. He would be invited [to top gatherings] by dint of his talent and personality. I think she took advantage of the opportunity that came her way. There was something inside of her that wasn't content with just being an actress. I mean, what would have happened after *Suits*? She wasn't getting any younger."

Despite such claims, it's indisputable that for the most part, Meghan and Cory's relationship was conducted with a veil of discretion on a day-to-day level. The pair would often stay in, indulging their love of good cooking and romantic nights at home. During Christmas 2015, the couple spent the holidays with Cory's parents in Ontario, where his mother, Joanne Vitiello, fell in love with her son's girlfriend. "She had no airs or graces," Joanne told David Jones. "She was very interested in being with the people she was with. She had a good sense of humor, and we were very fond of her."

Nevertheless, the relationship sputtered to a halt in April 2016. Speaking to David Jones in 2018, a smiling Cory evaded attempts to get him to spill the dirt on his former flame:

"I've got a lot of respect for Meghan and, from my end, to make it seem like I'm part of the story [of her journey to royalty] would seem self-serving and opportunistic," he said. "I'm pleased for Meghan. She's a great girl. There is no bitterness. I respect people's private and personal lives, and although she has put herself in the public spectrum, I still hold to that."

In the interview, Jones took the opportunity to ask the burning question: Was it he or Meghan who ended the relationship? Vitiello answered gently and deftly, "Ha ha! That's the one question you can't answer, huh? Well, you know what? I'll let the public forum debate that!"

PART FIVE

WHEN HARRY MET MEGHAN

The British media personality and breakfast television presenter Piers Morgan is one of the best-known faces in the United Kingdom. A former tabloid celebrity journalist who'd peddled celebrity dross for years, he was fired from the editorship of mass market tabloid the *Daily Mirror* in 2004, after admitting to having published fake photographs of British soldiers torturing Iraqi prisoners. A cheery social gadfly or duplicitous scoundrel, depending on your point of view, Morgan seems to positively revel in the online abuse and controversies his contentious comments generate, from attacking feminists and disrespecting trans people to his friendship with Donald Trump. (He even formally applied for the position of White House chief of staff in 2018.) In 2016, though, Morgan was one of the best-connected men in London. To get an idea of how Morgan's little black book contained just about everyone from the most distinguished of living legends to the flotsam and jetsam of celebrity Z-listers, wannabes, and professional idiots, just consider: Morgan was the man who had introduced Sir Paul McCartney to Heather Mills—a claim the latter denied.

At the end of June 2016, Meghan flew to London, after a week's holiday in Hydra, Greece, where she had arranged a hen weekend for her old college buddy Lindsay Jill Roth. With characteristic efficiency and taste, Meghan had organized a lovely few days of sun, wine, food, yoga, and relaxing, ahead of Lindsay's imminent wedding. As Lindsay's maid of honor, Meghan took her duties extremely seriously, joining Lindsay for wedding dress fittings, endlessly debating flower arrangements and caterers, and generally advising on the infinite list of tasks and jobs that accompany any well-heeled wedding.

Meghan had been immersed in this sort of stuff of late, as Rachel Zane had gone and got married on *Suits*. Fired up by the experience, Meghan was able to use her connections to make sure her friend's wedding, with its radiant maid of honor, went off without a hitch.

In London, Meghan had a few promotional duties to take care of, to remind the Brits that *Suits* was still very much a going concern when it came to Hollywood, as well as attending a meeting at Ralph Lauren, with whom Meghan was cross-promoting *Suits*. Meghan's key contact at Ralph Lauren was the aristocratic Violet von Westerholz, about whom Meghan quickly began gushing as being one of her favorite people. *The Tig* carried effusive tributes to von Westerholz, whose father happened to be Baron Piers von Westerholz, an old friend of Prince Charles. As kids, Violet and her sister Victoria had been skiing with the Royals on their annual Klosters trips and had kept in touch with the Princes. Violet and Victoria were keenly aware of Harry's recent public comments about wanting to settle down, stop falling out of bars, stop his trousers falling down in Vegas hotel rooms, and basically grow up.

On June 29, Meghan met with Piers Morgan for a drink at an upmarket pub in Kensington, the smart stomping ground for what the press rather unkindly dubbed Sloanes—posh British girls from old-money families whose loud, braying tones, fake tans, and Louboutins were a dime a dozen in that part of London. Meghan wanted to grill Piers on his connections and find out who was who and what was hot in London that summer. Piers was impressed with the star of *Suits*, one of his favorite television shows, commenting later that Meghan was "fabulous, warm, funny, intelligent, and highly entertaining." She and Morgan downed a few martinis and gossiped, before she jumped into a car and was driven over to Hertford Street, where her date for the evening was waiting in a private room.

Speaking to the press some years later, Harry recalled the moment he met Meghan. "I'd never watched *Suits*, I'd never heard of Meghan before. And I was beautifully surprised when I walked into that room and saw her and there she was sitting there. I was like, 'Okay, well I'm going to have to really up my game here. And sit down and make sure I've got a good chat.'"

According to a friend of Violet's, Meghan and Harry were bound to meet that summer, given the circles they were both moving in. "Meghan had been a part of the London social scene for a while and had slotted into the high society set really easily. And so, when Harry told Violet he was having trouble finding someone,

Violet said she might just have the perfect girl for him," said the source. Harry had been telling everyone how he wanted to stop dating and, instead, meet a potential wife. Violet knew that Meghan would click with Harry's charity and humanitarian causes and his innate desire to use his position for good and also, she would complement his vulnerable, lost soul as a strong, determined woman who was fizzing with motivation. In short, she could give the kindly but rather rootless Harry an invigorated sense of purpose. When Violet first suggested to Meghan that she meet the Prince, her first question was "Is he kind?"

Having been assured he was, she was intrigued and excited to meet a real-life Prince.

"One of the first things we started talking about when we met was just the different things we wanted to do in the world and how passionate we were about seeing change," Meghan said some time later. "I think that was what got date number two in the books, probably. I think very quickly into that, we said, 'We should meet again.'"

Following their dinner on June 29, the pair met up each day until Meghan flew back to Toronto on July 5. Something big had clearly happened between them. As Harry said later, "the stars were aligned."

But in a foreboding to how the early months of their relationship were to work, Harry was off to Africa for a month. He was excited about Meghan, clearly feeling a connection had been made. He told his brother and close friends how thrilled he was by Meghan. But despite this, he was still seen out and about the London scene, even going on a few dates with the model Sarah Ann Macklin. ("They got on," a friend blabbed, "But they're quite different. She is very clean living and barely drinks.") When Meghan Markle began shooting a new season of *Suits* in Toronto, Harry was texting her nonstop. A second meeting was in the cards. This finally happened in, of all places, Botswana.

"It was three, maybe four, weeks later that I managed to persuade her to come join me in Botswana and we camped out with each other, under the stars," Harry recalled. "She came and joined me for five days out there, which was absolutely fantastic. Then we were really by ourselves, which was crucial to me to make sure that we had a chance to get to know each other."

For her part, Meghan admitted, "For both of us it was a very authentic and organic way to get to know each other."

If you're going to fall in love, you might as well fall in love under African skies, in the luxury of a posh campsite in Botswana. They stayed in a tent in what Harry described as "the middle of nowhere."

If Meghan was unaware of Botswana's significance to her new boyfriend, she was quickly brought up to speed about how it had soothed him in the awful aftermath of Diana's death. Indeed, some years later when the pair wed, one of the diamonds on Meghan's rings came from the country.

Harry met a journalist, Klara Glowczewska, shortly before Meghan flew out to meet him. "I've been incredibly lucky to have been able to visit Botswana as many times as I have," he told her. "I feel rooted in Africa and everything about it. I've been lucky enough to visit Botswana for more than twenty years and I'm fortunate to be able to call it my second home."

Clearly, the romance of the location was key in bonding the pair together. "We camped out with each other under the stars," said Harry. "[We were] sharing a tent and all that stuff. It was fantastic." Over five days, Meghan gamely roughed it in the luxury surroundings of bush campsite Meno a Kwena, which is described as being the "ultimate tent and camping experience in Botswana." Situated between the Okavango Delta and the spectacular Central Kalahari Game Reserve, the encampment consisted of nine luxurious tents, all with en suite bathrooms that overlooked a river, a popular hangout for the local wildebeests, zebras, and elephants. It was idyllic. So impressive were the surroundings, so breathtaking the natural history and passionate the camp site's owner, Harry's old friend, conservationist David Dugmore, that Meghan refrained from posting anything online for the duration of her stay.

What a stay it was. Meghan, a stranger to the African plains, watched with increasing surprise as her new boyfriend began taking her around the reservation, discoursing knowledgeably on the local fauna and flora. He expounded at length about rescue projects designed to conserve and increase the local elephant and rhino populations. He took her deep into the Kalahari desert, where he introduced her to the local crocodiles, sunning themselves on the banks of the river. The new couple ate traditional African dishes at night and slept to the sound of zebras and elephants. All the while, the pair melted into each other's presence, deliciously and rapturously falling in love, under African skies.

By the time the holiday was over and the pair left to return to their respective lives, the love affair was blooming. Meghan told the BBC some years later, "I think that very early on when we were going to commit to each other, we knew we had to invest the time and energy and whatever it took to make that happen."

Harry was in no doubt that he had been struck with a thunderbolt by this girl from Hollywood who was totally unlike anyone he had dated before. The last few years had been a nightmare for him, lost and roaming the world, more often than not ending up in trouble—such as the time he was snapped naked playing pool one drunken night in Las Vegas. Or being caught out using racial slurs, among his fellow military recruits. Meghan was nothing like Harry, or indeed, his usual type, leggy blondes from moneyed backgrounds. Instead, she was an older, biracial, self-made woman, bursting with positivity, self-help mantras, yoga, wellness, and steely ambition. Whether it was her acting career or *The Tig*, her fashion collaborations for labels such as Reitmans or Ralph Lauren or her increasing number of charity and humanitarian causes, Meghan threw herself fervently behind whatever she undertook. For Harry, who had been more or less adrift since leaving the Army and was glumly contemplating a lifetime of service, playing second fiddle to his elder brother, the sudden appearance of Meghan, exploding like a firework into his life, was almost unbelievably astonishing luck. A friend, speaking to the British press, simply acknowledged: "Meghan has come along at the right time."

In October 2016, after four months of discreet dating, between London and Toronto, the inevitable happened. Meghan spoke later about how, thanks to military-level evasion, duplicity, and discretion, the couple had managed to avoid the spotlight. It had given them time to bond, get to know each other, and connect on a deeper level. It had also been invaluable for Meghan to get a sense of the world she would be a part of, should she decide to pursue the relationship. It's still up for discussion just how much Meghan was prepared for the unimaginable assault on her privacy and life that being with Harry brought. Unlike most young couples meeting and falling in love, Meghan and Harry had to be up front with each other. Harry had explained in detail to Meghan how her life would change. Meghan's friends, according to an interview she gave ITN's Tom Bradby in 2019, advised her to drop Harry, simply because loving him required turning her life upside down, not least abandoning her acting career. But all things considered, they had come to an understanding by the time they were tipped off that the press had finally tumbled to the romance and London's *Daily Express* newspaper was about to splash an exclusive about Harry's new love. They were in this for the long haul. The night before the Express's front-page story came out, the couple, who was in Toronto, quietly marked the moment with a glass of wine and a toast. Harry sighed and told Meghan: "Our lives will never be the same again."

"HARRY'S SECRET ROMANCE WITH A TV STAR," blared the front page of the *Daily Express* on the morning of Monday, October 31, 2016. The *Daily Express*, a midmarket tabloid that had never quite gotten over the death of Diana, gleefully informed its readers across the land, making them splutter in shock over their breakfast tea, that the third in line to the throne was now in love with " . . . the daughter of an African-American mother and a father of Dutch and Irish descent."

"They are taking each week as it comes and just enjoying each other's company," prattled the paper's source. "But it's fair to say . . . there's a definite chemistry between them. Harry has been desperate to keep the relationship quiet because he doesn't want to scare Meghan off. He knows things will change when their romance is public knowledge . . . at the moment they are just taking it a step at a time and seeing how things develop."

There was some irony in the paper printing that Harry was "desperate" to keep the relationship quiet because he knew how things would change when they went public. The day after the paper printed the story, Meghan opened her front door to find the world's media massed outside her house. Harry, with an expertise honed over a lifetime, had managed to give the press the slip and head back to London. But for Meghan, a new reality had dawned.

The headlines were relentless, as was the inevitable social media meltdown. Meghan might have been the star of one of a TV show in the States, but her profile was considerably lower in the United Kingdom, where she was seen as just another American starlet. Now she was shacked up happily with Harry on the grounds of

Kensington Palace, cohabiting in the tiny Nottingham Cottage and living in bliss with the third in line to the throne.

Of course, in addition to contending with the world media, Harry had another task—to meet with Meghan's parents. Then there was the rather prickly matter of his own family, for whom the words "American" and "divorcée" would arouse bitter memories of Queen Elizabeth's uncle King Edward VIII and Wallis Simpson.

More concern was felt in the Palace when the full extent of the dysfunctional Markle and Ragland families was revealed.

The couple had visited Los Angeles together in summer 2016, where Meghan introduced Harry to Doria. "She was bowled over by how down-to-earth and humble he is," revealed a source.

"Doria is very much a people's person and so isn't impressed by someone putting on airs and graces, and thankfully that couldn't be further from Harry's personality."

Meanwhile, Meghan's more delicate parental relationship, with her father, Thomas, also necessitated a nerve-racking meeting for Harry. They started to communicate in summer 2016, according to Meghan's half-brother, Thomas Jr.

"My dad knew about [the relationship] from the start," he told the *Daily Mail*. "He goes [to Toronto] once every couple of months—Meghan and her father are very close and they stay in close contact. He's pretty happy about Harry and he's extremely proud of her [Meghan]. They have an amazing relationship, they're very close and they always have been."

Prophetic words indeed.

***

Unlike the Royals, when the media discovered that Meghan's extended family of half-siblings on the Markle side had had rather colorful lives, their delight was unconfined. Meghan's half-sister Samantha (formerly Yvonne), now afflicted with MS, wasted no time in painting herself as a bitter and jealous woman. In November 2016, she began the first in a series of media appearances and interviews about her half-sister, with whom she had barely spoken in a decade. "I didn't feel a separation from her until I was in the wheelchair. The higher profile she became, she never mentioned me," she claimed. Announcing to *The Sun* newspaper that she was busy working on a book called *The Diary of Princess Pushy's Sister*, Samantha told the paper that Meghan was "selfish" and a social climber who was unsuited to being part of the Royal Family. "Hollywood changed her," she sniped. "I think her ambition is to become a princess. It was something she dreamed of as a girl when we watched the Royals on TV. She always preferred Harry—she has a soft spot for gingers." (Trevor Engelson himself was strawberry blond.)

Meghan's half-brother, Thomas Markle Jr., was more measured in tone when it came to the media, although he had a similar run of bad luck. In Oregon, where he worked as a window fitter, the father of two was no stranger to the authorities, mainly for alcohol-related mayhem.

In January 2017, he was arrested and charged with menacing, pointing a firearm at his girlfriend, Darlene Blount, and for the unlawful use of a weapon, after a drinking session at his apartment got somewhat out of hand. According to reports, the window fitter "grabbed a gun and pressed it to Blount's head, in an attempt to get her to leave the home." Speaking to the press the day after, his ex-wife Tracey Dooley, who had to come and bail her former husband out of the drunk tank at 3 a.m., charitably defended him. "Tom has had a little fame and publicity since Meghan started dating Prince Harry," she said. "He wants what's best for her. He is so happy and proud for her. They used to be very close but there has been some separation over the years. When he called, he sounded very sad and asked if I would help to get him out of jail."

Later that year, police were called again to the Markle Jr. home to intervene in a "domestic violence call." This time, Darlene was charged with fourth-degree assault and had to spend a night in the cooler at Josephine County Jail before being released. It wasn't the first time she had been charged with assault. Meghan retained a discreet silence. Harry was getting to know the in-laws all too well. As were the world's media.

The global media hysteria around Meghan and Harry was uncovering all sorts of titillating, juicy titbits. For instance, it was soon discovered that Meghan's racier scenes on *Suits* were available on pornographic websites, some real and some more explicit, clearly faked. They speculated on when Meghan's relationship with

Cory had actually ended and whether it was the presence of the Prince in Meghan's life that had ended it. Columnist Rachel Johnson, sister of UK Prime Minister Boris Johnson, elected in 2019, referred to Meghan's mother as being a "dread-locked African-American lady from the wrong side of the tracks," whose daughter's potential children could inject the Royal bloodline with "rich and exotic DNA." Meanwhile, as the persecution of Meghan and her circle intensified, Harry consulted with his family's advisors and tried to arrange private security for his girlfriend (who, very nobly, refused). While she was on-set at *Suits*, extra protection was drafted in to ensure the safety of the show's main star. That situation had become near-impossible too, following the revelation about Harry. Meghan knew that she could not continue playing Rachel Zane for much longer.

After a few weeks in which every possible scrap of information or gossip relating to Meghan was splashed online and in print around the world, Doria and Thomas and their families were plagued with reporters, and seemingly everyone who had ever met Meghan was offered eye-watering amounts of money to spill the beans. Some succumbed to the lure of the checkbooks, such as Meghan's estranged best friend, Ninaki Priddy. Priddy had fallen out with Meghan after the marriage to Trevor collapsed. Rumors flew around their circle as to why. Ninaki always maintained she was disgusted at the way Meghan had treated her spouse. Others claim, despite no corroborating proof, that a suspicious closeness had developed between Trevor and Priddy.

THIS IS NOT A GAME

The media onslaught prompted an unprecedented reaction from Harry, via the offices of Kensington Palace. In a furious statement, it was made clear that the Prince was "deeply disappointed" with the media attention and explicitly warned the press to lay off. "He knows reporters will say, 'This is all part of the game.' He disagrees. This is not a game—it is her life and his."

The Royals didn't issue such enraged directives to the press. It simply wasn't done. The motto "Never explain, never complain" had held good for generations. But no longer. Harry, acutely aware how media intrusion had played a role in extinguishing his relationships with Chelsy Davy and another flame, Cressida Bonas, not to mention their part in his mother's tragic death, had precious little patience with the press. He had to be constantly cajoled and persuaded into giving obligatory photo calls and press interviews, remembers Colleen Harris, the Clarence House press secretary during the Princes' teens. And now, when he had met the girl of his dreams, faked porn pictures were being sniggered over in the tabloids, and a rather unpleasant subtext was emerging around Meghan's mixed-race ancestry.

As reaction to the news of the relationship rocketed around the world and the extent of the Markle family's various peccadilloes became known, a certain degree of concern rose amid the courtiers and staff at the heart of the Firm. The fact that Harry had found love was a cause for celebration, true, but no one had expected someone like Meghan to bounce into the family. Meghan was American—and more noticeably, of mixed-race heritage. While the Queen is acknowledged to be above prejudice and bigotry, other senior members of the family have occasionally caused alarm with their statements and views. Americans are viewed with suspicion by the elder Royals.

As for race relations, Prince Philip, the Duke of Edinburgh, for instance, is a veteran in the art of foot in mouth. Over the course of a long and illustrious career of "plain speaking," he has, at various times, warned a British student studying in China he would get "slitty eyes" if he stayed in the country much longer, congratulated another British student in Papua New Guinea for not having been eaten by the locals, asked a Native Australian if he and his fellow Aborigines "chuck spears at each other," accused members of a Bangladeshi youth group of all being "on drugs," and, on the fiftieth anniversary of his own Duke of Edinburgh Awards (a youth activity scheme), announced that all young people were "ignorant."

Perhaps it is unsurprising that Meghan was on her guard as she became acquainted with the senior members of the Royal Family.

One especially telling incident occurred during the Royal Family's Christmas lunch in 2018, when Meghan joined about fifty members of the family, including Princess Michael of Kent, wife of Prince Michael of Kent, Queen Elizabeth II's first cousin. It was a big deal. This was Meghan's first-time meeting with much of Harry's family, and the rules had been broken for her. Usually, only married partners were invited to such an intimate gathering. But Meghan was at ease and relaxed, chatting with Kate, Prince William, Princesses Eugenie and Beatrice, and others. It was all copacetic until she was introduced to Princess Michael. The seventy-two-year-old Royal was wearing an eye-catching brooch on her coat when she arrived. Unfortunately, the accessory was a piece of Blackamoor jewelry, depicting Africans in subservient roles. Meghan and Harry registered the offending item but diplomatically said nothing about it. But despite her anguished protestations that the choice of brooch had just been a crazy coincidence, there is no denying Princess Michael has had previous form with ugly racist incidences. In 2014, she had allegedly told a group of black customers in a restaurant to "go back to the colonies," after complaining that they were being noisy. Princess Michael vehemently denied the story but then made matters worse by pointing out that she was so open-minded, she had once even "pretended to be an African." Again, Meghan kept a tactful public silence on the matter.

But there was an underlying elephant in the room, no matter how effusive Meghan's tinkling laughter, no matter how friendly William attempted to be, in his galumphing manner, or how chatty the Queen was. In December 1936, the King of England, Edward VIII, the uncle of the present Queen, gave up his throne and sovereignty over a global empire of half a billion people stretching around the world, so he could wed the woman he loved. In an era of deference, strict class hierarchy, blanket reverence from the media, and unquestioning loyalty from the overwhelming majority of people, this wasn't just a shock. It was a constitutional and social crisis, unparalleled in modern times.

The King had quit to be with an American divorcée, two words that, when combined, utterly shattered the staid British population's collective composure. Wallis Simpson was seen as a déclassée social climber, an opportunist exploiting a weak man enthralled by her power. Power, so people nudged and whispered, that owed much to her rumored skills in the boudoir. In the early 1930s, speculating on the sex life of the Royals was not something that was done, but it was said Wallis had mastered certain . . . *techniques*, if you will, which sated and fulfilled the King's more esoteric *tastes*, shall we say.

Of course, little was known for sure at the time, as to exactly what may have been going on behind Palace gates and under the regal bedsheets, but it was a damned good news story, and the nation was agog. But the national mood of shock and horror went beyond the ingrained insularity and misogyny of the day. There was real anger at the King's abdication, at what was seen as his dereliction of duty and the fact that he had been distracted from his God-given destiny by this . . . this . . . shameless divorcée from [whisper] *America*! Never, could a senior Royal be allowed to be swayed in such a way. Never, ever again,

This event, which shaped the course of the royal story through the twentieth century, is one of the reasons the Queen's long reign has been so stable. The Queen believes it is her destiny to fulfill the service of her people. She has reigned with dignity and all the conviction of a God-fearing woman, steadfast in her beliefs and unwavering in her faith. She will, of course, be the last Royal of our times to be cut from this cloth.

***

Kate remembered the sly comments all too well. The snide remarks, the laughter that would abruptly stop when she walked into the room. Most of William's friends were friendly, charming even, to her face. But she only had to hear a stifled snigger or a coughed "Doors to manual!" to know that she was the butt of the joke, yet again. For many of William's friends, the nouveaux riches, upwardly aspirational Middletons were hilarious. Their meticulous designer fashion, Barbour jackets, Range Rovers, and the shabby-chic country home. The apartment in trendy Chelsea, the perfect social diary of upper-class amusements and events—from horse racing to garden parties, the whole clan immaculately and appropriately attired, trailing amiably after the strident Carole. The fact that Carole and Michael, as far as many of the toffs around William's circle were concerned, were once cabin crew (not actually the case: Michael was a flight dispatcher) never failed to raise a sardonic braying chuckle or barbed comment. It was rumored that Camilla, a true blue-blooded British aristocrat, had found Kate's family hilariously nouveau riche at first but then came down hard on the Middletons, subtly influencing William to instigate the split between himself and Kate in 2007.

When Meghan came on the scene, Kate kept a diplomatic silence when her own gang began snickering at the brash, attention-soaking American. Rumors began floating around that Kate's friends would get together for raucous screenings of Meghan's pre-*Suits* made-for-TV Hallmark movies. These films, a common sight on the résumés of many TV actors and actresses, offer much in the way of unintended comedy, and Kate's gang reveled in the cheesy dialogue and hammy acting that was required. It's said that Meghan was even aware of the sniggers and took them on the chin, even when her cringeworthy lines were quoted back at her. (Obviously, none of those teasing Meghan would have publicly mocked Kate and William about the equally tacky TV movies pumped out by the likes of the Hallmark Channel about their romance.)

"We are very excited for Harry and Meghan," the Duke and Duchess of Cambridge said in a statement at the time. "It has been wonderful getting to know Meghan and to see how happy she and Harry are together."

But there was concern behind the scenes. William, whose deep bond with Harry had been a crucial mainstay of his life, was worried about his wayward younger brother. According to Royal biographer Ingrid Sewell, William and Kate felt Harry was rushing things.

"It was all so quick that William and Kate didn't have a moment to get to know Meghan, because Harry hardly knew Meghan," she said. "Of course, William and Kate would have quite naturally thought, 'Oh she's been married before, she's older than Harry, I hope she's going to make him happy.' Anyone would think that."

One of our sources reports: "Kate was always close to Harry and they always enjoyed a very playful, jokey relationship. However, she was nervous about meeting Meghan—mainly because she had heard and read and been told so much about her yet had not met her at that point . . . She had Charlotte with her and things flowed pretty naturally when the meeting took place. Kate offered Meghan tea, and Harry cracked a few jokes and quips. They were cordial and it was actually quite a formal meeting, hardly relaxed. Meghan smiled a lot and talked about her charity work, it was . . . well, afterward they called it a success."

But niceties aside, William's concern came from wondering whether his brother was quite sure he wanted this whirlwind of Californian energy and dynamism taking over his life. After all, Harry was still reeling from the ups and downs of the past few years, undergoing therapy and still processing his grief over his mother's death. For William, a man who had taken almost a decade to get around to finally marrying his own partner, caution and measured thinking was the key, as he liked to inform those around him.

For Harry, who had been subconsciously seeking a figure to replace the mother so cruelly torn from him at a vulnerable age, Meghan's confidence, commitment, drive, and ambition were irresistible. For the Royals, steeped in their characteristic blend of staid duty, austerity, and privilege, she was a dangerously unknown quantity. Having been yanked unceremoniously over the coals for their perceived callousness in the immediate aftermath of Diana's death, the family believed that they had modernized quite enough in recent years, thank you very much. But they hadn't counted on Harry falling in love with a woman who would not be cowed by the royal institution and who had accepted the impulsive Harry's invitation to a trip to Botswana, for only their third meeting.

"Harry's in Botswana?" Kate was reported to exclaim when she heard the news, aghast at the unseemly speed at which events were unfolding. Her discomfort echoed that of the man closest to Harry, who knew his erratic brother well enough to sense impending disaster looming.

Kate's womanly intuition made her warn Harry that he needed to go slow. She gently reminded him that he was dating someone with a completely different life, past, and career and it would take time, care, and attention for them to integrate. Harry's grandfather, Prince Philip, in typically blustery form, was much more direct and is rumored to have told Harry that one should "step out with actresses, not marry them." (One wonders how on Earth he had gained that knowledge.) Meanwhile, as far as anyone knows, the Queen retained her otherworldly silence, beadily observing Harry and Meghan's antics from her throne and most probably praying Harry wasn't following in his father's disastrous footsteps. As one courtier observed to *The Sun*: "A lot of people in the family objected. Who really knows what the concerns were? Was it Meghan's background? Her father and dreadful half-sister? Because she was an outspoken American? Divorced? But Harry stood up for Meghan very forcibly. He really loves her."

But it was William's quiet words of caution and carefulness that ignited Harry's fury. "William just wanted to stress that becoming part of the Royal Family is a massive undertaking and the pressure and scrutiny is unrelenting," said a source close to the brothers. "Was Meghan the right one?"

Harry didn't take well to William's words of caution, following his first meeting with Meghan at the end of 2016. Once she'd left, William reportedly warned Harry that they didn't know her intentions and her background. In response, according to a Palace insider, Harry "went mental" and accused his brother of trying to finish their relationship before it had started. Harry's rage was compounded when, allegedly, other senior Royals expressed their concerns to him, despite their superficially friendly reactions to Meghan. Nevertheless, the concern within the Palace staff wasn't all about Meghan's lack of suitability—some professed (quietly) quite the opposite opinion. At a gathering of senior family members, including Meghan, one well-placed aide remarked, "All their IQs put together would not equal hers."

One courtier said: "It's my opinion that Harry feels he couldn't protect his mother, so he's going all out to protect his wife. This is his way of atoning. He will brook absolutely no criticism of Meghan—and he is so sensitive he often sees criticism or negativity where there isn't any."

The Royals' unease may have also been prompted by Meghan's claiming that she wasn't especially familiar with the family before meeting Harry. Which was baffling, to say the least. "Because I'm from the States," she claimed to the BBC. "You don't grow up with the same understanding of the Royal Family—and so while I now understand very clearly there's a global interest there, I didn't know much about him."

But according to Ninaki Priddy, Meghan had been obsessed with the Royals from childhood. "It's like she has been planning this all her life," commented Priddy. "She gets exactly what she wants and Harry has fallen for her. Even when she was with Trevor, she told me she wanted to go and stay in London for at least a month . . . I wasn't shocked or even surprised to hear about Prince Harry."

Meghan's strategy of claiming she was more or less indifferent to the Royals was a peculiar tack for her to take. Aside from Priddy's claims to the contrary, Meghan, having grown up in Hollywood, would have been no stranger to the romance of the British Royal Family. Furthermore, as she was age fifteen or so when Diana died, a romantic like Meghan couldn't have failed to have been devastated by the tragedy.

While the media storm over their blossoming romance temporarily calmed in the wake of Harry's stern edict to the press, the Prince himself had other matters to deal with. The Queen had instructed Harry to undertake his first solo tour as a senior Royal, representing her at the independence anniversary celebrations in Barbados, Guyana, and Antigua. It was a chance for Harry to show how he had matured and grown in recent months. She needn't have worried—the trip was an unmitigated success, even when Harry was blindsided by what appeared to be a case of procurement, when the Antiguan prime minister introduced the Prince to a bevy of beautiful, bikini-clad models with a snigger, saying, "Whatever is done here stays here. So, don't worry." Harry was stunned, remarking to aides later he found the whole thing "pretty distasteful."

Whereas the Harry of old might well have made a grave error of judgment in Antigua when confronted with the opportunity to get friendly with the locals, now he had Meghan Skyping him nightly for progress reports and encouragement. The effect of her presence in his life showed—commentators on the tour noted how much more relaxed Harry seemed, how assured and calm, with one Royal journalist, Camilla Tominey, observing accurately, "With his American girlfriend Meghan Markle putting a spring in his step, it's fair to say Prince Harry has rarely been in better form."

Following a quick pit stop in Toronto to see Meghan, Harry returned to the United Kingdom with Meghan hot on his heels, joining him at his Nottingham Cottage hideaway in Kensington Palace.

That December, when Meghan was seen in public in the United Kingdom for the first time since the relationship became known, she was spotted sporting an "H & M" necklace (presumably not the budget clothing chain). Kate's posh friends had a field day, giggling behind their exquisitely manicured hands, at the tacky gesture, according to sources. Harry was showing her the sights of London—perhaps not the exclusive, tasteful locations that Meghan was more accustomed to, but taking her to the West End of London in the pre-Christmas mayhem to see the popular stage play *The Curious Incident of the Dog in the Night-Time*. A few days earlier, evidently having mugged up on this theater stuff that Meghan kept going on about, Harry had romantically taken her to see tourist favorite *The Lion King*.

Clad in matching beanie hats, the pair made their way through London's Shaftesbury Avenue, Harry excitedly pointing out the sights and lights on this, one of London's busiest thoroughfares, while Meghan kept her head down. Harry looked ecstatic.

"Harry has said his privacy is important to him," said the source. "They were clearly not afraid to be seen in public together. They are clearly crazy about each other and have told friends they are very much in love. Both Harry and Meghan obviously understand the intense interest in their relationship but are determined to enjoy time together without too much fuss."

Harry and Meghan also celebrated the season by buying a Christmas tree from the Pines and Needles tree farm in Battersea Park, where the owner, Sam Lyle, tickled at his Royal client, told *The Sun*: "You could have heard a pin drop—or a needle—when Prince Harry and Meghan walked into the store. They were completely charming together and blissfully unaware that our jaws had hit the floor. They chose a gorgeous Nordmann Fir and walked away after exchanging Christmas pleasantries."

A fellow customer, Gary Spence, said: "It was a bit weird seeing Prince Harry browsing the Christmas trees. I thought he'd go for the biggest one around, but he just wanted a little six-footer."

Though protocol prevented Meghan from accompanying Harry to the traditional Royal Family Christmas dinner, early in January they traveled to Tromsø in Norway, to see the Northern Lights. It was around this time that the makers of *Suits* came to a decision. Since Harry and Meghan went public, the media brouhaha over their star had gotten to the point it was making filming an impossible ordeal. Showrunner Aaron Korsh knew something had to give and so took the bold step of writing Rachel Zane out of the series. Her onscreen lover, Patrick J. Adams, understandably felt awkward about filming sex scenes with an actress who was dating one of the most famous men in the world. Meghan was gently let go from the series that had made her name.

As she slid further into the Royals orbit, she also had to give up another much-loved activity—her blog. Since inception, *The Tig* had grown into something of a big deal, with thousands of loyal followers lapping up Meghan's thoughts on everything from fashion to body fascism, gender issues, travel, and lifestyle. The winding down of *The Tig* as an independent platform for Meghan's personal expression mirrored the increased discretion she would need to draw over her views and opinions, now that there was a chance her relationship with Harry would become significant. As she closed the blog in March 2017, she bade a sad farewell to her readers, leaving them with that misty-eyed quote from Gandhi to "be the change you wish to see in the world." Her Instagram account was closed down too, prompting a wave of heartfelt farewells from her online gang.

The instruction to close the blog came from Harry. This ex-soldier—the man who had fought the Taliban in Afghanistan, who had braved the slings and arrows of global media attention and survived so much—now became a little mouse when he nervously approached Meghan and told her he had been advised that due to her outspoken views, she had to cease her constant social media activity. It was a warning sign as to the developing dynamic of the relationship, which was obvious to everyone apart from Harry. Meghan was incensed but diplomatically bit her lip and rapidly assessed the situation, deciding to pick her battles wisely. Within seconds, she regained her sunny composure, but Harry would have seen that flash of a temper she had long learned how to control—and would have learned to fear it.

Meghan knew that her relationship with Harry was still new and she was just learning how to fit in with his incredibly complex world. However, she made a mental note of the way Harry had handled the situation and filed it away for future reference.

In *The Tig*'s closing statement, she wrote: "What began as a passion project (my little engine that could) evolved into an amazing community of inspiration, support, fun and frivolity. You've made my days brighter and filled this experience with so much joy."

A source rather disingenuously suggested that the real reason for shutting the site down was her "busy schedule," balancing her charity work and television career, but it was easy to see what was really going on. What's more, Meghan was secretly fuming about having to delete the brand she had put so much effort into creating over the previous three years.

But Meghan was recalibrating herself. That much was evident to friends, who witnessed the transformation in Meghan's life as her romance with the Prince intensified.

Shortly after Meghan closed down *The Tig*, she accompanied Harry to the wedding of one of his closest and oldest friends, Tom "Skippy" Inskip. It was her first experience at a function of one of Harry's inner circle and would be an intensive crash course in how to navigate the world as a member of the global elite. The wedding was in Montego Bay in Jamaica, and the couple was staying in a lavish, seven-thousand-dollar-per-night villa. As soon as they arrived, the paparazzi were present, training their long lenses on the young lovers as they frolicked in the Caribbean waters. Harry was furious and dragged Meghan out of the line of sight, while she tried to calm him down. At the actual wedding event the next day, the pastor who married Tom and his bride, the Honorable Lara Hughes-Young, cheekily told Harry, "It's your turn next, Sir."

After a few precious days alone in an exclusive retreat in Negril, Harry and Meghan continued their transglobal affair, spending less and less time apart. Meghan would pop back to Toronto to visit her dogs and water the plants, before jumping back onto a London-bound flight to be with her paramour. He, in turn, was doing all he could to ensure Meghan was by his side as much as possible. In September 2017, he was due to host the Invictus Games in Toronto. When he flew to Toronto in March to attend planning meetings for the event, he stayed with Meghan and made it abundantly clear to everyone that come what may, he would have her at his side throughout. "Harry wants everything out in the open, for the days of skulking around to be over," commented a friend who was at the meetings. "He wants to show Meghan off as his future wife and the Games, which he has put his heart and soul into, will be the perfect platform to do that."

Meghan's elusive father, Thomas Senior, meanwhile, still hadn't met Harry. The press was combing his last known addresses, but the portly ex-lighting director seemed to have gone to ground. Meanwhile, Doria was speaking on most days to her daughter, keeping her grounded and connected to her roots as she navigated her first few months in the royal bubble.

In Britain, no royal relationship would be complete without a sporting kiss—taking place usually after the female half of the sketch had been seen adoringly supporting her man as he played polo, in a muddy English field. The typical polo match would see a flotilla of mud-spattered Land Rovers, Labradors gamboling about, horseboxes and stable girls, posh wives and families picnicking on smoked salmon sandwiches and champagne from large, shabby hampers while the men barreled around the pitch on horseback, swiping at one another. Harry and William were old pros at the game, and in May, the world got to see Meghan following tradition and really sealing the deal on the relationship with a smooch for Harry in the parking lot after a game at the Coworth Park Polo Club in Berkshire. Dressed down in dark glasses and a camel-colored jacket, Meghan boldly wrapped her arms around Prince Harry, who wore a white shirt, as the cameras clicked.

Later that month, despite the PDA at the polo, there were some red faces at the Palace and at the Middletons' GHQ in the country when it had to be explained that Meghan had not been invited to Kate's sister Pippa's wedding.

"People told her it's common in England for her to be a 'plus one'—Harry's 'date'—and for her to only attend the evening party," said a source. "However, Meghan was confused by this. Was she invited or was she not? How can you be half-invited to a wedding? Still, she got over the snub and chalked it up as just another of 'those British things' she didn't understand."

But Meghan also started to question—is it something to do with me? Am I being singled out? Do I really not fit in here?

Harry, of course, was not impressed. So much so, that he made a huge fuss about Meghan's presence being essential. He was so set on her going to the wedding, he pulled out all of the stops and made a hundred-mile round trip just to pick her up. A chivalrous move, but it meant Meghan still wasn't present to see the Duchess of Cambridge's sister marry James Matthews at St Mark's Church in the Berkshire village of Englefield.

Rumors had circulated about the possibility of Pippa holding a "no ring, no bring" rule, which would stop nonmarried couples from attending the wedding. But despite Meghan not being married or engaged to Harry, she finally attended Pippa Middleton's wedding reception regardless.

Perhaps Pippa was worried she could be upstaged by Harry's girlfriend, after noting the coverage from Skippy's wedding in March in Montego Bay. "She saw how all eyes were on Meghan rather than Lara," a source said.

Here, Meghan was, despite all her savoir-faire and worldliness, stumped by the intricacies of that anachronistic, lunatic structure, the British class system. To her face, everyone was charming, happy to meet her, making friendly chitchat, asking all the right questions, and congratulating Harry on his wonderful partner. Meghan was painfully unaware that every move she made was being analyzed and quietly judged. Having grown up in such rarefied circles, Harry would have been excruciatingly aware of this. To what extent he explained to Meghan that she was very much on trial by the upper classes is unknown. Most likely, she would have laughed off his concern that her social graces and etiquette were under the microscope, knowing she was her own woman and wouldn't change her behavior for anyone.

While the British public certainly enjoyed rebels crashing into the upper tiers of society—Diana is still seen as a saint by many, for the way she shook up the monarchy—the gentry still placed a great deal of weight on protocol and tradition. In these circles, nouveaux riches bores and rule breakers are simply not tolerated. Such individuals are brutally excommunicated in the most insidious manner, so subtly that in many cases, the offending party wouldn't even realize that they had been sent to social Siberia. They may still attend parties and events, there would be no superficial signs of discord or dislike—but there would be a definite undercurrent, perceptible only to those who were attuned to the faintest of glances and signals. That's not to say this ever actually happened to Meghan, of course, but it's known that a significant number of people in royal circles never embraced her at all. They saw Meghan as an interloper, without the pedigree and background deemed essential to match Harry's.

It is at this time Harry is said to have privately asked the Queen for permission to marry Meghan, a formality really, but crucial, given his position and Meghan's status as a foreign-born divorcée. The Queen saw how happy Meghan had made her grandson, how stabilized he now seemed—if somewhat deranged with love. And so she assented.

That August, Harry swept Meghan off to Botswana. Unlike their previous trip to the country, when no one knew about the pair's budding romance, this visit was keenly observed from afar as the beleaguered star-crossed couple sought refuge in the one place that brought peace and serenity to Harry. Back at the Okavango Delta, where they had stayed in 2016, with Kensington Palace and lodge managers declining to comment, the two could finally enjoy each other's company without the rest of the world looking over their shoulders every minute.

Harry and Meghan slept in a traditional thatched cabin with an outdoor shower and a carved wooden bed looking out over a lagoon where they would enjoy sunset cruises and fishing and where Harry caught a sharp-toothed catfish.

One local who saw the couple said: "They are like regular guys. They were just relaxed. You could see they were very happy together." The staff at the Lodge all knew "Mr. Harry" well—he had brought Chelsy to the same place in 2007. After a few days, Harry and Meghan were off, driving eight hours to Victoria Falls and the Tongabezi Lodge, on the banks of the Zambesi River. Despite the heartbreakingly beautiful scenery and solitude, this is not where Harry got down on one knee. It is, however, the place where he secretly sourced something incredibly valuable indeed—something that would soon be encircling a dainty finger.

Though the couple returned to London without a sparkler on Meghan's finger, bookmakers stopped taking bets on an engagement being imminent, and every royal watcher in the world knew it was now just a matter of time.

But this was also a turning point. Meghan was, said aides, starting to make Harry realize the power their relationship wielded. They had an announcement of value, so why not let people wait and speculate? Stir them up into a frenzy. Meghan had always been a canny operator, Harry less so. Meghan saw the enormous power their dual presence had and understood that if she manipulated this immense asset they had, the sky would be the limit! While Harry has always claimed to loathe the press, Meghan was basking in the attention—this beat anything that had happened on *Deal or No Deal*!

Meghan knew that this period, before she was ready to allow Harry to announce their engagement, would be the window of opportunity for her to tie up loose ends and capitalize on her unprecedented fame and power as a single woman on the cusp of marriage.

To that end, she arranged to fulfill one of her girlhood dreams, and in September, she graced the cover of *Vanity Fair* magazine. It is doubtful whether *Suits* actress Meghan Markle would have achieved this rare honor, but royal princess-in-waiting Meghan was going to grab the chance, all the same. It was extraordinary, and a sign of things to come. Usually, prospective royal brides were silent ahead of their marriages, demure, dutiful, and discreet. Even rebels like Di or Sarah Ferguson wouldn't have imagined preempting the accepted protocol of things by spilling all in a revealing interview before their engagement had even been announced. But here was Meghan, doing just that.

In her gushing interview with *Vanity Fair*'s Sam Kashner, Meghan alternately told it like it was, or simpered cutely. "We're a couple," she informed Sam, while cooking him supper in her Toronto home. Then she managed to flag up the imminent engagement to one of the world's best-selling magazines, while sweetly affecting a deep need for privacy. "We're in love. I'm sure there will be a time when we have to come forward and present ourselves, and have stories to tell, but I hope what people will understand is that this is our time. This is for us. It's part of what makes it so special, that it's just ours. But we're happy. Personally, I love a great love story."

As they ate, Meghan underlined the burden of her song, in case Sam had missed it. "We're two people who are really happy and in love. We were very quietly dating for six months before it became news, and I was working during that whole time, and the only thing that changed was people's perception. Nothing about me changed. I'm still the same person that I am, and I've never defined myself by my relationship."

That last line rang alarm bells over at Buckingham Palace, where courtiers and Palace officials gulped discreetly as they scanned the article. More drama was clearly incoming. Further panic was occasioned by the cover, which saw Meghan showing off her shapely shoulders, unencumbered by the inconvenience of clothing. There was a collective intake of breath over the photographs and the magazine headline "She's Just Wild About Harry!" The photographs were among the last taken by the late Peter Lindbergh, who, shortly after shooting her, personally told me what a natural Meghan had been in front of the camera and how little encouragement she had needed to come alive for his lens.

A Royal expert who saw the photos opined thus: "It's Meghan, the nearly-royal rebel. It is a beautiful and very natural portrait of her. However, her shoulders are bare—it looks as though she could be topless. This is not a way anyone associated with the royal household should present themselves."

Needless to say, copies of the magazine were banned from the Palace, and great lengths were gone to ensure the Queen never saw it. A Palace insider admitted that "Harry received a very stern call from his father about this. It was unbecoming, he felt this was the wrong thing for Meghan to do. Charles started to suspect that Harry couldn't control his fiancée. It started to dawn on him that she was someone who would put up a fight when it came to royal protocols. He also started to realize that despite what Harry was telling him, he was secretly enjoying this. Harry was reveling in the upset he was causing and—as he always had—been the rebellious one, who can't be controlled."

"Just like his mother," Charles would surely have muttered to himself.

Some sources claimed Meghan wanted to announce their engagement in the interview, but Harry talked her out of it. But the damage had been done, and the Royal hackles had been raised about this mouthy broad. As one source wearily said, "I think it is a mistake. You can hardly bleat about privacy if you choose to do such things. Ultimately, to make a call on whether this was a good or bad idea, one has to question who this interview actually benefits, and what it achieves."

Christopher Andersen, whose book *The Day Diana Died* had topped e-book charts, told the *Daily Beast*: "For Harry a large part of Meghan's appeal is that she breaks—make that shatters—all precedent when it comes to royal brides. She is a television actress, she is American, she is biracial, she is divorced. The fact that Meghan is the last person Britain's establishment would choose for him to wed makes her that much more irresistible to the renegade prince. Like Kate Middleton, Meghan has played her cards right. She seems utterly unflappable despite all the hounding by the press, and like Kate has demonstrated a remarkable amount of patience. The consensus now in royal circles is that a royal wedding is inevitable, and it will probably take place next spring. There's no turning back, really at this stage."

At the launch of the Invictus Games in Toronto at the end of September, Meghan was on home turf but, even here, found herself on the receiving end of a huge snub on the opening night. She sat several rows behind Harry, who was cajoled into a VIP box with Justin Trudeau, US First Lady Melania Trump, and various other presidents and dignitaries. This was Harry's event, and he couldn't even get his own girlfriend into the VIP box? Meghan put on a brave face but was truly put out.

However, she took a little comfort in the fact that she knew that had she sat with Harry, it would have made her the center of attention and taken away from the real reason of the day, which was to celebrate the fantastic servicemen. Also, several news outlets noted that per royal protocol, the Prince was not allowed to sit with her until they were engaged. For once, Meghan took a cue from Kate's playbook by sitting aside to offer support while also letting her boyfriend be the focus of the day.

Two days into the games, a Royal press officer surprised photographers by suddenly alerting them to keep cool during a game of wheelchair tennis and not leave their places. Sure enough, a ripple of amazement made its way around the stadium as Harry and Meghan strolled in, hand in hand, dressed casually, laughing and joking with each other and taking their places courtside. Meghan was wearing a "husband shirt," as she had described it on *The Tig*, designed by her friend Misha Nonoo (it had sold out within minutes of being featured on the blog). Former President Obama, Joe Biden, and his wife Jill also all showed up to hang with Harry at the finale to the wildly successful event, where the Prince took the mic to thank the participants, the crowds, and Toronto for making it such a memorable games. "You have delivered the biggest Invictus Games yet, with the most incredible atmosphere, making our competitors feel like the stars they are." It was a milestone for the competing athletes and the Invictus project, but for that moment, all eyes were on Harry, standing in the VIP enclosure next to a beaming Doria Ragland and her daughter. Harry leaned over and kissed Meghan, to astonished and delighted applause.

Game on.

***

On the morning of November 27, 2017, Kensington Palace issued an official statement:

> *His Royal Highness The Prince of Wales is delighted to announce the engagement of Prince Harry to Ms. Meghan Markle. The wedding will take place in spring 2018. Further details about the wedding day will be announced in due course. His Royal Highness and Ms. Markle became engaged in London earlier this month. Prince Harry has informed Her Majesty The Queen and other close members of his family. Prince Harry has also sought and received the blessing of Ms. Markle's parents.*

Not to be outdone, a joint statement was released by Meghan's parents, Thomas Markle Sr. and Doria.

"We wish them a lifetime of happiness and are very excited for their future together." Meghan had reached out to her father, by now living in Rosarito, Mexico. Thomas Sr. now lived a reclusive life, changing his number and residence frequently. Meghan spoke to him, alerted him of the coming engagement, and warned him he would now be chased by the world's media. Harry had also called him, to politely ask him for his daughter's hand in marriage.

The Queen and Prince Philip weighed in with an assurance that they were "delighted for the couple and wish them every happiness."

That afternoon, the world's media massed at Kensington Palace to meet the couple and have them pose for their official engagement photos.

The royal couple held their photo call in the Sunken Gardens, one of Diana's favorite places. Harry, looking stiff and nervous, was gently steered into place by a perky-looking Meghan, who held his hand reassuringly throughout. When asked by the press how they felt, Harry simply replied: "Thrilled."

"Very glad it's not raining!" Meghan piped up, showing she was already a pro at the British habit of making small talk about the weather. "I'm so very happy."

When asked when he knew she was the one, Harry said with a shy smile, "The very first time we met."

Then the couple walked out into the garden, holding hands. Meghan, wearing a white coat by Line The Label, reassuringly stroked her nervous fiancé's arm as reporters asked them for details on the proposal. Was it a romantic proposal, Harry was asked? "Of course it was!" he responded tersely, while Meghan softened the reply with a beaming "Very."

Of course, everyone wanted to see the ring, which Harry had designed himself. The center stone was a diamond from Botswana, while two outside diamonds had, touchingly, been sourced from Diana's collection.

That evening, the BBC broadcast the official engagement interview with the couple, by renowned broadcast journalist Mishal Husein, who had been specially selected by Harry and Meghan in light of her campaigning work to ensure gender equality at the BBC. It was a warm and fuzzy chat—light years from Charles and Diana's awkward, stilted conversation on their engagement day, much more relaxed even than William and Kate's rather wooden engagement interview. Harry told Mishal he had proposed to Meghan one evening at home in Nottingham Cottage, while roasting a chicken for Meghan. This became a big story in itself. Why on Earth did Harry take the knee while cooking up a roast chicken supper at home? Had he bent down to inspect the bird in the oven when Meghan walked in unexpectedly? Did he get a cramp and had to come up with a quick excuse? We will never know.

"It was just an amazing surprise," Meghan cooed to Mishal. "It was so sweet and natural and very romantic; he got on one knee."

(Pundits quickly assumed that the chicken recipe Meghan had dug up in an interview the year before, by Ina Garten, was the one they had been using on the night in question. It was a simple dish, but an old favorite of Meghan's and, if prepared according to Garten's instructions, loaded with lemon, garlic, thyme, butter, and onions. The surefire winner is now known worldwide as "Engagement Chicken." So excited was Garten to hear of her recipe inspiring a royal marriage, she took to Twitter to congratulate the pair, wryly pointing out the romantic properties of her chicken recipe.)

Harry spoke movingly of his mother, how she would have been "thick as thieves" with Meghan and how having two of her diamonds on the wedding ring ensured that she would be there to "join us on this crazy journey." "The stars were all aligned," Harry famously observed, of his whirlwind romance. "It was this beautiful woman who just sort of literally tripped and fell into my life, I fell into her life." They also revealed Meghan would give up acting to focus on causes close to her heart, working alongside her husband-to-be.

"I know that she will be unbelievably good at the job part of it," said Harry.

The stage was set for the wedding in May 2018, confirmed for St George's Chapel in Windsor. Meghan had made her way into the Firm.

Had Meghan Markle dreamed that from the moment of her engagement, she would be living a nonstop life of glamour and decadence, her first engagement as a Royal fiancée put to rest any such romantic notions. On the morning of December 1, 2017, she undertook her first official royal engagement in the prosaic surroundings of Nottingham, in the Midlands. A historic city, most famous for claiming to be home of Robin Hood, it produced thousands of eager people lining the streets to catch a glimpse of the glamorous new Royal-to-be as she accompanied Harry to an AIDS charity care center. There were echoes of Diana everywhere that day, from the absolute pandemonium on the streets to the patients in the center who were impressed with Meghan's natural ease with them. They remembered Diana's groundbreaking embrace of an AIDS sufferer in the early 1980s, when the illness was widely feared and misunderstood, and the huge impact the sight of her hugging and comforting the patient had on the public. While Meghan didn't do any hugging, one prominent UK columnist, Jan Moir, positively reviewed the day, declaring: "Meghan Markle was not born to be a princess, but she moves with ease in her brave new world."

***

Ahead of Christmas 2018, Harry came up with a cunning plan to soothe any ruffled feathers Meghan had caused at the highest level of the family, by editing together a YouTube compilation of clips of Meghan in *Suits*, to play to the Queen and Prince Philip. His editing skills must have been extremely judicious, as the Queen broke protocol to green-light Meghan's appearance at the family Christmas.

"WHAT MEGHAN WANTS, MEGHAN GETS"

Christmas with the family was Meghan's first major challenge after the engagement. Prince Philip and the Queen kept their misgivings to themselves and tried to forget Harry forcing them to watch *Suits* and invited Meghan to the first event of the Royals' festive calendar. At the annual staff party at Windsor, the family celebrated hundreds of royal staff, from courtiers to footmen, butlers to gardeners. This year, there was one member-to-be of the family everyone was dying to meet. Meghan circulated regally around the room, drawing hard-won approval from the cynical staffers. "She asked everyone their name and what they did—she was a natural," commented one member of Palace staff.

Harry mentioned later that there was "plenty" that he had to explain to acclimatize Meghan to the myriad traditions and rituals of the Royals' Christmas, but overall, she had done a "fantastic" job. This in contrast to Diana, whose sighing unhappiness and sulky boredom at family gatherings rarely went unnoticed.

The couple spent the holiday at William and Catherine's home, Anmer Hall, two miles from Sandringham, where they played with the couple's children, George, four, and Charlotte, two.

"We had an amazing time," Harry said. "We had great fun staying with my brother and sister-in-law and running around with the kids. Christmas was fantastic."

But there was a hint of unease as well in his comments. "I think we've got one of the biggest families that I know of, and every family is complex as well," he said pointedly.

Harry may well have been referring to rumblings of disquiet behind the scenes at Anmer Hall. The unusual step of welcoming Meghan into the family fold for the holidays at Sandringham was unprecedented—even faultlessly behaved Kate hadn't been afforded that privilege prior to being married to William, despite their years of courtship and her gradual immersion into the royal bubble. Harry felt that despite the Queen's generous invitation to Meghan, there was a distinct coolness on the part of William and, by extension, Kate. That was beginning to bother him.

Biographer Katie Nicholl wrote: "According to one of the princes' mutual friends, there was a fallout [at] Christmas when Harry told William he didn't think his older brother was doing enough to welcome Meghan into the family. Harry felt William wasn't rolling out the red carpet for Meghan and told him so. It was only resolved when Charles stepped in and asked William to make an effort. That's when the Cambridges invited the Sussexes to spend Christmas with them."

Nicholl wrote that tensions between the brothers had been growing in the run-up to Christmas. "Kate and Meghan are very different people," she said, quoting a source. "While they don't have a lot in common, they have made an effort to get along. But any issues are between the brothers."

Royal commentator Angela Mollard also observed the delicate tensions at the heart of William and Harry's relationship at this time: "William is a very dutiful man. He himself, in his relationship with Kate, when that had been going on for many years, he had to question himself, whether or not this relationship was going to last the distance. Now, we're always very protective of relationships, particularly in that phase that we call the limerence phase in the first three years when we're deeply infatuated. It takes three years for it to soften out to a normal relationship. They haven't got to that point, and in a sense, they didn't have the time to get to that point."

But William's advice only served to get Harry's back up. Meghan's rebel persona meant that he was always alert for any implied or explicit disrespecting or snubbing of his beloved. And as the Christmas period, with all the significance it entailed for the newly engaged couple, progressed, William's sense of unease and worry at Harry's increasing hostility continued to fester.

Meanwhile, Christmas was looming. The three-day celebrations at Norfolk's Sandringham House kicked off with the Royal Family assembling on December 20 for a family lunch. Meghan had to quickly figure out who should be bowed and curtsied to in the prelunch frenzy of greetings. For what seemed like hours, everyone genuflected or bowed as tradition and rank dictated. Meghan had to curtsy to the Queen, Kate, and the Countess of Wessex. That ordeal done, she was seated between Charles and Peter Phillips, with whom she "pulled crackers" and, per tradition, shared the corny jokes hidden inside of the holiday confections' packaging. "She was obviously a bit nervous at first, but soon relaxed, with Harry's help as he introduced her to everyone and then she really enjoyed it," a source said.

For Harry, Meghan, Kate, and William, Christmas day itself started with a light breakfast at Anmer Hall before everyone headed off to St Mary Magdalene church for the morning service. A crowd had gathered to wave to the Royals, in freezing cold, wind, and rain. Of course, Meghan was the focus of attention, and she managed to wave, smile, and stiffly curtsy when the Queen arrived by car. Back at the main house, the Christmas feast was served and eaten in ninety minutes flat, as tradition dictates: everyone has to stop eating the moment the Queen is finished, then, rather surreally, they troop into the living room to watch the Queen's speech at 3 p.m., like any other family up and down the land.

During the days that follow, the men of the family usually stride forth to the Norfolk fields, where specially bred pheasants wait to be massacred during the traditional Boxing Day shoot. William and Harry loved shooting, but this year, one of the brothers was conspicuously absent. The press cheekily wondered if a foreign influence was exerting some subtle pressure here. As it turned out, Harry was in London, where he was guest-editing the BBC's morning radio news program *Today*. The broadcast had been arranged before the engagement was announced, and naturally his impending marriage had ramped up anticipation among listeners and BBC producers. The show was a success: Prince Charles, boxer Anthony Joshua, and former president Barack Obama were interviewed in between items on climate change, youth violence, the military, conservation, and a topic that Harry would become increasingly vocal about, mental health issues, especially for young men.

Despite the success of the show, Harry inadvertently offended the Markle family when, in the interview with Obama, he described the festivities he'd just enjoyed at Sandringham with Meghan and the Royals. "She's getting in there," he said of Meghan's success with the family. "I suppose it's the family she's never had."

The Markles, usually divided, came together in their indignation at Harry's comments. First up was Samantha Markle, who angrily pointed out that Meghan "has a large family who were always there with her and for her." Not to be outdone, once he'd emerged from his latest hangover and keen to sell another story to the press, Thomas Jr. weighed in too, with admirable sorrow: "My father made sure that she had what she needed to be successful and get to where she is today."

The family's internecine squabbling continued to unfold, a dysfunctional and unedifying backdrop to the carefully packaged, slick romance presented in London. Samantha had been threatening for ages to write her book, *The Diary of Princess Pushy's Sister*, but now she appeared on television, crying and begging Meghan to invite her to the wedding (Meghan relented and did so). And Thomas Sr. himself was finally tracked down by an intrepid British journalist, to his Mexican perch, where he admitted he was "delighted" by Meghan and Harry's wedding. Rather more talkative was his son, who proudly demanded his dad attend the wedding and give the traditional father-of-the-bride speech, saying: "He has to know he is just not representing his family, he is representing America."

More arguments ensued, with Thomas innocently passing Meghan's phone number to Samantha, Meghan complaining to Doria, Doria reprimanding Thomas, Thomas getting annoyed with Doria as well as at Meghan's refusal to make friends with Samantha. To complete Meghan's migraine, Thomas Jr. got arrested for being drunk and disorderly again. To top it all off, Ninaki Priddy sold her life story to the papers. No wonder Harry and Meghan's smiles were looking increasingly glazed as the wedding rumbled down the line toward them.

British media, deep in the grip of Meghanmania, speculated endlessly on how the wedding would play out. Rumors abounded that Meghan was planning a "very feminist wedding by turning various traditions on their head." These reports struck icy horror into the hearts of crusty old courtiers at the Palace. "I've heard that Meghan wants her mother to walk her down the aisle, which would be a sweet moment," said a friend of the couple's, before adding menacingly: "While Meghan and Harry will always be mindful of traditions and the views of their elders, the day is ultimately *about them and what they want to do.*"

Samantha helpfully chimed in again too, claiming Meghan's father, Thomas Markle, had to walk her down the aisle. And then another character from the never-ending drama of the Markle family appeared: Samantha's ex-husband warned Prince Harry and Meghan to avoid inviting her, saying that the "fame hungry" ex-model was never as close to Meghan as she claimed she was. "Harry and Meghan need to know the truth about her," he pontificated helpfully. "She's the last person who should be at Windsor Castle." The papers were ecstatic.

Meanwhile, closer to home, conflicts were emerging over preparations for the wedding. Per tradition, Meghan could choose her jewelry from the Queen's collection. She initially wanted an emerald tiara. But no one knew exactly where it came from, the likeliest source being Russia. It was vetoed, and Meghan was invited to pick out another piece.

But Meghan was insisting on the emerald tiara. This was said to have "upset" the Queen, which is Royal-speak for "the Queen hit the roof." Despite being summoned by the Queen and told to chill his lady out, Harry allegedly told courtiers and staff before the wedding, "What Meghan wants, Meghan gets." It was to become a familiar refrain over the next few months.

TEARS AND TIARAS

In the lead-up to Harry's wedding to Meghan, the Royals very much recalled the chaos and trauma of Edward's abdication and therefore made every effort to welcome the woman who, it seemed, had finally brought Harry some happiness and stability. Since his military career had come to an anticlimactic end, Harry had found himself without much purpose or ambition. Since childhood, he had been made to feel constantly inferior to his brother, who was groomed to be the King from babyhood. He knew he was the "spare." The only one who seemed to love him unconditionally, unjudgmentally, for his mischief and spirit, who would always defend him from the grind and misery of constant public view and comment, was dead. In Meghan, he had found someone, at last, who would look after him, bolster his ego, curb his excessive tendencies, and allow him to find himself and a sense of purpose. And of course, this would come at a price.

The preparations for the wedding clearly showed the Royals who were in charge—and it wasn't them. On one notorious occasion, Kate was said to have been left "in tears" during a bridesmaids dress rehearsal session with Princess Charlotte. In a moment of tension, the issue of their respective children's titles had come up, and it allegedly unleashed a torrent of pent-up emotions.

Alexis Slifer, a presenter on the Canadian show *Talko*, claimed to have seen a video said to be secretly recorded by a courtier in which Meghan raged about the fact that any children she and Harry would have would be "only" bestowed a Lordship: "Meghan was going off about Prince William and Duchess Kate's children. They're being given His and Her Royal Highness titles while Meghan and Harry's children are only going to be Lords. People think that she's having a meltdown because the only reason she married Harry in the first place was to get those titles."

"We are talking about Meghan Markle being exposed for who she truly is," continued Slifer. "Ever since she has been involved with the Royal Family there has been drama at every corner. People act like they don't even like Meghan— which is possibly why they created this video in the first place, because they don't even like her."

As tensions rose, the royal staff was thwarted and baffled by Meghan's insistence on controlling every aspect of the big day. She ruled that the day had to reflect the sparkly "fun, laughter, and love" of their "fairy tale," which meant Meghan was making constant demands, rejecting various solutions and plans, and ignoring traditions and customs. Harry was growing increasingly "petulant and short-tempered" in the buildup to the wedding, as writer Robert Jobson described. "Meghan had her heart set on a tiara with emeralds and Prince Harry went spare when they were told she couldn't wear it," said a source. "It prompted the Queen to speak to Harry. She said, Meghan cannot have whatever she wants. She gets what tiara she's given by me."

To staff and family, some of whom had known and cared for Harry since infancy, his words now rang like a mantra of encroaching horror, like a drumbeat of ever-increasing dread and fear: "What Meghan wants, Meghan gets. What Meghan wants, Meghan gets." When the Queen learned that he was still acting up over Meghan's demands, despite her earlier warning, that was that. He was summoned again to her presence and, in no uncertain terms, "put firmly in his place." The Queen also issued a stern admonition to Meghan to behave and stop complaining about the "musty" smell of St George's Chapel, the wedding venue. Meghan had been making a fuss about the ancient chapel's pleasant smell of wood and dust and had been trying to order in stacks of her favorite Jo Malone candles to scent it. The Queen wasn't having any of it. "The Queen also questioned why Meghan needed a veil for the wedding, given it was to be her second marriage," said an insider. "The message from the Queen was very much Meghan needed to think about how she speaks to staff members and be careful to follow family protocols."

With the reports of the upset Queen already making the rounds of royal circles, the rest of the staff at Kensington Palace was now walking on eggshells, wary of exciting Harry's wrath. This meant they were unprotestingly contending with

Meghan as she bounced out of bed each morning for her 5 a.m. spirulina smoothie (a type of cyanobacteria, often referred to as blue-green algae), her soothing morning yoga, and, as one insider described it, her email "bombardments" of staff. What is typical in Hollywood was clearly not the norm in the "household," where there is an established hierarchy, a fixed, tried-and-true "way of doing things," according to a source.

Meanwhile, not to be outdone, across the Atlantic the rest of the Markles were reliably doing their best to create as much mayhem as possible. As Samantha made endless television appearances, raking in plenty of appearance fees while she speculated sourly on her half-sister's imminent entrée to the Royals, the rest of the family turned on her. "She has dogged on Meghan forever," Samantha's mother, Roslyn, told the *Daily Mail*. "She has never liked Meghan, and she's always been jealous of her."

Samantha was also busy tweeting her disgust that she and other family members had not been invited to the wedding, as Meghan's parents had been the only two members of the family to have received invitations.

"Out of respect, tradition and humanitarianism, the #Markles should be invited if 2000 complete strangers are invited," Samantha wrote on Twitter. Meanwhile, *In Touch* magazine carried an interview in which she criticized her half-sister for not helping their father financially. "If you can spend $75,000 on a dress, you can spend $75,000 on your dad," Samantha hinted gently. A few days later, TMZ claimed wheelchair-bound Samantha had suffered a broken ankle and fractured knee, in what her boyfriend described as a "paparazzi confrontation" on a road in Florida. Her flourishing media career was sadly put on pause. But this was not to be the last the world would hear from the lively Samantha.

THE WEDDING WALK THAT WASN'T

Perhaps it was a newfound sense of fraternal concern and family unity that caused Thomas Markle Jr. to return to the royal fray. Whatever the case, he felt the need to express sadness and surprise that somehow he hadn't been invited to the wedding of the half-sister with whom he had barely been in touch with for years. After some thinking, Markle Jr. decided to eschew the usual means of reaching out to new family members ahead of a wedding and instead penned a discreet open letter to Harry, via global media.

"It's not too late," he wrote. "As more time passed [*sic*] to your Royal Wedding, it became very clear that this is the biggest mistake in Royal Wedding History. Meghan's attempt to act the part of a princess like a below C average Hollywood actress is getting old. My father will never recover financially from paying Meghan's way, nor emotionally from disavowing him. Meg is showing her true colors."

A week later, baffled at Harry's lack of reply to his earlier letter, Thomas Markle Jr. penned a second billet-doux, this time a conciliatory one to his half-sister. Again, just in case the mail to Kensington Palace was slow, he published it on an international media platform. "Meg, I know that I'm not perfect, nor is anyone else in our family, as I'm sure you have read by now," he wrote in the letter, published by *In Touch*. "But good, bad or perfect, we're the only family that you have. It does hurt my feelings not getting invited to your wedding, along with the rest of the family. But it's not too late to send me an invite along with your entire family."

Unbelievably, even this heartfelt appeal failed to penetrate Kensington Palace. Meanwhile, the charm offensive continued, when in another public appeal for their half-sister's attention, Samantha said she had a present she would love to give Meghan. "I searched the world for something that I thought was really senti-mental, and I'd like to give it to her in person. But if not, I will certainly send it," she told gossip website TMZ. Pressed to divulge what present she had bought, Samantha replied coyly, "Well, then it wouldn't be a surprise—right?" Any hope that Meghan might tune into TMZ to witness this heartwarming message and respond with squeals of "Oh, you shouldn't have!" was dashed with more silence from London.

While all this drama was unfolding, Meghan and Harry were apparently close to a breaking point, which explains why he went to such great lengths to ensure his bride-to-be could have everything she wanted on her big day. But below stairs at Buckingham and Kensington Palaces, staff were merciless in their private mocking of Meghan.

A source said: "Some of the staff don't seem to want to give Meghan a chance. Harry is besotted and understandably extremely protective of her."

Commenting on the drama in the countdown to the wedding, a very well-placed source said: "Understanding the Palace way, the deference, the politics and the fact that there's a pecking order, is taking a while for Meghan to get her head around. She is quite opinionated, and Harry has got very dictatorial of late, which hasn't made things easy at times."

The final blow to Meghan came when her father, torn apart by his family and his own conflicted feelings for his daughter, participated in a bizarre stunt, orchestrated by none other than Samantha. In the days leading up to the wed-ding, a surreal drama of Shakespearean dimensions was played out that threat-ened to sink the good ship Markle once and for all in the world's eyes.

The drama began on May 4, when Kensington Palace issued a statement announcing that Thomas would be at the wedding to walk his daughter down the aisle. "Mr. Markle will walk his daughter down the aisle of St. George's Chapel," it read. "Ms. Markle is delighted to have her parents by her side on this important and happy occasion." The statement also revealed that Thomas and Doria would arrive in the country on the week of the wedding, allowing time for the Royal Family to meet them.

But a few days later, disaster struck. On May 12, London's *Mail on Sunday* revealed that photographs of Thomas apparently preparing for the wedding were in fact staged. The pictures, which showed Thomas engaged in activities such as being measured for his suit or googling Harry, had been carefully choreographed. At Samantha's urging, Thomas foolishly worked with a paparazzi agency to set up the pics, something the confused and beleaguered man subsequently told TMZ that he did in an attempt to "recast" his image, after photographers "ambushed" him several times and took "unflattering" shots of him.

Two days later, on May 14, Thomas told TMZ that he had decided not to attend the wedding after all. Now his own official mouthpiece, he explained that he'd suffered a heart attack the previous week, and was not fit to travel internationally

The news was greeted with shock and sadness in London. That night, Kensington Palace released a statement about the situation. "This is a deeply personal moment for Ms. Markle in the days before her wedding," a palace spokesman said. "She and Prince Harry ask again for understanding and respect to be extended to Mr. Markle in this difficult situation."

But the drama was far from over. The very next day, Thomas said Meghan had contacted him about the paparazzi photos and apparently convinced him to come to the wedding and walk her down the aisle. Although he had just suffered a heart attack, he said that he would come once he got the OK from his doctors.

Now the Palace reformed its plan and prepared to welcome the father of the bride. All seemed well. But then, only a few hours later, Thomas announced that his medics had scheduled his surgery for May 16, meaning he would now be absolutely unable to attend the wedding.

The next day, Meghan released a statement via Kensington Palace, whose Twitter feed was fast resembling that of a daytime telenovela instead of a royal communications channel. "Sadly, my father will not be attending our wedding," Meghan said. "I have always cared for my father and hope he can be given the space he needs to focus on his health. I would like to thank everyone who has offered generous messages of support. Please know how much Harry and I look forward to sharing our special day with you on Saturday."

Months later, Thomas admitted that he was still making money from paid interviews. "I'm going to defend myself and I'm going to be paid for it. I don't care," he told a documentary crew. "At this point, they owe me. The royals owe me. Harry owes me. Meghan owes me. What I've been through I should be rewarded for." Suffice it to say with less than three days to go until the wedding, there was no father of the bride in sight. At Harry's request, Prince Charles very splendidly stepped in to walk Meghan down the aisle. "I asked him to, and I think he knew it was coming, and he immediately said, 'Yes, of course, I'll do whatever Meghan needs and I'm here to support you,'" Harry said in a documentary. "For him, that's a fantastic opportunity to step up and be that support, and you know he's our father, so of course he's going to be there for us."

A nation breathed a sigh of relief and Charles began pacing around nervously. Now, with all that settled, Kensington Palace tweeted a stern statement of intent: "This wedding, like all weddings, will be a moment of fun and joy that will reflect the characters and values of the bride and groom."

THE POWER OF LOVE

When the day finally arrived, the ceremony didn't take place in historic, venerable Westminster Abbey, where Will and Kate sealed the deal back in 2011. Instead, Harry and Meghan opted for St George's Chapel on the grounds of Windsor Castle, an intimate venue with a capacity of eight hundred people, compared with Westminster's two thousand. Its apparent mustiness had been dispelled, to Meghan's satisfaction, with candles from Diptyque. And so it was to host a truly epochal wedding, unlike anything the Royals had seen before.

After all the fuss, dramas, family fights, tears, and tantrums, it all worked out in the end. Everyone got their first glimpse at the bride when she traveled to the chapel with Doria, the pair having spent the night before at the exclusive Cliveden House. On arrival, Meghan greeted her wedding party. Young pageboys Brian and John Mulroney—the twin sons of her best friend, Jessica Mulroney—held the sixteen-foot-long train as she made her entrance, applauded by a sparkling array of guests including the Queen, Prince Philip, the Prince of Wales, and the Duchess of Cornwall.

As Meghan walked up the aisle on his father's arm, Prince Harry's nervous, tense expression gave way to a huge grin. Meghan wore a simple, elegant Clare Waight Keller for Givenchy dress, crisp and white with a bateau neckline and a dramatic veil. Her hair was in a low bun, her makeup was minimal, and a smile stretched from ear to ear. As Prince Charles steered Meghan over to Harry, the latter leaned over and whispered in his father's ear. "Thank you, Pa," Harry said, before turning to Ms. Markle and saying, "You look amazing. I'm so lucky." Meghan was clutching a bouquet that featured flowers picked by Harry, just before the wedding. Blooms in the bouquet included sweet peas, lily of the valley, astilbe, jasmine, astrantia, and forget-me-nots, which were Princess Diana's favorite. Like all royal wedding bouquets, it included a sprig of myrtle, which dates back to the wedding of Queen Victoria.

The vows had been written by the bride. As with Kate, the traditional promise to "obey" had been dropped. "I, Meghan, take you, Harry, to be my husband, to have and to hold from this day forward; for better, for worse, for richer, for poorer, in sickness and in health, to love and to cherish, till death us do part; according to God's holy law. In the presence of God I make this vow." Harry's vows echoed those of his new wife.

Then, in case anyone thought this was going to be just another royal wedding, came the highlight of the day: a show-stopping sermon from Bishop Michael Curry. The first black bishop in the Episcopal church all but set the ancient chapel roof on fire with a sermon, "The Power of Love," that had the audience eating out of his hands. Indeed, at one point, he cheerily instructed everyone to raise their hands, at which point there were serious fears Prince Philip would spontaneously combust in fury. Everyone survived, despite visible eye rolls from some of the staider guests.

With windmilling arms, the Bishop stepped up and testified in a captivating, jubilant voice:

> There's power in love. Love can help and heal when nothing else can. Love can lift up and liberate for living when nothing else will. And the love that brings two people together is the same love that can bind them together. Whether on mountaintops of happiness and through valleys of hardship.
>
> This love, this is the way of Jesus. And it's a game changer. Imagine our homes and families when this way of love is the way. Imagine our neighborhoods and communities when love is the way. Imagine our governments and countries when love is the way. Imagine business and commerce when this love is the way. Imagine our world when love is the way.

The chapel erupted in slightly baffled applause, many just thankful the speech was over. Harry was spotted, gobsmacked, uttering the single word *Wow*. If the royal rebel had been planning to disrupt the centuries of tradition that accompanied royal weddings, he could not have found a greater disrupter than Michael Curry. The bishop had been allocated five minutes and cheerfully spoke for fourteen. As he got into his stride around the five-minute mark, the Queen retained her Buddha-like otherworldly calm. But as he excitedly approached the ten-minute mark, she coughed warningly. At one point, she was noticed pointedly checking her watch.

This was followed by a gospel choir singing "Stand by Me," another first for a royal wedding.

Truly, this was the wedding of a modern, diverse couple leading the way into a very different future for the Royal Family. Meghan and Harry, now the Duke and Duchess of Cambridge, were delighted. With around 1,900 guests invited to the Westminster Abbey service and a global television audience estimated at two billion people, Prince William and Kate Middleton's wedding had been a major production. Yet Harry and Meghan showed that weddings of second siblings in the Royal Family aren't always understated.

Following their wedding ceremony, Prince Harry and Meghan went on a horse-drawn carriage procession around Windsor. They waved, smiled, and kissed each other as they traveled through the town and back up the Long Walk in the spring sunshine. The crowds lining the route cheered the radiant couple in delight.

At the Queen's lavish lunch party for the newlyweds, the cake was revealed. In yet another break from tradition, the cake was supplied by American baker Claire Ptak, owner of the Violet Bakery, an old favorite of *The Tig*. Unlike the comfortable predictability of Kate's 2011 fruitcake confection, this was a lemon elderflower cake with buttercream frosting, decorated with fresh flowers. The plan for the cake, Ptak described to *Town & Country* magazine, was always going to be unorthodox. "We discussed that they wanted something very unique and outside the box; they didn't feel that there should be any kind of constrictions to do something within tradition," she said.

That evening, a boisterous reception was held at Frogmore House. The couple arrived in style, in a silver-blue Jaguar E-Type Concept Zero, which had a plate numbered 190518 in recognition of their wedding date. Meghan, now Duchess of

Cambridge, had changed into a second wedding dress, a high-neck, sleeveless Stella McCartney gown. She paired it with Aquazzurra shoes and Diana's emerald-cut aquamarine ring, while the new Duke of Cambridge sported an American-style tuxedo.

The six hundred invited guests included Sir Elton John and his husband, David Furnish; George and Amal Clooney; and an eye-catching transatlantic contingent including several members of the cast of *Suits*. They feasted on pea risotto and pork belly, as well as slabs of wedding cake and copious quantities of champagne. Harry took to the floor to make an emotional speech in which he moved his wedding guests to tears when he praised his new wife, saying they made a "great team" and that "I can't wait to spend the rest of my life with you." Predictably, Meghan again upended tradition here, by standing up to make a speech (not usual for brides) in which she thanked the Royal Family for welcoming her and especially, to Charles for being so caring of Doria. "That's something a lot of people don't know," Camilla murmured in earshot of guests: "Just how kind he is."

Loads of toasts followed, with guests enjoying a special cocktail featuring ginger (in honor of Harry's red hair) and rum (not that Meghan was Jamaican) named "When Harry Met Meghan." Late-night talk show host James Corden served as emcee, introducing various speeches and keeping the comedy vibes going as the party loosened up.

Wedding guest Peter Fearnhead, cofounder of African Parks, told the *Sunday Telegraph*: "When Harry and Meghan came in, they stood on the podium and Prince William introduced them. Prince Charles made a really gracious speech, it was amazingly endearing. He's got a wonderfully dry sense of humor."

Charles's speech gently ribbed his younger son about his childhood antics and included a very informative anecdote about changing Harry's diaper. He didn't mention Diana at all. More emotionally, he described how moving it was to watch his little boy get married and finished by saying, "My darling old Harry, I'm so happy for you."

William struck a poignant note by reminding guests how proud Diana would have been of the way her younger son had turned out. But as the booze flowed, William and close family friend Charlie von Straubenzee got revenge for Harry's merciless mocking of his brother at his wedding party, with an ear-burning recital of fraternal tiffs and pratfalls. Harry had visited the van Straubenzees' family home in Cornwall almost every summer since he was a boy, surfing, relaxing, and exploring local attractions, including cider and pretty girls. So Charlie van Straubenzee and William had plenty of embarrassing anecdotes to share with the audience. Charlie's brother, Tom, and "Skippy" Inskip then took to the stage, once the older members of the assembly had left, with some cruder nods to Prince Harry's playboy past. However, there had been strict instructions to downplay Prince Harry's pre-Meghan Las Vegas trips.

William put an end to their recounting of increasingly lurid anecdotes by coughing gently into the slightly shocked silence before hammily asking if any of the guests could play the piano.

Sir Elton John waddled importantly to the stage and kicked off his set with Diana's favorite, "Your Song," before playing "Tiny Dancer," "Circle of Life," and "I'm Still Standing." "He was incredible. It became like a miniconcert in the reception area," said one guest. "Some people were even crying."

A close friend of Harry's told the *Sunday Times*: "As Elton John was playing, dowagers were sent flying as guests raced to the front to dance." The friend described the reception as "so much more relaxed than William and Kate's, just like a lovely, family wedding." Soon, the atmosphere changed, and DJ Sam Totolee (who also performed at Pippa Middleton's wedding) started banging out house anthems, a "drinks of the world"-themed bar was available, and candy-floss and "dirty burgers" were offered as midnight snacks.

After the reception ended, boozed-up guests headed to the trendy A-list hangout the Chiltern Firehouse to carry on the night. Other A-listers who attended the wedding held an "after, after party" at the bar in Marylebone at around 1 a.m.

As the party faded into the night, Harry and his wife retired to their quarters so Meghan could be up early for her yoga and the pair could begin the first day of their married life—a life that would forever change the monarchy.

At least one source, speaking to this author, worried that the star-splashed nuptials didn't bode well for the future. "The wedding, with A-list stars, was showbiz," said the source. "The whole point about showbiz is that it's not real. It's make-believe. It won't sustain you—and therefore the marriage won't last. The

House of Windsor hasn't quite disintegrated, but there's little doubt the Royal Family is fraying at the edges."

And everyone is asking the same question—is this a Markle-driven debacle?

WINDSORS & LOSERS

Harry and Meghan's wedding in 2018 put them on top of the world and made them without doubt the biggest celebrities on the planet. Little would anyone at the time know that it would also represent the absolute pinnacle of their success, and only twenty months later the whole thing would come crashing down as they made their calamitous, shocking exit from the Royal Family, thumbing their noses to both of their families as they decided they knew better and that a Hollywood lifestyle would be more suited to them and their family.

Not for Harry and Meghan anymore was the stuffy old institution of monarchy, ceremony, and service, forged through hundreds of years by the noblest minds the United Kingdom had to offer.

The pull of the silver screen, the making of a quick buck, and the glamour of celebrity proved enough to drag them away.

After Harry and Meghan stepped back, the public's focus was once again returned to Prince William and Kate—stoic, reliable, and after the flash in the pan of Harry and Meghan, once again the favorite royal couple.

By now, William, Kate, and their growing brood were becoming a familiar sight to royal watchers around the world. The birth of their third child, Louis, in 2018 had brought another sign of the changing dynamic in the Royal Family. For the first time, thanks to the Queen's amendment of the laws of accession to the throne, Princess Charlotte remained fourth in line to the throne, instead of being trumped by her new brother. Month by month, the visibility of the Cambridges began to edge on that of the Queen. Charles and Camilla jokingly referred to themselves as Gladys and Fred, the pensioner couple happy in each other's company, sedately making the rounds of the country. They were the caretakers of the monarchy as the elder generation finally begin to settle down and put their feet up.

The Queen and Prince Philip, now each well into their nineties, are applying the brakes on their public appearances, after over half a century of royal duty. Philip is now fully retired. Although the Queen—as has been seen during the trials and tribulations of Megxit—is still very much the boss, she has focused her energies on keeping up with the causes and events that are closest to her heart. Otherwise, with some degree of relief, she has let Charles and the family, although wisely not the wayward son Andrew—forced to step down from royal duties— pick up the slack.

During the past decade, the Palace has been working discreetly behind the scenes, to rotate the "center of royal gravity" away from the monarch to Charles and Camilla, en route to the Duke and Duchess of Cambridge, as one source put it. The Palace has been quietly reassembling the vast complicated network of responsibilities, obligations, day-to-day jobs, and commitments into a new model for the next era. The process has been discreetly going on for years. So much machinery needs to be recalibrated, so much logistical legwork remains to be undertaken, especially given the rupture caused by the sudden departure of the Sussexes.

When William finally assumes the role he has been groomed for since birth, he will no doubt seek to modernize and reassess the role of the monarchy as Britain progresses through the first half of the twenty-first century. Will he over-see the House of Windsor's dwindling from titular head of the nation, as it was in its Elizabethan heyday, to harmless sideshow? A ceremonial bit of window dress-ing to keep tourists happy?

Certainly, those who argue for the whole damn lot of 'em to be abolished have had quite a bit of ammunition over recent years. The controversies and upsets we have witnessed over the last decades of Elizabeth's rule mean that George, Charlotte, Louis, Archie, and their peers will look to their elders and ancestors— Meghan, Harry, Andrew, Diana, Camilla—and question the very nature of their identity and purpose. In what kind of world will they come of age? Will the Brits' inexplicable sentimentality and deep-rooted fondness for their Royals still course through the nation's veins? We can only speculate.

For now, the gradual easing of the Queen's schedule means the nonagenarian is relinquishing more and more of her routine duties to Charles. Dispensing honors, conducting investitures, undertaking exhausting long-distance overseas tours—Charles is your man. He also has more or less taken over the day-to-day political business that was once the preserve of the monarch, such as the Privy Council, accompanying his mother to the State Opening of Parliament and routine meetings with government ministers, as well as receiving foreign and Commonwealth representatives.

William, Kate, and their three children's home at Kensington Palace will increasingly become the base of the Royals, as the Queen and her administration sail slowly and regally into the sunset. William and Kate will take on more and more royal responsibilities as their children grow up and Charles himself starts to feel the strain of spending his time squashed into an airplane seat, eating rubbery chicken and petits fours, and groaning softly to himself, destined for yet another royal reception at an airport somewhere. Over the years, his occasional lapses into irascibility or impatience have been embarrassingly well documented, whether it be his hot mic gaffe in Klosters in 2003, groaning about what a "dreadful" man the BBC correspondent was, or being caught describing Chinese officials as "terrible old waxworks."

But Charles has already built a substantial legacy in Britain. He was making impassioned pleas for sustainability and climate-change awareness long before these subjects were discussed in the mainstream, let alone the height of fashion as they are now. He has been ridiculed for his beliefs, misjudged and pilloried for the breakdown of his marriage, and he has had to tolerate the abuse and denigration he received throughout the 1990s, following his divorce from Diana and then again after her death, all while raising their teenage sons.

Since his marriage to Camilla, he has been rehabilitated in the public's gaze, thanks in large part to his warm and loving relationship with his two sons. Shattered by the death of their mother, they turned to their father for comfort and support and found it in abundance. Burying his own complex and tormented feelings about Diana, encompassing a very human mélange of guilt, grief, anger, and love, Charles did his best with his boys, though he knew full well one was going to either usurp or succeed him—and the other was not going to have much of substance to do at all.

This was always going to be a fatal imbalance in the relationship between

William and Harry. Laudably, Diana did all she could to raise them as "normally" as possible, showering them equally with love and attention. But she couldn't change their destinies, which couldn't have been more different. From birth, Harry was "the spare:" barring an unthinkable series of deaths or calamities, his life was going to be spent in the shadows. William was going to be King.

With the acrimonious departure of Harry and Meghan to live what is most likely to be a life reminiscent of Edward and Wallis Simpson, William's young clan is settled, assured, and ready to take over the mantle of being Britain's "first family." King William's steady, unflappable character will be supported by his loyal and devoted helpmeet, Queen Catherine, and their brood of young Princes and Princess, who look set to enjoy the kind of tranquil and secure childhood their father didn't have.

Many speculate that depending on timing, Charles may clear the way for his son to directly jump on the throne and begin the William epoch immediately, for the sake of the Royals' long-term future. William knows this and typically is prepared. He has no doubt been discussing this scenario with Kate since their courtship. Secure in her love, wisdom, and steadfast loyalty, he has established a trusted, respected inner core of advisors and courtiers. The outwardly jovial, self-deprecating everyman is a shrewd and sharp strategizer and planner. He is experienced enough to know when successful leadership means lots of listening and learning.

Whereas William's future is set in stone, Harry has needed a purpose and direction. His tragedy was to be born an energetic, lively, and restless soul, at odds with his historical position in the family, number two son, the spare. This has caused him heartache and deep insecurity and unhappiness over the years. The only time Harry has been in his element and free to realize his vast potential was in the Army. But due to who he was, he was thwarted from engaging as fully as he would have liked. Much to his chagrin, he was destined to spend the rest of his life doing charity work (which he genuinely does love), travel (ditto), and the rest of the time, behaving badly. This was the downward spiral Harry was on before Meghan. The angry drunken Prince, the wayward lost soldier, the confused, fragile man with no idea who he was or, indeed, why he was.

Meghan, as has been extensively explored, changed all that. Unlike Kate, who reinforced, supported, and understood William's destiny from the outset and devoted herself to fitting into that narrative, Meghan offered Harry a way out. Whatever her motives may be, she shone a light in Harry's world; she showed him it didn't have to be this way.

"Harry's life was upended when his mother died," said a source, explaining how the death of Diana led to his unique bond with Meghan. "It has helped, or hindered, his taste in women. He has always liked women who have strength and opinions of their own. This is the latest manifestation of his rebelliousness. But no one ever expected it would tear the monarchy apart, as it has."

In Meghan, Harry was excited to find a woman who, unlike his previous partners, was an old hand at celebrity and showbiz and knew only too well how to come a long way on a modest amount of innate talent. Harry was born into fame and global celebrity and came to loathe it. Meghan aspired to it and then came to weaponize it.

"Image has always been everything to Meghan Markle," said a friend. "It's now more important for her than ever before because with the Queen's money no longer pouring in, she needs income."

A former friend put it more bluntly: "Meghan has always been fascinated with the creation of a 'brand.' I do not believe she married Harry with that solely in mind, but it was a determining factor. In Harry, she found someone who was fragile—and who she could control and manipulate. She married two objects of desire. As Harry said before the wedding, what Meghan wants, Meghan gets— and he's very, very keen on making her happy, I think to the detriment of himself."

For better or worse, Meghan showed Harry how he could isolate and exploit the millstone around his neck, his royalness, while living his "best life." Together, they established themselves as an entirely new kind of Royal Family—untethered from the Firm. The tensions, conflicts, and differences between William's vision of the future and theirs will create a new monarchy that we can't imagine.

Remarking on the uncharted territory, one source said: "Never before has a member of the British Royal Family been for sale—to cash in on their profiles. That's what it actually is. When others have flirted with this, it has ended in disaster. Look at Prince Andrew and Jeffrey Epstein. Sarah Ferguson. Even

Princess Diana. One shady business deal and the House of Windsor could become, at a minimum, corrupted—or at worst it comes, crumbling down. This is the Queen, Prince Charles', and Prince William's worst fear—and was a key topic at the Sandringham summit of the Firm in January 2020, designed to decide the future role of the Sussexes. With Harry and Meghan on the loose, they're susceptible to rogues and renegades. That strikes the fear of God into the Firm." (The Duke's friendship with Jeffrey Epstein, an American financier and convicted sex offender, produced a steady stream of criticism and eyebrow raising. Virginia Giuffre [then known by her maiden name Virginia Roberts] asserted that she had sex with the Duke on three occasions, including on a trip to London in 2001 when she was seventeen, and later in New York and on Epstein's Little Saint James hideaway. She alleged Epstein paid her fifteen thousand dollars to have sex with the Duke in London. Flight logs show the Duke and Giuffre were in the places she alleges the sex happened. The Duke and Giuffre were also photographed together with the Duke's arm around her waist and included Epstein's alleged pimp, Ghislaine Maxwell, standing in the background. Prince Andrew also orchestrated a plan for Jeffrey Epstein to pay off nineteen thousand dollars' worth of his ex-wife's debt.)

Germaine Greer, who in 2018 predicted Meghan would leave the Firm and take Harry with her, has, more recently, wondered aloud about Meghan's motives. "All I can think is she'd better be in love," she said in a recent interview. "If she's been faking it all this time, oh boy, what misery." She went on to opine: "If they escape from the jurisdiction of the Firm and they do things on their own initiative, the outcome is likely to be disastrous."

Said one of this author's sources: "This is all Meghan, I am convinced—remember Harry did say, 'Whatever Meghan wants, Meghan gets.' Meghan clearly wants to have her cake and eat it. There is absolutely no way Harry would disrespect his grandmother in such a way. Sadly, Meghan has completely removed him from family and friends. He is now surrounded by Meghan's courtiers, helping to complete the 'brainwashing.' This will not end well, mark my words. It will end in divorce."

Of course, the less cynical explanation is that Meghan really does love Harry. Just because she's a woman who is opinionated, sassy, sexy, and accomplished doesn't mean she has a malicious intent. This woman has fought and struggled her way to success, despite truly awful family problems, poverty, and racial and gender prejudice. Leaving the Royal Family at a time of her choosing was simply what needed to be done. It upset the old gray suits at the Palace? Sorry, not sorry, as some would suggest. Meghan behaved in ways Harry simply didn't dare. And he will be in thrall to this for the foreseeable future. She is his one survival strategy for his greatest dream—a life forever free of being a Royal. The Prince formerly known as a Prince.

EPILOGUE

Their bags might have been heavy, but Prince Harry and Meghan Markle's spirits were light as they departed on a commercial flight from the United States to Canada on February 14.

The casually dressed duo—Harry wore jeans, a gray sweater, and a cap, while Meghan rocked a striped button-down, a black cardigan, and black flats—were all smiles as they carried their own luggage and made their way to a waiting car.

It had been less than two months since the couple shocked the world and reverberated through royal ranks with their plans to step back from their engagements and embark on a new life outside of Britain with their soon to be one-year-old son, Archie.

On the surface, all seemed well.

But Harry and Meghan were to soon realize cutting royal ties would take its most dramatic turn yet.

***

A month before landing in Canada, while delivering a speech at a dinner for Sentebale, the HIV and AIDS charity he created in 2006 to honor the memory of his late mother, Princess Diana, in London on January 19, Harry took the opportunity to address attendees, "not as a Prince, or a Duke, but as Harry," he said.

The red-headed royal's tone was unusually somber and emotional as he revealed that he and Meghan had "no choice" but to step down as senior members of the royal family.

"When I lost my mum twenty-three years ago, you took me under your wing," Harry told the captivated crowd. "The decision that I have made for my wife and I to step back is not one I made lightly. But there really was no other option."

A day earlier, the Queen had released a statement from Buckingham Palace announcing that the senior-most youngest royals had been essentially cut off from the royal family.

The missive came after the couple expressed their desire to start splitting their time between the United Kingdom, Canada, and the United States. But the matriarch of the Windsors—staunch in tradition and values—was unwilling to let Harry and Meghan straddle the line between royals and commoners, so she effectively forced them out of the Firm completely.

What's more, Elizabeth delivered a strict edict: Harry and Meghan must pay back the Sovereign Grant money they spent on renovating their UK home, Frogmore Cottage, and she wanted the pair to start paying rent and upkeep for the estate, which they'd wanted to keep to use when Harry made trips to his home country.

"Harry and Meghan were extremely hurt by the Queen's decision to force them to step back even further than they had wanted," said an insider.

"They feel outed. But it's one of those all-or-nothing situations, and Harry accepts that."

So, they soon adjusted to their new life—*and what a life it was.*

Mille Fleur is a French Country–inspired five-bedroom house on Vancouver Island in Victoria that the couple has been borrowing from an unnamed billionaire. It was there where Meghan and Harry spent the holidays. Now, they began to settle into a routine with little Archie. According to reports, friends had also come from California to visit them, like former *Suits* costar Abigail Spencer and actor Janina Gavankar, who took a picture of Archie that they featured on their holiday card. Meghan also hosted longtime friend and trainer Heather Dorak for a girls' weekend. Otherwise, the actress was spending most of her time at home with Archie and the nanny, and only headed out for walks or hikes when the weather allowed.

But Meghan was soon to unleash her long-desired plan.

***

Meghan had made it obvious she clearly had no plans to retreat into total obscurity. The glitter of Hollywood gold was calling—again. So, Meghan and Harry began to feast their eyes on a new home: a fifteen million dollar one in Malibu, California that would put them close to her mom, Doria Ragland.

As the Firm had initially feared, the couple began to use Meghan's Hollywood connections to stay in the Tinsel Town mix.

"They are in touch with a number of LA power players and are looking forward to hosting dinner parties with the likes of George and Amal Clooney and big-time movie producer Jeffrey Katzenberg," said one insider, at the time.

For Harry, he might not be used to paying his own way—but he was said to be looking forward to doing it for the first time in his life.

"He didn't even understand what a mortgage was until a few years ago," joked one friend. "But he'll be able to cope with financial independence." (While he and Meghan will no longer receive public funds for royal duties, Harry's dad, Prince Charles, will still offer monetary support, according to the palace.)

Meghan was also said to be happy to teach him about what she considered to be "the real world."

"She doesn't come from millions," said the insider. "Meghan's worked hard to get to where she is today." There would seemingly be no shortage of moneymaking opportunities, either. Meghan signed a deal with Disney and did voice-over work for a film for Disney Nature, *Elephants*, to benefit the charity, Elephants Without Borders.

"Meghan loves the idea of being the breadwinner," noted another source. "She has no plans to do another show like *Suits*, but Harry's been encouraging her to do more voice-over work, writing, producing, and directing in her free time."

It's obvious: Together, Meghan and Harry could no doubt take Hollywood by storm.

"It doesn't take a genius to work out that the Sussex's can easily make millions—or even a billion—from being a brand," said one source.

What's more, Princess Diana's former butler, Paul Burrell, predicted his former bosses' youngest will likely shine outside of William's shadow. "I doubt he'll miss being a royal," said Burrell. "Yes, he was born a prince, but his long-term ambition is to be known as a humanitarian, like his mother."

Said a source:

> Harry is determined to make it in Hollywood. Just as much as Meghan,
> he'll focus on producing documentaries about charities but wants
> some screen time too. We'll see him on camera, mostly as a spokes-
> man. He's not trying to be the next Brad Pitt or anything. He under-
> stands it's a risky venture. Harry knows Hollywood is fickle. He wants
> to get things right from the beginning and if all goes well, he'll use the
> exposure to shine a light on worthy causes. With Harry and Meghan,
> it's not just about making a fast buck—there has to be a purpose behind
> their work.

Within a few weeks of Harry and Meghan moving into their new Los Angeles
home, the rebellious royals had already adopting a distinctly LA lifestyle: Harry
had been enjoying the near-constant sunshine and had even taken up yoga. "After
practicing a few times, he's become an avid yogi," an insider told *Us Weekly*.

But before they could embark on California dreaming, there was one final official royal engagement.

***

It certainly wasn't the warmest of welcomes.

Harry and Meghan were seated in the second row at Westminster Abbey for
the annual Commonwealth Service on March 9 when Prince William and
Catherine, Duchess of Cambridge, arrived and headed to their own seats, situated
directly in front of the rebellious couple.

Though Meghan said hello and gave a quick wave, and Harry flashed a warm
smile, Kate barely glanced in their direction. Harry's brother, William, offered a
quick head nod, then he and his wife turned their backs on Harry and Meghan
and sat down.

The tense reunion was a fitting end to Harry and Meghan's farewell tour—and
one that solidified the ongoing feud between the brothers and sisters-in-law.
"There was definitely tension in the air," an onlooked said. "It was really
awkward."

It seemed their final appearance as royals couldn't end soon enough for Meghan and Harry. "Meghan thought Kate might make more of an effort, but she didn't," said one onlooker, who added, "Their 'Fab Four' days are well and truly over."

Meghan wasn't taking the ice-out too hard—because she had become used to it.

Her brief return to the United Kingdom with Harry was met with mixed reactions: Their entrance at the Endeavor Fund Awards on March 5 was accompanied by raucous boos, but they got a standing ovation two nights later at the Mountbatten Festival of Music. Through it all, Meghan maintained a near-constant megawatt smile.

"She looked and felt amazing," said a friend. "She has no regrets and is looking forward to returning to her peaceful life in North America."

In fact, said an insider, she felt like she's gotten the last laugh: "It was sweet revenge for Meghan to come back and be herself, and not have to do things the official royal way or tip-toe around anyone."

If that meant ruffling some royal feathers, so be it. She reportedly upstaged Camilla, Duchess of Cornwall, by posting Instagram photos of her visit to the National Theatre the same day the Camilla gave a speech about domestic violence. "That was the final straw for Camilla," added the source, who said that though Camilla has never been Meghan's biggest fan, she couldn't believe she stole her spotlight. "She was livid."

The insider said Meghan also broke protocol when she entered an event and "barged right past" the Duchess of Cornwall, who was hosting. "The way Camilla sees it, she's the future queen of England, and Meghan should be more respectful."

While back home, Harry did a better job of keeping the peace—at least with the Queen.

He sat down with his grandmother for a four-hour heart-to-heart. "Harry was very emotional," a palace aide later confided. "He cried and apologized for the way things went down."

The meeting was positive but intense, the aide added.

"The Queen told Harry that it's her greatest wish for him to remain in England," added the insider. "She left him with no doubt that while she'll respect his decision, it would be wonderful if he'd change his mind. She basically pleaded with him not to leave, and to come home as soon as possible if he had to go."

One thing was certain after Meghan and Harry's farewell tour—they had no plans to return to the United Kingdom beyond the Queen's invitation to join her at Balmoral for a visit with her great-grandson, Archie, over the summer.

That was until an unprecedented health crisis would rock the world: The greatest pandemic in living memory.

**

Come April 2020, like many across the world, Harry would become personally effected through the spread of a silent killer. The former royal, having moved to LA, became trapped as his UK family was exposed to the dangerous and deadly virus, called COVID-19 (or coronavirus).

Late one night, Prince Charles called to tell his son he'd tested positive for the deadly virus. Harry was overcome with emotion. "It hit home for him that Charles and the Queen aren't going to be around forever," said a source.

At the time of publication, fortuitously the Queen had avoided coronavirus as she remained under lockdown at Windsor Castle, even though she was considered at high risk for exposure. After all, a staffer at Buckingham Palace was infected; and she met with British Prime Minister Boris Johnson shortly before it was confirmed that he also tested positive for the virus—and came perilously close to dying.

"Harry's biggest fear is not being there if his grandmother were to die," said a source.

On the home front, Meghan was doing her best to help Harry cope. "She gets that he's in a tricky situation with his family," the insider said. "She's assuring him that once things go back to normal, he'll love their new life in LA"

While holed up in a gated community in Malibu, a source said, they've also looked at permanent pads in Bel Air and Hidden Hills. "Meghan wants to take him hiking and talks about the local polo club and how much he'll love surfing," the insider said.

But as she held onto the California dream, there was still tension at home over

Harry feeling so torn. "Like any household right now, there are ups and downs," a source said. "To Harry's credit, he has tried to shield Meghan from his stress. So, he'll confide to friends in the UK over the phone.

"On top of it all, he's got cabin fever. It was far from an ideal situation. Harry's gone from being excited about the move to feeling secretly tortured."

***

Fortuitously, Harry's got enough on his plate to keep him busy.

He remains the dutiful dad: tending to Archie and meeting with his advisors to discuss upcoming projects. The couple just hired Catherine St-Laurent as chief of staff for their forthcoming charity foundation, which is set to be announced later in 2020.

Across the pond, Harry's also doing his best to stay in constant contact with his loved ones, including talking to the Queen once or twice each week, according to a source. He and Prince Charles have been communicating often too.

"Charles found a great deal of comfort in their conversations while he was recuperating," the source said.

But sadly, the turmoil hasn't helped bridge the gap between Harry and Prince William. "They speak, but it's awkward," said another confidant, adding that Harry and Meghan haven't talked to Kate at all. If anything, the latest crisis has only added to William's anger at his younger brother for jumping ship. "He's hurt that Harry isn't in London to support the family amid the coronavirus outbreak."

With the Queen and Prince Charles out of commission, Kate Middleton and Prince William pitched in to pick up the slack. Before retreating to Anmer Hall—their country residence in Norfolk—with children Prince George, Princess Charlotte, and Prince Louis, they met with health workers on the front lines battling the coronavirus.

Things, as have been well documented, have been tense among the former "Fab Four" for quite some time, and the coronavirus development certainly hasn't helped matters.

"William and Kate feel screwed over," said a royal insider, noting that the couple will likely have double the workload now that Harry and Meghan won't be showing face at many official engagements. "They think it's unfair that Harry and Meghan still get to reap the rewards of being part of the royal family without having to put in any effort."

While William was aware of Harry's intention to start spending more time in North America, he and Kate expected the transition to be a gradual one.

"No one was prepared for this," the insider explained. Kate is said to be "panicking over how she'll juggle the extra responsibilities with family life"—especially during the pandemic of taking on the burden of ensuring elderly members of the Firm are safe, secure, and healthy.

Said a source:

> Harry misses his brother and Kate, but there's too much mud under the bridge at this point for any meaningful communication. They're cordial, but that's about as far as it goes. Meghan isn't as fazed as Harry about not being close to his relatives, perhaps because she grew up in a broken home. She's survived estrangement, so she believes Harry will too.

As for Prince William and Kate:

> They think it's pathetic how Meghan works Harry like her own personal puppet. They've resigned themselves to losing the Harry they once knew for the foreseeable future.

***

For now, Harry and Meghan have no choice but to hunker down in their new American home, the country with the largest outbreak of COVID-19. Fortuitously, they have a team of security guards and household help working around the clock.

"Harry and Meghan have read about all that can happen to celebrities in LA and they don't want to take any risks, especially with Archie," said the insider. "It's not cheap. The security team's going to cost them a fortune—millions and millions of dollars."

On March 29, in the grip of the pandemic, President Donald Trump tweeted his refusal to foot the bill for their security, writing: "It was reported that Harry and Meghan, who left the Kingdom, would reside permanently in Canada. Now they have left Canada for the U.S. however, the U.S. will not pay for their security protection. They must pay!" To retort, Meghan and Harry quickly released a statement saying they had no plans to ask the US government for assistance.

But while Harry's doing his best to protect the people inside his house, he can't do much about what's happening outside.

"It's a terrifying time," said the source.

"There's a big part of Harry that wishes he were still in the UK so he could be with his family there. He doesn't ultimately regret moving, but he knows the timing couldn't be worse. Of course, neither he nor Meghan could have foreseen the tragic events that have unfolded around the world … but that doesn't make it easier for Harry—who is now officially an outcast—to be away from his loved ones when they need him the most."

***

In the end, and despite all of the drama, this hasn't exactly been the fresh start Harry was hoping for. He and Meghan were forced to flee Vancouver Island, British Columbia, before its borders closed due to growing concerns over COVID-19.

"He's overwhelmed with guilt over not being closer to home while this is going on," said one insider. "He feels totally helpless."

For Meghan, being physically cut off from the rest of the world could be what she wanted, all along, predicted one former friend: "This could have the unintended but perfect way to hit reset for their family."

The truth is, the outbreak of COVID-19 proved Harry to be just like every single one of us. It might have provided a kind-of self-isolation from the rigors of royal hood, but it couldn't stop the feelings of being frightened and numbed with anxiety about one's own health and that of their loved ones, especially when so many across the world have died.

If, at the end of this book, you thought you knew the Harry and Meghan story, you're wrong. Due to the havoc-wreaking effects of COVID-19, it's perhaps just the beginning of a whole new chapter, full of tangential unanswered questions.

How will the pandemic end?

Will Harry return to the United Kingdom—and an ailing family?

Can the Queen persuade him to return to his former royal role?

Can Meghan ride gunshot—again?

Or will Harry make a big introduction to showbiz?

Perhaps most intriguingly, there is one coda to this story which suggests that the world's—and the British especially—fascination with Harry and Meghan isn't quite done yet, lockdown or no lockdown.

On April 20, as the pandemic hit its peak in the United Kingdom, the Duke and Duchess of Sussex sent an extraordinary—and unprecedented —open letter to the editors of the four leading British tabloid newspapers, the *Sun*, the *Daily Mail*, the *Mirror*, and the *Express*. In a lengthy attack on the press, they declared a new policy of "zero engagement" and that from now on they would not respond to any inquiries from journalists from those newspapers ... except when necessary through their lawyers.

The couple also said they will no longer "offer themselves up as currency for an economy of clickbait and distortion" and accused the press of printing stories about them that are "distorted, false, or invasive beyond reason."

If the letter was supposed to draw a final line under the Megxit saga, it has done anything but. The following day every single one of the major British newspapers ran a Harry and Meghan story—including the four tabloids specifically named by the couple. None were positive.

It's apparent: This story is not over yet.